MODELS OF
INTERNATIONAL COLLABORATION
IN SOCIAL WORK EDUCATION

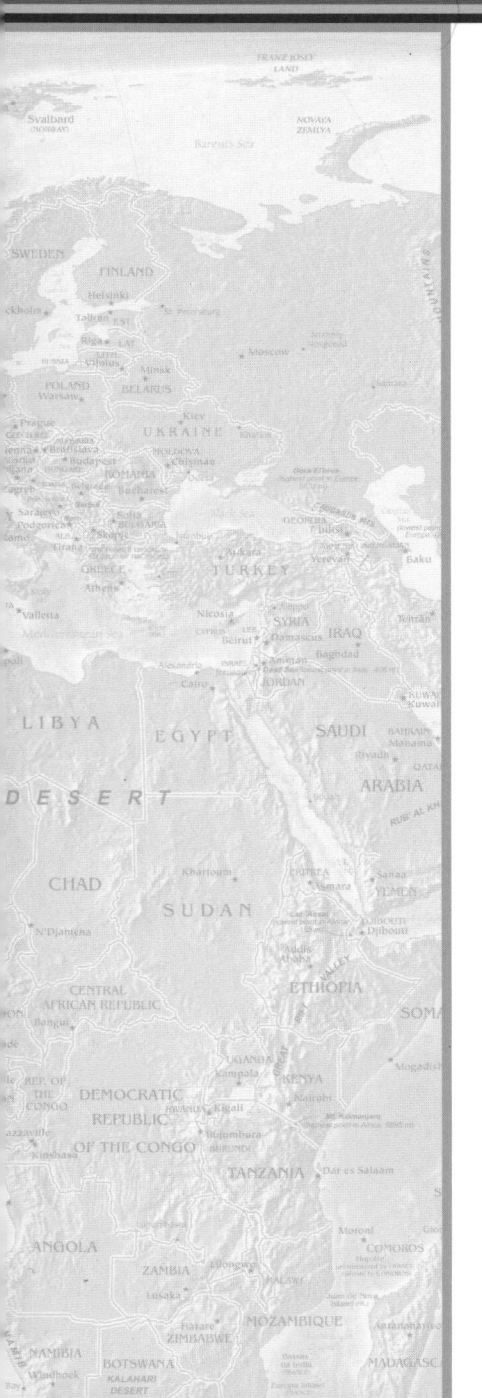

EDITORS   LYNNE M. HEALY • YVONNE ASAMOAH • M.C. "TERRY" HOKENSTAD

D1294840

COUNCIL ON SOCIAL WORK EDUCATION • ALEXANDRIA VA

Council on Social Work Education
1725 Duke Street, Suite 500
Alexandria, VA 22314-3457

Printed in the United States of America

Models of International Collaboration in Social Work Education

ISBN 0-87293-095-5

CONTENTS

PREFACE

The founders of the social work profession were strong advocates of international exchange and collaboration. In a paper at the first International Conference of Social Work held in 1928, Eglantyne Jebb issued a call for "constant contact between social workers on an international intellectual basis" (Jebb, 1929, p. 651). The importance of interuniversity collaborations as a form of this international intellectual exchange has inspired us to compile *Models of International Collaboration in Social Work Education*.

When we began writing this book, social work education in the United States was governed by a curriculum policy statement that included no requirements for international knowledge. Its preamble, however, did acknowledge cross-national cooperation: "Effective social work programs recognize the interdependence of nations and the importance of worldwide professional cooperation" (CSWE, 1994). The acknowledgement coincided with a period of expanding cross-national contact in social work education, as schools in North America and Europe were called upon to provide assistance to fledgling programs in the former Soviet bloc countries. These activities, in turn, led to increased interest in international collaboration.

As our work neared publication, a new curriculum policy statement, the Educational Policy and Accreditation Standards (EPAS), has been adopted by the U.S.-based Council on Social Work Education (CSWE). This statement more boldly addresses international knowledge and competence. A particularly important new component requires programs to prepare students to "recognize the global context of social work practice" (CSWE, 2001). While there are a number of paths to this outcome, cross-national collaboration and international exchange programs can play an important and dynamic role.

As the case studies in this book illustrate, international exchange and collaboration can contribute by enriching faculty and student understanding of global issues and diverse cultures. These exchanges may result in new content and new perspectives for the curricula of the participating schools. Through consultations and the exchange of ideas, technology transfer often occurs, which leads to successful adaptations of innovations from the partner school. Another exciting outcome of some collaborations is a program of joint research and publication. Occasionally, a collaboration even enhances or provides services to agencies or directly to clients. In these diverse ways, international exchange programs make important contributions to participants' understanding of social work in its global context. Such projects also ensure that students address the related learning outcomes specified in EPAS: to gain knowledge of international issues in social policy and to understand the global interconnections of forces of oppression.

There was fear that the fallout from the September 11th, 2001, terrorist attacks would lessen support for international exchange. Yet, a survey conducted by the Institute for International Education (IIE) of 600 international education professionals, representing colleges and universities throughout the United States, showed that institutions of higher education continue to demonstrate strong support for maintaining and developing international linkages (IIE, 2001). Asked whether international educational exchange was more or less important in light of the September 11th attacks, 43% of respondents answered that it is more important; 55% reported no change in importance; and only 2% said it is less important. We concur with the president of IIE, who said that "this is a time when our world needs more international exchange, not less" (IIE, 2001, p. 2). We hope our book will provide encouragement for increased exchange.

This publication is intended primarily as a guide for social work educators in the United States and Canada who are seeking to initiate or enhance international collaborative projects. Therefore, we have selected case studies of exchanges involving a U.S. or Canadian partner. The editors believe that collaboration between schools in developing countries, often referred to as South-South collaboration, can be highly beneficial; however, we have not included examples of such collaborations here because our target audience is the North American social work education community. We selected cases involving international partners from diverse countries and have included projects involving Central America, the Caribbean, Asia, both Eastern and Western Europe, and Africa. We regret that only one case has an African component and there may well be good examples that we did not discover in our search for contributors. Although these projects involve both MSW and BSW programs, there is greater representation at the master's level. One case study specifically describes a joint doctoral program. We balanced our desire for diversity with the selection of collaborations that had demonstrated some longevity, sustainability, mutuality, and institutional impact. More will be said about these elements in the chapters that follow.

These case studies provide important examples of various types of collaboration. Authors were asked to describe their project's activities and to suggest lessons that can be learned from their experiences. Theoretical material on collaboration and a literature review that provides background on social work and inter-university linkages are discussed in chapters 1 and 2. Case authors were specifically requested to minimize their discussions of the literature in order to avoid repetition.

This volume has been made possible by our contributing authors. We were fortunate to find 11 solid examples of international collaboration in social work education. Each author or set of authors has done an excellent job presenting their experiences and the lessons they learned that can be used by others. Several of the chapters are jointly authored by educators from both of the institutions that participated in the collaboration. We appreciate the extra effort that was required for these joint submissions. We also would like to

acknowledge our colleagues on CSWE's International Commission for their encouragement and inspiration.

Several people provided invaluable assistance with the publication. Pamela Harrison, from the University of Connecticut School of Social Work, managed the manuscripts for us and provided secretarial expertise in compiling the volume. Her ongoing work over the past 2 years helped greatly in moving the volume along to publication. Theresa Wilson and Marianne Thompson, both of the Mandel School of Applied Social Sciences at Case Western Reserve University, assisted with the preparation of several chapters of the manuscript. Michael Monti, CSWE's director of member programs, conferences, and publications, was encouraging and helpful to us in every step of the process. We also thank the anonymous reviewers for their insightful comments.

Lynne M. Healy
Yvonne Asamoah
M. C. "Terry" Hokenstad

REFERENCES

Council on Social Work Education. (1994). *Curriculum policy statement*. Alexandria, VA: Author.

Council on Social Work Education. (2001). *Educational policy and accreditation standards*. Alexandria, VA: Author.

Institute of International Education. (2001). *Interest in international educational exchange remains strong in the aftermath of September 11th according to IIE survey* [Press release issued November 13, 2001]. Retrieved July 30, 2002, from http://www.iienetwork.org.

Jebb, E. (1929, July). International social service. In *First international conference of social work* (vol. 1, pp. 637–655). Proceedings of the First International Conference of Social Work, Paris, France.

ONE

International Collaboration in Social Work Education: Overview
Yvonne Asamoah

Exchange programs, institutional linkage agreements, joint research ventures, and many other types of collaboration between schools of social work on different continents have increased considerably in the past decade. The realities of global interdependence and globalization have fueled the growth of interest in collaboration and are potent factors in the future of international exchange. Participation in international collaborations has been shown to increase individual awareness and knowledge of global issues, to enhance cross-cultural competence, and to strengthen the capacity of social work education to contribute to the building of the social work profession at home and throughout the world. As most North American universities and colleges now embrace the ideology of internationalization and globalization in their missions, the participation of social work in international ventures is a new criterion for relevance within the institution. Thus, the time is right for a guide to international collaboration in social work education.

Collaboration can be simply defined as "a mutually beneficial and well-defined relationship entered into by two or more organizations to achieve common goals" (Mattessich & Monsey, 1992, p. 39). Razack (2002), in her recent review of international exchanges in social work, suggests that educators have not always thought through the educational and practice implications of these collaborations. This volume presents models of international collaboration for social work education in the form of case studies of successful and varied examples. The intent is to assist social work educators in thinking through the elements of sound international linkages and to guide their efforts to establish educationally relevant and mutually beneficial collaborations. Because this volume is written primarily for a North American audience, all of the case studies include one partner from the United States or Canada. We hope that the experiences discussed will be relevant

to readers in other countries, even though exchanges in other parts of the world may have different characteristics. Most of the cases included reflect collaborations that involve exchanges of faculty or students in addition to other resources. Some represent creative attempts at cross-cultural coalition building among various institutions, including both universities and noneducational organizations. Although some of the cases are collaborations between social work programs, other linkages involve multiple disciplines. The case studies also represent the full range of levels of social work education, from BSW to doctoral programs. Efforts were made to include cases with partners from diverse countries, as the authors highlight the significance of the cultural, political, and social contexts within which the collaborations take place and explore the extent to which these different environments pose challenges to successful outcomes. Before describing the contents of the book, I will discuss the importance of international collaboration in the context of globalization, provide a brief history of such efforts, and present the goals and potential benefits of international collaboration.

WHY COLLABORATION? THE GLOBAL CONTEXT

Current international exchanges occur within the context of increasing globalization. Globalization is a significant force of the late 20th and early 21st centuries. While the growth of a world economy is the most commonly referenced hallmark, there are many other dimensions of globalization, including human migration, international travel, intercountry communication, the spread of cultural influences, and environmental interdependence. *Foreign Policy* magazine points out that although some countries are "more globalized" than others, even the least globalized "are being drawn together by new forces beyond their ability to control, whether it is global warming, the spread of infectious disease, or the rise of transnational crime" ("Measuring Globalization," 2001, p. 8).

Ife (2000) suggests that globalization has been understood primarily as an economic concept. He notes, however, that it is too simplistic to think of this concept as the development of a single world market in which nation states and cultural differences will become irrelevant under an all-encompassing economic system. The market is not the best mechanism for equitably meeting human need. Instead, the fallout from economic globalization may be glaring disparities between rich and poor nations and individuals. Poverty and social injustice have no geographic boundaries and remain a threat to large segments of the world's population. Therefore, Ife argues that social conditions have to be taken into account along with economic policy if we are to develop a global civil society that safeguards human rights. Social work can have a fundamental role in this effort. However, recognition of the social components of globalization is a precondition for action.

New social problems have emerged as a result of globalization and enduring problems have intensified. As mentioned above, some parts of the world are experiencing increased poverty and deprivation. Migration—voluntary and involuntary—of large numbers of people results in dislocation and problems of adaptation: increased ethnic conflict and violence occur as a result of the tensions accompanying economic, political, and social integration (Midgley, 1997). According to Prigoff (2000), without alternatives in place, the global economic system as currently operated is likely to marginalize and exclude a majority of the world's population from participation in productive economic activity and its rewards. The further exploitation of people, especially women and children, is likely.

In addition to recognizing these issues, it is important not to overlook the increase of positive actions designed to address global problems. The United Nations (UN) has sponsored world conferences and world summits to bring governments and nongovernmental organizations (NGOs) together to discuss issues including social development and poverty, the status of women, children's issues, and human rights. Declarations, plans, and programs of action have been adopted and promulgated. Regional political alliances, integration of world and regional markets, and advances in telecommunications have resulted in a confluence of cultures working to adjust to a new reality (e.g., Ayton-

Shenker, 1995; United Nations Development Program [UNDP], 1999, 2000). While globalization creates opportunities for economic exploitation and exacerbates some problems, it also provides chances for confronting many of the world's most pressing issues (Annan, 1999).

Many authors have called for the involvement of social work, first to recognize the realities of the globalized context, and then to fulfill its mandate as a profession committed to the ideals of human rights and social justice on a global level (e.g., Asamoah, Healy, & Mayadas, 1997; Canadian Association of Social Workers, 2000; Elliot & Mayadas, 1999; Healy, 2001; Healy & Asamoah, 1997; Hokenstad & Midgley, 1997; Jones & Kumsa, 1999; Kendall, 1994; Mary, 1997; Midgley, 1997; Prigoff, 1999, 2000; Ramanathan & Link, 1999). Similarly, the need for university education to take the lead in promoting the global perspective and entering into international collaborations is widely recognized. The *World Declaration on Higher Education* that emanated from the 1998 World Conference on Higher Education stated that "quality...requires that higher education should be characterized by its international dimension: exchange of knowledge, interactive networking, mobility of teachers and students and international research projects" (United Nations Educational, Scientific and Cultural Organization, UNESCO, 1998, article 11, b). In her article on a social development linkage project, Mericourt asserts that "internationalization is fundamental to the pursuit of academic excellence, the enrichment of the University culture, and the contribution of the University to its international community" (2001, p. 46).

International collaborations are increasingly recognized as an important component for internationalizing education. As stated in the preamble to the *World Declaration on Higher Education*, "international cooperation and exchange are major avenues for advancing higher education throughout the world" (UNESCO, 1998). Mericourt further states that "partnerships and strategic alliances are vitally important in positioning modern universities to become contributors to an increasingly interconnected and globalized world" (2001, p. 46).

HISTORY AND TYPES OF COLLABORATIONS

International educational exchanges have a long history in secondary and higher education generally and in social work specifically. The Institute of International Education was founded in 1919. Less than a decade later, at the First International Conference of Social Work in Paris in 1928, many speakers hailed the importance of international interchange to the development of the profession. The International Committee of Schools of Social Work was initiated at the 1928 conference and soon began a series of periodic international seminars to bring educators together (Healy, 2001). The Fulbright Program, established by the U.S. government in 1948, has promoted faculty and student exchanges for more than 50 years. It is interesting to note that among its broad goals is the creation of "understanding among people and cultures not accustomed to communicate at ease and thereby contributing to world peace" (Altbach & Teichler, 2001, p. 9). Academic exchange efforts intensified after World War II, in part as strategies to secure allies in the Cold War and to assist in development efforts for new nations. Social work was active in a number of these exchange programs. The greatest emphasis from the 1940s through the 1960s was on sending Western consultants to developing nations to assist universities starting social work programs, and on hosting students from Asia and Africa in U.S. and European schools.

Many of these early exchange models are most accurately described as one-way consultations without a true exchange component, and some models lacked cultural relevance and sensitivity. However, there are notable exceptions and some of the early arrangements are laudable prototypes representing "ground-breaking" firsts for international collaboration in social work (Kendall, 1994). These developmentally focused programs often involved multiple levels of interaction among schools of social work; government agencies; overseas ministries; local, national, and international NGOs; and the UN. Their success put social workers in demand as consultants and advisors all over the world. Through their involvement with UN programs and member countries, these consultants made significant contributions to social policy and to the formulation of social work education worldwide.

International social work professional organizations, such as the International Association of Schools of Social Work, the International Federation of Social Workers, the International Council of Social Welfare, and the Inter-University Consortium for International Social Development, have played and continue to play important roles in fostering international linkages among social work and social development programs and personnel. The international conferences sponsored by these organizations provide important opportunities for networking, often spawning collaborations. National social work organizations, including the Council on Social Work Education and the Canadian Association of Schools of Social Work, along with the National Association of Social Workers and the Canadian Association of Social Workers, have also been involved in international linkages.

Regional efforts to foster collaboration and exchange have gained momentum in the past few decades. Most significant are the programs of the European Union, which will be briefly described below and again in the final chapter. The majority of collaborations reflected in the social work literature are examples of university-to-university or social work program-to-program exchanges. Over the past several decades, these have included projects covering a wide range of countries, industrialized and developing, and many facets of exchange (e.g., Abrahams & Shera, 1984; Asamoah & Beverly, 1988; Deslauriers, et al., 1984; Laforest, Naltchayan & Bilodeau, 1984; Mericourt, 2001; Traub-Werner, Shera, Rodriguez Villa, & Tello Péon, 2000; Tsang, Yan, & Shera, 2000; Whitmore & Wilson, 1997).

Types of Collaboration

The most prevalent types of international collaboration are study-abroad programs and other exchanges of faculty and students between academic institutions. These programs differ in duration and in terms of the nature and degree of student, faculty, and institutional involvement. They range from short-term visits of a few weeks to a semester or a year in another country. Traditional student-exchange programs emphasize immersion in another culture and often include residence in a family's home. The Experiment in International Living and American Field Service have run such programs for many years and the Council of International Programs for Social Workers and Youth Workers is also an important contributor.

Some student exchanges are more work or project focused. They may involve students working abroad, joined by student colleagues from local institutions, and may be sponsored by a non-social work institution such as the Habitat for Humanity and Crossroads Africa programs. There is a growing interest in international field placements as a form of cross-cultural learning, as a way for social work students to internationalize their education, and for some, as preparation for careers in international development. Learning about cultures other than one's own, however, does not adequately define cross-cultural learning. True cross-cultural learning allows students to transcend their original cultural conditioning to view human life more objectively and sensitively (Ramanathan & Kondrat, 1994). Well-organized and well-coordinated international field practica build in this type of learning. Educationally sound international field practica require extensive prior planning involving all participating institutions or agencies. The availability of adequate funding for both the international linking institution and the student is critical to the success of these placements.

Lyons and Ramanathan (1999) outline various models of field practice in international settings and discuss appropriate rationales for undertaking such placements. Of particular importance is their discussion of institutional arrangements that foster or impede successful international field practica. They call for the reconsideration of expected outcomes of such placements in order to take advantage of the unique opportunities offered. The evaluation of student performance, for example, might emphasize the ability to adapt and organize learning in a different setting, rather than the specific practice skills of the home institution.

Student exchanges for field placement or academic study can be a means for profound learning in cross-cultural and international understanding. Indeed, these situations are often life-changing experiences for the participants. The benefits of student exchange, however, are largely individual, not institutional. There may be few strongly collaborative components between the educational institutions, and often, especially in social work, the potential ripple effects that might result when students share exchange experiences through class discussions may be muted by planning such an exchange late in the student's program.

Institutional exchange relationships have the advantage of wider impact. Through faculty and materials exchange, students and educators who do not travel can still be exposed to the international relationship. Still others can be involved in collaborative research. A recent study shows that study-abroad experiences for faculty—even short-term ones—had a multidimensional impact on teaching (Sandgren, Ellig, Hovde, Krejci, & Rice, 1999). Specifically, these short immersion experiences are "likely to produce dramatic and enduring transformative change in participants and their teaching" (p. 55). The changes observed went beyond the addition of international content to instructors' courses, although this did occur. Faculty

reported increased self and social awareness, new consciousness of the dynamics of teacher-student relations, and changes in teaching style (Sandgren et al., 1999). When faculty are involved in exchanges, then, the ripple effect should be considerable. Therefore, most of the case studies in this volume describe institutional collaborations; in most, faculty and student exchanges are components of the collaborations along with other activities.

Consultative collaborations are prevalent as a form of faculty exchange. Lessons learned from the past have prompted current consultations to be nonobtrusive, to have clear expectations of mutuality and trust, to be based on viable partnerships, to show respect for indigenous models of social work and existing social institutions, and to be culturally sensitive and culturally relevant (see chapter 2 for an elaboration). Attention to process and the subtleties of communication in a different language and tradition are critically important. Although some faculty collaborations involve a partnership between two social work schools, others involve wider coalitions either within the university systems or within the wider community, including social welfare agencies, NGOs, and local government departments in the host country. Faculty activities can involve teaching in the host institution, joint development of teaching materials, program development including the development of degree programs, curriculum design, joint research and publication, and training for community groups.

The majority of collaborations involving North American partners state learning about difference and developing respect for diversity as goals. In contrast, a series of collaboration programs initiated by the European Union was part of a wider scheme to foster Europeanization through educational exchange. The initial project was the ERASMUS program, later replaced by SOCRATES. These institutional arrangements encouraged student exchanges among European institutions. The idea was "harmonization": the use of exchange to move toward more uniform standards, courses, and structures among social work (and other) programs in Europe (Lyons, 1996) to ultimately promote professional mobility across borders. In other words, exchanges were funded to make social work education more similar. In most of the North American examples discussed in our volume, collaborations were created to benefit from diversity.

Rare but interesting is the use of collaboration to bring change to a specific area of practice. Dominelli

(2000) describes a six-university, four-country educational exchange project focused on child welfare practice. Between 1997 and 2000, this European Union–Canada project placed a total of 44 students in international field placements in child welfare, in addition to sponsoring faculty and practitioner exchange visits and joint publications. By focusing on a single practice area, the participants hoped that learning different approaches to child welfare would introduce seeds of change into practice and policy. The project stands out in both its size and the scope of its goal to influence child welfare policy and practice.

The revolution in electronic communication has facilitated collaborative efforts. Apart from instant access to information on other cultures and programs at foreign institutions through the Internet, email can make assisting and expanding a collaboration easier and can allow for continuous contact. Social work educators' burgeoning interest in this area is expected to increase its use in international exchange (see Estes, 1999). In her article on "globalization from below," Johnson (1999) describes how distance-learning techniques can facilitate interaction between students in different countries. The interesting email partnership she pioneered is portrayed in our concluding chapter, along with an elaboration on other uses of technology for exchange. While very promising, this technology is not available on as wide a scale as needed internationally, and the realities of unpredictable conditions and limited technological support may prove frustrating for potential partners. However, some countries in continents outside North America already have the necessary technology and are looking for linkage partners.

Some have suggested that the growth of international Internet-based distance education and the increasing use of technology will mean that fewer students will study abroad in the future. However, if professors become more involved in the design and the delivery of education for students from diverse countries, "perhaps academic staff will need to be more mobile so that they can better transmit international knowledge and understanding to students" (Altbach & Teichler, 2001, p. 20).

GOALS AND POTENTIAL OUTCOMES OF COLLABORATIONS

In planning and developing a collaborative project, it is important to identify the goals and expected benefits or outcomes. As noted above, these outcomes can include individual advantages for participants, institutional benefits, and in some cases, impact beyond the participating institutions, even systemic change.

One of the main goals of international collaboration is to prepare students and faculty to function more effectively in a global society and to respond more appropriately to issues generated by a global economy described earlier in this chapter. Another more long-standing goal is the development of knowledge, attitudes, and skills required to work cross-nationally and cross-culturally at home with different populations. Many programs involving student and faculty exchanges identify the sensitizing of participants to issues of social and economic justice worldwide as a goal. A related outcome for exchanges involving North American students and faculty is increased awareness of the effects of Western policies on the welfare of people in the global South. As the concept of international civil society takes hold, helping students (and faculty) understand the rights and responsibilities of "global citizenship" is an emerging and important goal of exchanges (Drover, 2000; Hokenstad & Kendall, 1995; Lorenz, 1994; Olsen, 1996; Sarri, 1997).

Altbach and Teichler (2001) posit that a paradigm shift is occurring in international collaboration that is moving the emphasis from experiences to competencies. They argue that "the traditional commitment to the 'exchange paradigm,' which supported the basic concept of exchange as a value in itself, is being eroded" and is in danger of being replaced by a "competition paradigm" that will force a hard look at measurable results (p. 21). The traditional and long-standing goal of many international exchange programs has been to increase international understanding. Although this is still a crucial element, it may be viewed as less important than the goal of preparation for the globalized world of work. The "traditional ideal of a cultural experience has been superceded by the goal of obtaining knowledge useful for the new internationalized professions of the postindustrial era" (Altbach & Teichler, 2001, p. 17). As social work institutions consider international collaborations, a range of possible goals and outcomes exists, then, from the more traditional goals of cross-cultural experience to the newer concept of using exchange to prepare for professional functioning in the global era.

The U.S. Department of State, Bureau of Educational and Cultural Affairs (USDOS), has identified a set of important and more specific benefits to be derived from international linkages between academic institutions:

1. Strengthened teaching, research, administrative, and public service capacity for all partner institutions;
2. Establishment, expansion, or reform of educational programs;
3. New pedagogical models and educational materials;
4. Collaborative research; and
5. Outreach to local communities and relevant professional, nongovernmental, and government entities (USDOS, 2002).

These outcomes are reflected in the case studies in this volume and more broadly in the goals that international collaborations in social work have sought to achieve. Among these goals are the following:

- Building a cadre of leadership in the social welfare field in the host country;
- Restructuring social work education to increase its relevance to the social situation in the host country as defined by that country;
- Conferring status on social work as a profession both within the university and within the community at large;
- Helping front-line workers to be more effective in community development through "train the trainers" educational programs;
- Expanding the coverage of global issues by Western schools of social work through interaction with international partner universities;
- Increasing regional mobility of social workers through education, exchanges, and other activities;
- Increasing the cultural competence of the students and faculty of all participanting institutions;
- Developing a specific product, such as a new or joint degree program;
- Developing tools and skills for cross-national comparisons in policy, practice, and research; and
- Promoting mutual learning, hopefully in all cases.

These goals are operationalized in many ways, including exchanges of curriculum materials; joint work on new teaching materials and teaching techniques; collaborative research projects; joint conferences, seminars, and workshops; for-credit study tours; and field-placement exchanges. These activities and their institutional impact are discussed in depth in the case studies.

Regardless of the goals and means used, we believe that collaborations and exchanges will play increasingly

critical roles in raising the profession's global awareness and profile within the university in the 21st century. Additional attention is needed to ensure that students in all countries will benefit from international learning and exchange.

It may be particularly important for faculty in the United States to expand participation in international collaborations. A 14-country study of university professors found that "the American professoriate is the least committed to internationalism" (Altbach & Lewis, 1998, p. 1). Only slightly more than 50% of U.S. faculty said that connections with scholars in other countries are important; the lowest percentage for the 13 other responding countries was 78%. U.S. faculty also study and conduct research in other countries far less often than the faculty from the other participant countries. Only 35% of U.S. respondents had gone abroad for scholarly work in the 3 years preceding the study; this compares with 53% of professors from England, 75% of Swedish professors, and 93% of professors from Israeli universities. In summary, U.S. faculty spent comparatively little time collaborating with colleagues from other countries. Yet, the United States educates more foreign students than do other countries and receives many visiting scholars and researchers. This situation suggests the danger of "a neocolonialism characteristic of an earlier era," as many U.S. academics seem to view internationalism as a "one-way process" (Altbach & Lewis, 1998, p. 3). The authors of the study conclude, as do the editors of this volume, that "what is needed are programs that promote faculty and student exchange" (p. 3).

Midgley (1992) predicted that through international exchange "social work will increase its knowledge base and test and refine its practice methods, share innovations, and develop into an internationally recognized profession" (p. 13). To realize this potential, there must be increased participation. Even more importantly, collaborations must be based on sound principles and careful planning.

IMPLEMENTING AND EVALUATING A COLLABORATION

The successful collaboration, as demonstrated by the models in this volume and in the literature, has three essential ingredients: (1) sustainability; (2) mutuality, with each partner contributing and benefiting in a meaningful way; and (3) the ripple effect that comes from institutional commitment and involvement that goes beyond that of a few individual faculty members.

Sustainability allows the collaborative partners to benefit from this experience and make improvements over time. Mutuality ensures that the partners are invested in the exchange and will benefit equally, although not necessarily in the same way. Institutional commitment ensures that support will be sufficient to sustain the program for the period agreed upon without compromising the goals and objectives. Without administrative commitment, appropriate arrangements may not be made to give faculty sufficient time to devote to the collaboration. If the institution is not committed, the collaboration may be too dependent upon the devotion of a particular faculty member, resulting in the collapse of the project if that person leaves. International partnerships require energy and investment in organizing, facilitating, and sustaining the program. Faculty need administrative support in order to provide the required time and effort.

Possibilities for sustainability need to be set out at the beginning of a collaboration project and built into the model. Otherwise, support may not be allocated and the project may become a one-time program. The parties should also discuss and plan how they will ensure mutuality in order to prevent domination by one partner. A formal contract or partnership agreement is helpful and should include plans for both sustainability and mutuality.

Ideally, an evaluation component should be built into the project from the beginning and should be designed to receive feedback from all participants. The contract or agreement is useful for evaluation because it provides a basis either for ongoing assessment or final assessment after the project concludes. Evaluation should focus on the critical factors of mutuality, sustainability, and ripple effect. Ripple effect is an important consideration in program evaluation. It is the impact that might not have been anticipated, but which provides benefits to the participating institutions, faculty, and students, or which positively influences curriculum development, organizational development, local and indigenous organizations, or the local community. Evaluation of this effect can be taken into account and built into the model if the project is continued or replicated.

Successful collaborations depend upon how seriously organizers consider and address the factors discussed above (Healy, Maxwell, & Pine, 1999; Ramanathan & Link, 1999). Chapter 2 will elaborate on these factors, drawing on research in interorganizational theory to provide additional support.

THE MODELS

The models in this volume are examples of existing programs or those undertaken and completed in the past decade. They reflect and report on the criteria the editors thought would be useful for educators wishing to establish collaborative programs. These models are not intended to be an exhaustive representation of the various programs currently in existence or from previous years. They do demonstrate creative ways of establishing collaborations across international boundaries.

The editors asked the case study authors to cover the following elements:

- Reasons for establishing the collaboration (i.e., the instigating factors);
- Goals of the collaboration;
- Issues of common interest between the collaborating institutions;
- A description of what was exchanged during the relationship (e.g., faculty, students, teaching materials, program development ideas);
- Institutional support and efforts to institutionalize the collaboration by either or both participants;
- Challenges in achieving mutuality and a description of how mutuality was built into the collaboration;
- Results (i.e., what impact the collaboration had for both institutions and their personnel;
- The evaluation component, if any;
- Prospects for the future of the collaboration;
- Lessons learned (including an analysis of factors that contributed to success and those that could have been improved); and
- Possibilities for replication by others.

Preceding the cases, in chapter 2, Lynne Healy focuses on the theoretical issues related to collaboration and suggests possible theoretical frameworks for guiding these efforts. She notes that although international exchange relationships are fundamentally agreements and relationships between organizations, rarely do schools of social work consider organizational theory when making decisions about initiating such programs and maintaining them. Her examination of relevant theory on interorganizational relationships, exchange, and collaboration illuminates factors that have fostered successful collaborations and impeded others. She states that mutuality is the cornerstone of a successful exchange program and the foundation for the future development of international social work. Citing Midgley's (1981) classic criticism of the export model of social work described as "social work imperialism," Healy notes the negative impact these models had on the development of locally relevant forms of social work, particularly in developing countries. Healy also describes the tangible and intangible resources involved in an exchange; the importance of access, legitimacy, and reputation; goal-setting; and the interpersonal and cultural factors relevant to successful linkages. This chapter also examines the concepts of institutionalization and sustainability—two criteria the editors considered important in selecting the models for this volume.

Chapters 3–13 are case studies of educational collaboration. The linkages described involve students, faculty, or both and resulted in a variety of tangible outcomes.

Chapter 3 by Rosemary J. Link and Gabi Čačinovič Vogrinčič describes an exchange between the Department of Social Work at Augsburg College, in Minneapolis, Minnesota, and the School of Social Work at the University of Ljubljana, Slovenia that is part of a college-wide formal exchange. The program is interdisciplinary and involves departments of education, business, philosophy, and social work.

This exchange clearly demonstrates mutuality and emphasizes a maximum role for student involvement. The program has been in existence since 1996, and its success has depended heavily on a strong mutual institutional commitment. Despite the remarkable differences in the environments and culture of Slovenia, which gained its independence from the former Yugoslavia in 1991, and Midwestern Minneapolis, the commitment to mutual learning, as opposed to exportation of consulting skills, made this program a success. The case demonstrates how a formal agreement between institutions can outline the specific components of the project and specify the responsibilities of each party. This example also shows the benefits of a built-in review process. Of particular interest are suggestions for working with a country identified as "in transition" and suggestions for navigating the nuances of cultural sensitivity. Careful attention is given to the process of establishing a collaboration in an area identified as a "hot spot." Enlightening lessons are learned as both institutions struggled to produce social work practitioners who would serve as global citizens.

The intricacies of Asian–U.S. collaborations have perhaps received less attention in the literature than collaborations involving other continents. Peter C. Y. Lee's discussion in chapter 4 describing a project involving Tunghai University in Taiwan and San Jose State University in California makes an excellent contribution toward filling that void. The conceptualization of this collaboration began prior to the formation of the first Sino-American Conference on Social Welfare Development in 1981, and this project has continued for 2 decades. The author examines what he regards as the misguided Western consultative assistance for establishing Asian social work programs in the 1970s and 1980s, and proceeds to describe Taiwan's search for professional social work training that is culturally relevant. He draws significant contrasts between the philosophy, sociocultural values, behavior, and problems facing social workers in Western countries and the Asian-Pacific region. The need for a Western-oriented social work solution to all problems is not a given. Considering the harsh social and economic realities faced by so much of the world's population, Lee argues that persons involved in international collaborations must be prepared to adopt a social development approach that cuts across populations, is not clinically oriented, and focuses on the development of an entire society.

The objectives of this collaboration involved identifying curricular needs in both countries, exchanging faculty and students, conducting joint research, and bringing together U.S. and Chinese social welfare administrators and educators to address major issues in the Chinese community in Taiwan. Lee attributes the long-standing success of this collaboration to consistent international funding, technological support, organized training, professional exchanges, and frequent conferences that bring together faculty, government officials, social welfare scholars, NGO representatives, and practitioners.

Chapter 5, by M. C. "Terry" Hokenstad, analyzes a collaboration that grew out of the upheavals in Eastern European countries following the end of the Cold War. This collaboration is between the Department of Social Policy and Social Work at Eotvos Lorand University (ELTE) in Budapest, Hungary and the Mandel School of Applied Social Sciences at Case Western Reserve University (CWRU), in Cleveland, Ohio, and involves the exchange of educators. The linkage reflects the emergence of a new era in Eastern European–U.S. relations that has fostered increased political and economic interaction and an environment conducive to expanding international contact, including exchanges in education and research. While Eastern Europe's recent switch to a free market economy has brought increased economic opportunity, it has also spawned problems requiring the assistance of professionally trained social workers. This social transition that occurred in the 1990s provided an ideal opportunity for developing a collaboration.

Benefits extended beyond the institutional affiliation because ELTE's Department of Social Policy and Social Work provided national leadership for the establishment of the social service professions during the 1990s. Funding by the U.S. Information Agency enabled faculty members from ELTE and CWRU to make 12 exchange visits between 1991 and 1996. Their objectives included providing international teaching expertise at both universities in social policy, human development, and research, offering consultation in the expansion and enrichment of CWRU's curriculum, and promoting scholarship in international and comparative social policy and social work. Ripple effects of this exchange had an impact on the several colleges and universities offering social work education in Hungary, and increased the global awareness of the students and faculty at CWRU. A major contribution of this chapter is the description of factors necessary for a successful collaboration.

Chapter 6 by John A. Maxwell and Lynne M. Healy describes what the authors label a "true partnership:" the ongoing linkage between the Department of Sociology and Social Work at the University of the West Indies, Mona Campus (UWI), in Jamaica, and the University of Connecticut School of Social Work (UConn), in West Hartford. Although this is a collaboration between an institution in a developing country and a North American university, it was not conceived nor implemented as a North to South consultation project. The ongoing project has lasted about a decade and features varied and sustained activities and accomplishments. The identification of a common issue of interest, West Indian migration, is a key element of this partnership. It complements two other linkage goals: the mutual interest in increased publication and research and UConn's goal of increasing outreach to the Caribbean American population in Connecticut.

Positive outcomes include the exchange of faculty resulting in seminars and workshops for students and faculty at both institutions, workshops for area practitioners, shared teaching materials, curriculum development, joint research, joint presentations at national and international conferences, joint publications, and a for-credit study tour. Although efforts were targeted at the MSW level, the BSW program at UWI also benefited as

UWI faculty teach at both levels. Through the interactions, UWI faculty have gained increased access to opportunities for conference presentations and publications. Recently, *The Caribbean Journal of Social Work* was launched and a textbook is likely to be a by-product of a conference held in Jamaica in 1999. Institutional benefits to UConn include curriculum enrichment, enhanced reputation in the West Indian community, increased national and regional visibility, and enhanced faculty productivity.

Chapter 7 by Terry Saunders Lane, Ole Langsted, and Lee H. Staples is the only case in this collection that illustrates a partnership between institutions in two wealthy industrialized nations—Boston University, in Massachusetts, and the National Danish School in Aarhus, Denmark. The collaboration has lasted over 10 years, from 1989 to the present, and it demonstrates the ways that social work educators and students from two wealthy countries can engage in mutual learning. The exchange included regular week-long study programs for faculty and students, lectures by visiting faculty at both schools, and field placements for Danish students in Boston human service agencies.

The project was initiated by Boston University as a way of deepening its focus on international social work. Goals emphasized the development of knowledge, attitudes, and skills. The knowledge component concentrates on social work practice and professional issues. Attitude goals relate to student self-awareness through cross-cultural learning, and it is anticipated that the emphasis on knowledge and attitudes will lead to skill development in cultural competence. There is also a strong emphasis on ethics. While both countries are industrialized, their welfare policies and practices are quite different, providing opportunities for cultural learning and practice for both groups of students.

Although limited funding for students resulted in inadequate enrollment in some years, the collaboration has thrived due to the personal commitment and dedication of the organizers and the mutual institutional supports. The program's longevity has allowed the organizers to benefit from experience and make improvements every year. Major mutual benefits include the exchange of knowledge, the development of curricula, and the emergence of strong friendships. The authors discuss key factors necessary to replicate this type of exchange.

Chapter 8 by Doreen Elliott, Catheleen Jordan, Manuel Ribeiro Ferreira, Santos H. Hernández, and Héctor Luis Díaz describes the Joint Doctoral Program in

Social Work and International Comparative Policy between the University of Texas at Arlington and Universidad Autónoma de Nuevo León, Monterrey, Mexico. This program is an excellent example of international collaboration in doctoral education and clearly demonstrates issues of mutuality in program development and implementation. Initiated in the fall of 1997, this 57-credit dual-degree program specializes in international comparative social policy; it was also the first doctoral program in Mexico. Major goals for this program include preparing future leaders in social work to deal with complex social problems at local, state, national, and international levels, and the production of scholars competent in research, evaluation, and critical analysis. Student exchange is the cornerstone of the project and all students take courses both in Mexico and Texas; graduates receive degrees from both universities.

A critical factor in the success of this program is the financial support of both universities. A binational doctoral faculty is charged with the responsibility of program management, evaluation, and follow-up. The authors describe their extensive evaluation of the program, which should be very helpful to other educators contemplating establishing this kind of linkage.

The chapter contains a thoughtful analysis of the challenges to program development and implementation, some of which are inevitable given the bilingual nature of the program, the different educational philosophies and practices at the two institutions, and the financial burden for students. Plans are under consideration to expand this collaborative effort into a trinational program that would include Canada.

Chapter 9 by Julia A. Guevara and Ruth S. Ylvisaker presents a different type of collaboration by describing and contrasting two models for providing students with relevant learning: a Home Model and a Host Model. This chapter enhances this volume because the partnership involves BSW students. The two linkages discussed are between Grand Valley State University (GVSU), in Allendale, Michigan, and NGOs in El Salvador, and between GVSU and the University of Natal in Durban, South Africa.

In the Home Model, social work faculty have the responsibility for directing academic learning and direct service experience in collaboration with nongovernmental social service agencies in the host country. This model is unique because most schools of social work provide international experiences through linkages with an institution of higher education. The nature of the current social upheaval in El Salvador made linkage

with such an institution there unfeasible, thus GVSU formed linkages with a number of NGOs. In this service-learning model, students have to undertake work that is meaningful to the community. The model was piloted in El Salvador and has been replicated in Ireland and Albania. It requires students to engage in a comparative study of social work between countries while contributing hands-on work hours. Part of the experience involves a live-in stay with a host family for both students and faculty. This chapter examines the positive benefits and limitations associated with NGO linkages.

In the Host Model, faculty collaborate with the university directors of an established international program. Social welfare comparisons are made between countries while students have a direct service experience in their field of choice in an international setting. The linkage described is between GVSU and a 6-week International Winter School at the University of Natal. Students alternate between the classroom and service learning in social agencies.

Although direct exchange of students or faculty is not the focus of either of the above models, collaboration between host and hosted is important for their success. The authors examine the benefits the two models have provided for GVSU students, the collaborating agencies, and GVSU as an institution. Future plans call for efforts to help South African students undertake service learning in the United States.

The model described by Robert Constable, Regina Kulys, and W. David Harrison in chapter 10 starts with individual faculty members initiating a collaboration and seeking support of their university as needed. This consultative model relies on individual expertise as well as support from a variety of organizations. Over a period of 9 years, from September, 1991, the authors developed the Vytautas Magnus University Center for Professional Social Work Education in Kaunas, Lithuania. The Center involved diverse governmental, religious, and private agencies in Lithuania and universities in the United States and Lithuania. Its initial purpose was to "educate the educators"—leaders and developers of social work. A master's degree program has been established and 11 of the graduates are at various stages of doctoral study.

Social work had never existed as a profession in Lithuania. Concepts of practice became clearer as the program developed and as the authors worked to establish a balance between direct practice with individuals and families and social development. It was a challenge for members of the complex network comprising the Center to work together, and these foreign consultants helped provide the continuity for the program to develop. The program's sustainability is a result of the delicate balancing act between university, governmental, and private sectors and the mutually understood boundaries that had to be maintained to develop outcomes everyone could support.

Support from the authors' own universities in the form of scholarships, sabbaticals, leaves of absence, and other tradeoffs helped to sustain the Center, but not without some difficulties for the U.S. faculty. The complexities of the overseas consultants' role in developing local leadership while potential local leaders prefer to depend too heavily on the consultants' expertise present serious, but not uncommon, dilemmas to the U.S. participants.

An important contribution of this chapter is the description of the Lithuanian students' struggle to reconcile the social work values they were learning with the oppressive practices in social agencies in which they were placed. Another is the assessment of how Western faculty coped and thrived in an educational environment in which culturally different students were struggling to become professional social workers. Official transition of the program to Lithuanian leaders and full incorporation into the Vytautas Magnus University took place in May, 1997. The authors describe the steps necessary to maintain consultative contact with the program as graduates move into high-level positions in Lithuania.

Chapter 11 by Wes Shera describes a collaborative project between a Western university and a ministry-based school of social work. This interinstitutional co-operative program between the University of Toronto Faculty of Social Work, Ontario, Canada, and the Sri Lanka School of Social Work, in Colombo, Sri Lanka, is not unlike many consultations that emerged in English-speaking former colonies in the 1970s and 1980s. The project's overall objective was to increase the capacity of the Sri Lanka School of Social Work to contribute to the country's development efforts and to increase the capacity of the Canadian social work educators to provide appropriate technical assistance for these efforts. The social development model was mutually agreed upon as the guiding framework. Beginning in 1983, mutual efforts included a planned program for the development of social work education, upgrading curriculum within the context of social development needs in Sri Lanka, strengthening diploma-level training, planning for master's-level training, and

analysis and evaluation. The project was funded by the Canadian International Development Agency (CIDA), UNICEF, the Ministry of Social Services in Sri Lanka, and the University of Toronto Faculty of Social Work.

The objectives were achieved through the use of Canadian social work educators as consultants, ongoing evaluation, orientation programs, joint workshops, development of indigenous teaching materials, and the provision of advanced educational opportunities for Sri Lankan faculty. The author describes the nature and advantages of short- and long-term consultations and presents a six-stage framework identifying required activities that were focal points of the collaboration.

In international work much occurs that is beyond the control of the program—including major upheavals and disasters rarely encountered in North America. The author describes how these contextual variables can affect the outcome of the most well-planned collaboration. Documentation of program activities and the impact of this linkage provides a valuable resource for anyone wishing to replicate this model. The long-term beneficial effects of this program are still in evidence.

In chapter 12, author Maureen Wilson analyzes a successful South-North development partnership between the University of Calgary in Alberta, Canada and the Escuela de Trabajo Social at the Universidad Centroamericana, in Managua, Nicaragua. The partnership, funded by CIDA, reflects how social work redefined its philosophy and activities in accord with the political events of the late 1980s through the early 1990s. This new role was based on Paulo Freire's methodology of popular education and popular participation, which stressed activism on behalf of the poor and promotion of social change.

The 5-year project was designed to enhance Nicaragua's ability to effectively plan, implement, and evaluate social policies and community-based programs. Strengthening the country's only school of social work was seen as the mechanism for the development of the human resources necessary to carry out the plan. Planning and development were implemented through a participatory process reflecting a shared philosophy of "accompaniment," which clearly identified the Nicaraguan partners as the owners and controllers of the process and the "outsiders" (Canadian partners) as accompanying their process. Implicit in the concept of accompaniment are the concepts of "empowerment" and "participation" and attention to these ideas was considered critical in accounting for the project's success. The on-site presence of Canadian partners who shared both the process of goal implementation and the vicissitudes of daily life in a society in transformation greatly facilitated mutual learning. The author describes how the external environment played a role in project implementation. Political and economic disorder, daily survival issues, and the struggles of the social work program to maintain its position in the university under conditions of restructuring hindered the realization of some of the projects' goals.

Program activities included academic upgrading, curriculum development, public education, and the creation of a Social Action Documentation Center that houses collections on Latin American social work, social policy, and related areas—a valuable resource for faculty, students, program graduates, NGOs, and members of the community. The author discusses the unanticipated spin-offs from the project and direct and indirect benefits to Canadian students, faculty, and the academic community at large. She also outlines a set of practical principles that will help make Southern partners genuine agents of their own change process, rather than passive recipients of development assistance, thus avoiding "professional imperialism."

Chapter 13 by Wayne Evens, Marjorie J. Malkin, Mizanur R. Miah, Ivan Nikolov, Kathleen Welshimer, Sue Tebb, Patsy D. Tracy, and Martin B. Tracy depicts a multi-institutional collaboration between two coalitions—one in Russia and one in the United States. The social work program at Southern Illinois University at Carbondale (SIUC) was interested in establishing a relationship with academic institutions and social service agencies in Russia for faculty and student exchange, possible practicum placement sites, and joint research projects. Russian social workers hoped to use this collaboration as leverage for institutional development and funding. A memorandum of understanding between the Togliatti Social and Economic College, in Togliatti, Russia, and SIUC, later to include the Institute for Teacher Re-Training and Staff Development in Education, in Samara, Russia, facilitated the project.

The model was a "meeting of peers" rather than a teaching model. The roles of the U.S. coalition were to consult with the Russian partners in determining their own needs and in planning curricula, and to coteach lectures, seminars, and workshops. The authors outline the basic philosophy and principles that guided the interaction and describe the process by which broad-based coalitions, encompassing academic institutions, government and nongovernment agencies, nonprofit

social service agencies, and other professionals, in Samara Oblast, Russia, and the United States evolved. The U.S. coalition continues to expand, currently embracing NASW and other academic institutions. Strong institutional support and direct and in-kind funding contributed to the project's success. The first Russian–American Summer University, in 1998, drew in a wide range of professionals. The authors describe the steps leading up to this successful educational experience, specify the issues that presented obstacles to mutuality, and offer a prescription for replication of this kind of institutional collaboration.

The Russian participants have benefited through exposure to new teaching methods, techniques, and ideas. Recently awarded training grants, including one with an exchange component, will help sustain this effort. The experiences of the U.S. academic participants informed their teaching and research, broadened their perspectives on practice and service delivery, and enriched the curriculum at SIUC.

The concluding chapter by M. C. "Terry" Hokenstad examines the models of collaboration presented in this volume in the context of increasing global interdependence. First, he points out the societal and environmental forces that influence international exchange, and then he reviews the various types of collaboration using examples from the previous chapters. Particular attention is given to program focus and objectives, but program activities and sources of financial support are also considered. The principles of mutuality, sustainability, and ripple effect are reexamined based on this review. According to the author, the lessons learned from the collaborations presented in this volume should help us to design more effective exchange programs. The chapter concludes with a look at the future of international exchange in social work education.

To borrow the words of Altbach and Teichler (2001), "we are convinced that the communication and interaction among students, scholars and researchers remains of importance—indeed is central in the environment of the 21st century" (p. 5). We hope that the following chapters will assist educators in developing and strengthening international collaborations.

REFERENCES

Abrahams, C., & Shera, W. (1984).The Canada/Sri Lanka social work education linkage project. In D. Kimberley, (Ed.) *Beyond national boundaries:*

Canadian contributions to international social work and social welfare (pp.4-22). Ottawa, Canada: Canadian Association of Schools of Social Work.

Altbach, P. G., & Lewis, L. S. (1998). Internationalism and insularity: American faculty and the world. *Change, 30*(1), 1-4. Retrieved July 26, 2002, from the InfoTrac database.

Altbach, P. G., & Teichler, U. (2001). Internationalization and exchanges in a globalized university. *Journal of Studies in International Education, 5*(1), 5-25.

Annan, K. A. (1999). *Facing the humanitarian challenge: Towards a culture of prevention.* New York: United Nations Department of Public Information.

Asamoah, Y. A., & Beverly, C. C. (1988). Collaboration between Western and African schools of social work: Problems and possibilities. *International Social Work, 31*(3), 177-193.

Asamoah, Y., Healy, L. M., & Mayadas, N. (1997). Ending the international-domestic dichotomy: New approaches to a global curriculum for the Millennium. *Journal of Social Work Education, 33,* 389-401.

Ayton-Shenker, D. (1995). *The challenge of human rights and cultural diversity: United Nations background note.* New York: United Nations Department of Public Information.

Canadian Association of Social Workers. (2000, July). Social work and globalization [Special issue]. *Canadian Social Work, 2*(1).

Deslauriers, J. P., Dunberry, G., Gendron, J. L., Lefrançois, R., Malavoy, M., Perron, J., & St. Martin, N. (1984). Expérience d'échange interuniversitaire France-Québec. In D. Kimberley (Ed.), *Beyond national boundaries* (pp.23-41). Ottawa, Canada: Canadian Association of Schools of Social Work.

Dominelli, L. (2000). *International social work placements: The European Union-Canada exchange on child abuse, protection and welfare.* Unpublished Manuscript.

Drover, G. (2000, July). Redefining social citizenship in a global era. *Canadian Social Work* [Special issue], *2*(1), 29-49.

Elliot, D., & Mayadas, N. (1999). Infusing global perspectives into social work practice. In C. S. Ramanathan & R. J. Link (Eds.), *All our futures: Principles and resources for social work practice in a global era* (pp. 52-68). Belmont, CA: Brooks/Cole.

Estes, R. (1999). Informational tools for social workers: Research in the global age. In C. S. Ramanathan, & R. J. Link (Eds.), *All our futures:*

Principles and resources for social work practice in a global era (pp. 121-137). Belmont, CA: Brooks/Cole.

Healy, L., Maxwell, J., & Pine, B. A. (1999). Exchanges that work: Mutuality and sustainability in a Caribbean/U.S.A. academic partnership. *Social Development Issues, 21,* 14-21.

Healy, L. M. (2001). *International social work: Professional action in an interdependent world.* New York: Oxford University Press.

Healy, L. M., & Asamoah, Y. (1997). *Global perspectives in social work education: A collection of course outlines on international aspects of social work.* Alexandria, VA: Council on Social Work Education.

Hokenstad, M. C., & Kendall, K. A. (1995). International social work education. In R. L. Edwards (Ed.), *Encyclopedia of social work* (19th ed., pp. 1511-1520). Washington, DC: NASW Press.

Hokenstad, M. C., & Midgley, J. (Eds.). (1997). *Issues in international social work: Global challenges for a new century.* Washington, DC: NASW Press.

Ife, J. (2000, July). Localized needs and a globalized economy: Bridging the gap with social work practice. *Canadian Social Work* [Special issue], *2*(1), 50-64.

Johnson, A. (1999). Globalization from below: Using the Internet to internationalize social work education. *Journal of Social Work Education, 35,* 377-393.

Jones, J. F., & Kumsa, A. (1999). Professional growth in the global context. In C. S. Ramanathan & R. J. Link (Eds.), *All our futures: Principles and resources for social work practice in a global era* (pp. 206-218). Belmont, CA: Brooks/Cole.

Kendall, K. (1994). The challenges of internationalism in social work: Past, present and future [Keynote address]. In *The global-local link: International challenges to social work practice* (pp. 3-11). West Hartford, CT: Center for International Social Work Studies, University of Connecticut.

Laforest, M., Naltchayan, M., & Bilodeau, G. (1984). Une expérience de coopération. In D. Kimberley (Ed.), *Beyond national boundaries* (pp.66-86). Ottawa, Canada: Canadian Association of Schools of Social Work.

Lorenz, W. (1994). *Social work in a changing Europe.* London: Routledge.

Lyons, K. (1996, July). *Education for international social work.* Presented at the Joint World Congress of the International Federation of Social Workers and the International Association of Schools of Social Work, Hong Kong.

Lyons, K., & Ramanathan, C. S. (1999). Models of field practice in global settings. In C. S. Ramanathan & R. J. Link (Eds.), *All our futures: Principles and resources for social work practice in a global era* (pp. 174-192). Belmont, CA: Brooks/Cole.

Mary, N. L. (1997). Linking social welfare policy and global problems: Lessons learned from an advanced seminar. *Journal of Social Work Education, 33,* 587-597.

Mattessich, P. W., & Monsey, B. R. (1992). *Collaboration: What makes it work.* St. Paul, MN: Amherst H. Wilder Foundation.

Measuring globalization. (2001). *Foreign Policy,* 1-11. Retrieved April 3, 2001, from the InfoTrac database.

Mericourt, B. (2001). Unequal but mutually beneficial partnerships in social development: A case example. *Social Development Issues, 23*(3), 43-49.

Midgley, J. (1981). *Professional imperialism: Social work in the third world.* London: Heinemann.

Midgley, J. (1992). Challenge of international social work. In M. C. Hokenstad, S. K. Khinduka, & J. Midgley (Eds.), *Profiles in international social work* (pp. 13-27). Washington, DC: NASW Press.

Midgley, J. (1997). Social work in international context: Challenges and opportunities for the 21st century. In M. Reisch & E. Gambrill (Eds.), *Social work in the 21st century* (pp. 59-67). Thousand Oaks, CA: Pine Forge.

Olsen, G. R. (1996). Public opinion, international civil society, and North-South policy since the Cold War. In O. Stokke (Ed.), *Foreign aid towards the year 2000: Experience and challenges* (pp. 333-354). London: Frank Case Co.

Prigoff, A. (1999). Global social and economic justice issues. In C. S. Ramanathan, & R. J. Link (Eds.), *All our futures: Principles and resources for social work practice in a global era* (pp. 156-174). Belmont, CA: Brooks/Cole.

Prigoff, A. (2000). *Economics for social workers: Social outcomes of economic globalization with strategies for community action.* Belmont, CA: Brooks/Cole.

Ramanathan, C. S., & Kondrat, M. (1994). Conceptualizing and implementing a social work overseas study in developing nations: Politics, realities, and strategies. *Social Development Issues, 16*(2), 69-75.

Ramanathan, C. S., & Link, R. J. (Eds.). (1999). *All our futures: Principles and resources for social work practice in a global era.* Belmont, CA: Brooks/Cole.

Razack, N. (2002). A critical examination of international student exchanges. *International Social Work, 45*(2), 251-265.

Sandgren, D., Ellig, N., Hovde, P., Krejci, M., & Rice, M. (1999). How international experience affects teaching: Understanding the impact of faculty study abroad. *Journal of Studies in International Education, 3*(1), 33-56.

Sarri, R. (1997). International social work at the millennium. In M. Reisch & E. Gambrill (Eds.), *Social work in the 21st century* (pp. 387-395). Thousand Oaks, CA: Pine Forge.

Traub-Werner, B., Shera, W., Rodriguez Villa, B. M., & Tello Péon, N. (2000). International partnerships: A Mexico-Canada social work education project. *Canadian Social Work* [Special issue], *2*(1), 184-197.

Tsang, A. K. T., Yan, M. C., & Shera, W. (2000). Negotiating multiple agendas in international social work: The case of the China-Canada collaborative project. *Canadian Social Work* [Special issue], *2*(1), 147-161.

United Nations Educational, Scientific and Cultural Organization. (1998). *World Declaration on Higher Education.* Retrieved November 10, 2002, from http://www.unesco.org/education/educprog/wche/declaration_eng.htm

United Nations Development Program. (1999). *Human development report 1999.* New York: Oxford University Press.

United Nations Development Program. (2000). *Human development report 2000: Human development and human rights.* New York: Oxford University Press.

U.S. Department of State, Bureau of Educational and Cultural Affairs. (2002). *Educational partnership programs.* Retrieved August 2, 2002, from http://exchanges.state.gov/education/partnership/

Whitmore, E., & Wilson, M. (1997). Accompanying the process: Social work and international development practice. *International Social Work, 40*(1), 57-74.

TWO

A Theory of International Collaboration: Lessons for Social Work Education

Lynne M. Healy

Schools of social work often enter international collaborative relationships due to serendipitous factors. Certainly they rarely, if ever, consider organization theory in making decisions about initiating exchange programs and maintaining these relationships. International collaborations, however, are fundamentally agreements and relationships between organizations. In this chapter, a brief examination of relevant theory on interorganizational relationships, exchange, and collaboration is provided to illuminate factors that have been found to encourage or impede successful organizational collaborations. A brief analysis of the ways in which these principles apply to social work education programs will follow, including alternative perspectives on the controversial issue of "social work imperialism" in intercountry relationships.

Relevant literature in the field of interorganizational relations includes writing on exchange theory, on interorganizational coordination and interdependence, and a fairly extensive emphasis on collaboration. Some of this research has been conducted in human service settings but relatively little is specific to university or educational programs.

DEFINITIONS AND ELEMENTS OF EXCHANGE AND COLLABORATION

Classic interorganizational exchange theory defines exchange as "any voluntary activity between two organizations which has consequences, actual or anticipated, for the realization of their goals or objectives" (Levine & White, 1961, p. 588). Exchange is an economic concept involving the assessment of costs and benefits to be incurred or gained as a result of the interorganizational activity. As such, parties can be expected to remain in exchange relationships only when the perceived benefits outweigh the costs.

Various resources are involved and are usually transferred from one organization to the other. Reid (1969) points out, however, that the transfer of resources is not necessary for exchange to occur; instead, one organization may use its resources in ways that satisfy the goals of another organization.

One-Way Versus Mutual-Exchange Relationships

In this volume, mutuality is promoted as a cornerstone of productive and sustainable exchange relationships. Yet, mutuality is not always achieved, and in fact, is often difficult to attain due to inequalities between partner institutions. Research shows, not surprisingly, that exchanges in which one partner perceives benefits from interacting while the other does not will have higher levels of interaction than pairs in which neither perceive benefits, but lower levels than exchanges in which both or all partners perceive a benefit (Schmidt & Kochan, 1977). Furthermore, the highest levels of interaction and satisfaction are between partner institutions showing symmetrical and substantial interdependence (Schmidt & Kochan, 1977). "Optimally, the benefits received are equal or equally valued, although partners may receive different 'commodities' from the exchange" (Healy, 2001, p. 263). Thus, mutuality, or at least the perception of mutuality, of benefit is key to successful collaboration. As expressed by Wimpfheimer, Bloom, and Kramer, (1990) "every party. . . has to perceive itself a winner" (p. 93).

Coordination, Interdependence, and Collaboration

Coordination and interdependence are related concepts. Coordination can be defined simply as joint or cooperative programming, often undertaken to avoid duplication of services. Viewed systemically, coordination includes elements of comprehensiveness of service, coherence and compatibility, and the demonstrated ability to work together (Aiken, Dewar, DiTomaso, Hage, & Zeitz, 1975). These characteristics are more common for service coordination projects, but they could be demonstrated in a joint venture between educational institutions to offer a continuum of educational services or related field practicum experiences through exchange. A more general definition of coordination is offered by Taylor-Powell, Rossing, and Geran (1998): "coordination is a deliberate, joint, often formalized relation among parties involving communication, some planning and division of roles, and longer term goals" (p. 5). Although some sharing of resources is involved, authority and decision making remain with the individual organizations.

Interdependence is a state achieved when each participating organization in a linkage perceives that it can achieve its goals most effectively through participation with the other partner or partners (Reid, 1969). Thus goal attainment becomes dependent upon the exchange and linkage relationships. A school of social work that offers a program of international field placements, for example, can only achieve that goal through working partnerships with one or more institutions in another country. Disrupted linkages would impede goal attainment.

The more recent interorganizational literature emphasizes collaboration and views it as a higher order relationship than coordination. Collaboration is defined as "a mutually beneficial and well-defined relationship entered into by two or more organizations to achieve common goals" (Mattessich & Monsey, 1992, p. 39). Although collaborations can be either extended or brief, the term usually refers to a more durable relationship. Among the characteristics of an exchange that is a true collaboration are comprehensive planning, well-defined communication channels, a common vision, shared risks of resources and reputation, and mutual authority over matters relevant to the collaboration (Taylor-Powell et al., 1998; Mattessich & Monsey, 1992). A successful collaboration must also remain flexible, dynamic, and ready to change in response to its environment. This characteristic is demonstrated in several of the case studies, as initial plans were reshaped in response to external conditions, such as the civil unrest in Sri Lanka (see chapter 11).

What Is Exchanged

In collaborative relationships, a variety of tangible and less tangible resources may be exchanged by the partners. In educational programs such as those described in this volume, the resources exchanged fall into three categories: material resources, including books, equipment, or even funds; expertise, including personnel; and a less tangible category that includes access, reputation, and legitimacy.

Books, educational videotapes, and journals are often sent from one partner to another in an exchange. Especially when one partner is disadvantaged in terms of access to social work resources, the more advantaged partner is likely to send materials to assist in library development, faculty research, or student instruction. Expertise is commonly exchanged in a number of ways, including faculty exchanges for short or long visits; on-site or long-distance consultation on course development, administrative problems, or other educational issues; and exchanges of course outlines, field education guidelines, and other educational information. Materials and expertise can also be exchanged to enhance the partners' knowledge of each other's social welfare systems, in order to inform teaching or research.

Access can be a particularly important resource in an exchange relationship. Partners may be able to assist each other with access to opportunities for publication, participation in conferences, research opportunities including joint research ventures, and organizational memberships. The provision of links to these opportunities may be more important than material resources in an exchange. In service-providing agencies, interagency referrals are key exchange resources. While this is less relevant in educational exchanges, some referral may occur. Students may be referred to one program by the other, especially if the partners provide different levels of education. Several of the case studies in this volume report that faculty members from one school enrolled in the doctoral program at the partner institution.

Reputation and legitimacy are also important elements in an international exchange (Rogers & Molnar, 1975). A newly developing social work program will enhance its own legitimacy through linkage with a prestigious university or an established program that enjoys a good reputation in the profession. Additionally, a social work school seeking to gain recognition for its international program will gain this legitimacy only if it can establish and maintain one or more international institutional linkages. Thus, prestige and reputation can be "transferred" from one partner to another in an exchange relationship.

VARIABLES FACILITATING OR IMPEDING COLLABORATION

Interorganizational research suggests a number of variables that can facilitate collaborative relationships or hinder their development. Some of these variables are fairly simple and obvious, while others involve complex elements of organizational and even national culture and interpersonal relations. From an extensive review of case studies, Mattessich and Monsey (1992) identified 19 factors that affect the success of collaborations. This sizable list encompasses factors related to the environment, collaboration membership, process and structure, communication, collaboration purpose, and resources. Although the list is too extensive to be fully covered, selected variables will be discussed below.

Opportunities for Contact

Not surprisingly, opportunities for contact and the proximity of the partners are positive forces in successful exchange relationships (Taylor-Powell et al., 1998; Gray, 1985). Thus, in developing a collaboration, partners should consider how ease of travel and communication, including factors such as cost, time zones, and availability of electronic communications technologies, will affect their prospects for success. In addition, partners might examine what additional opportunities for contact may exist, such as meetings at conferences. Research has found that "extra-organizational" contacts between representatives of collaborating organizations are likely to enhance their exchange, as such contacts provide additional opportunities to become familiar with the partner and to discover common ground for collaboration (Mattessich & Monsey, 1992; Halpert, 1982; Beatrice, 1990). This suggests the importance of the friendships that many educators report developing out of their exchange relationships.

Organizational Factors

Characteristics of the participating organizations also facilitate or hinder collaboration. Some of these characteristics are within the control of the partners, but others are fixed organizational factors. Formalization—the extent to which an organization runs by rules and standard procedures—and administrative autonomy are examples of the latter, while goal relevance is an example of a factor that the partners can control. Formalization leads to predictability, which may aid collaboration; it may also impair a program's capacity to enter into less formal and more flexible relationships. The degree of administrative autonomy for the social work program within its host university will shape the program's ability to freely enter into exchange agreements. Programs with greater autonomy can make less encumbered decisions; however, theory suggests that a high degree of organizational autonomy leads to

cautiousness in entering collaborations unless there are strong incentives for doing so (Maxwell, 1995).

Drawing upon their work on child welfare agency collaboration on the U.S.-Mexican border, Padilla and Daigle (1996) view formal agreements as both a positive and a negative in the implementation of a collaboration. Ideally, they recommend that formal intergovernmental agreements be developed at multiple levels, including the national level. They recognize, however, that operating at a less formal and lower level gives human service providers considerable latitude in program innovation. Thus, although there are substantial barriers to human service collaboration at the national government level, informality has allowed significant cooperation at local levels in various states. Nonetheless, Padilla and Daigle (1998) recommend the following steps in developing a successful international collaboration: forming working relationships, structuring formal agreements (where possible), identifying and securing needed reciprocity, and creating systems for exchanging information. These steps are applicable to educational exchanges as well as service-oriented programs.

Goals and Goal Relevance

Collaborations are enhanced when partners share a vision of what they want to achieve. In addition, the formulation of concrete and attainable goals and objectives has been found to increase the likelihood of success for a partnership (Mattessich & Monsey, 1992). These goals should include several that can be reached in a relatively short timeframe, as it has been found that "interim successes and a compelling reason for stakeholders to remain committed to the process are imperative" (Reilly, 2001, p. 72).

Partners will be more likely to remain committed to a collaboration if the goals of the collaboration are relevant to their own organization. As social work programs shape exchange agreements, they should pay attention to the relationship of exchange goals and organizational goals. The more the collaboration can be linked to core organizational objectives, the deeper the investment will be for the participants and the greater the likelihood that the collaboration will be supported and sustained (Mattessich & Monsey, 1992).

Interpersonal and Cultural Factors

Personnel Factors. Although collaboration projects are interorganizational relationships, they are also interpersonal relationships between the participating individuals. Therefore, personnel factors are critical. Maxwell (1995) identified a set of personal characteristics that lead to successful interorganizational exchange: high levels of interpersonal trust, openness to new learning experiences and comfort with risk taking, willingness to share decision making, a positive feeling about the personnel of the partner organization, and a "cosmopolitan ethic." The "cosmopolitan ethic" connotes a type of world-minded openness that leads to valuation of international exchange and makes learning from others possible. It is particularly important for U.S. faculty and students involved in international exchange, as studies have documented that they tend to be less globally-minded than other scholars (Altbach & Lewis, 1998).

As the emphasis on interpersonal trust would suggest, continuity in personnel is important to collaborations. High staff turnover can be problematic in sustaining any collaboration, particularly an international exchange (Taylor-Powell et al., 1998).

The Impact of National Culture. Individuals' orientation to trust, group decision making, and risk taking are shaped, in part, by the influences of their national culture. The concept of national culture has not received much attention in social work, but it is critically important in international relationships. Using trust as an example, Maxwell (1994) pointed out that "interpersonal trust is not just related to an individualistic value system. National cultures vary substantially in their tendency to trust or distrust other people" (p. 9). Thus, a relationship between an institution from a high-trust culture and one from a low-trust culture would be challenging. In this and other aspects of interpersonal orientation and attitude, relationships between individuals from different cultures can be difficult.

The Dutch scholar Geert Hofstede has studied variations in national cultures for more than 20 years. Early in his research, he identified four dimensions along which national cultures differ: power distance, uncertainty avoidance, individualism-collectivism, and masculinity-femininity (Hofstede, 1980). Later, a fifth dimension was added, long-term versus short-term orientation (Hofstede, 1993). Partner differences on any of these dimensions will make successful collaborative relationships more challenging—and, for those from cultures low in uncertainty avoidance—more interesting.

The national culture of the United States is characterized by small power distance, low uncertainty avoidance, fairly high masculinity, short-term orientation, and the highest rating on individualism of any of the 40 countries rated by Hofstede (1980). Canada shows similar characteristics, with only modestly lower ratings on individualism and masculinity. Thus, North Americans in general accord less deference to formal power, favor informality in relationships, and are able to tolerate ambiguous situations and some level of risk taking in relationships. Although male-female differences exist in all societies, dominant culture in the United States and Canada reflects masculine culture, defined as emphasis on materialism and on "tough values like assertiveness, performance, success and competition" (Hofstede, 1993, p. 90). Combining these characteristics with the strong valuation of individualism, which suggests independence, initiative, leadership, and an emphasis on the "I" over the "we," North Americans can be expected to encounter cultural dissonance in relationships with colleagues from collectivist orientations. The low power distance orientation may lead North Americans to ignore deference to formal power important in foreign institutions; the preference for informality can be misinterpreted as rudeness.

Obviously not all citizens share the attributes of their "national culture" and Hofstede's findings are generalizations. However, these ideas often ring true and should be considered in an analysis of relationship difficulties between personnel from dissimilar cultures.

EVALUATION: MEASURING SUCCESS AND IMPACT OF EXCHANGES

Counting Contact and Joint Activities

Empirical studies of exchange and collaboration projects have often relied on the simple counting of events as the prime measure of success. Frequent communication and contacts are associated with a successful collaboration, as seems relatively obvious. Thus, as international exchange relationships are implemented, programs should track the frequency of their communication and face-to-face contacts. A long hiatus or reduction in contact may signal stagnation or a reduction in the perceived relevance of the relationship.

Aiken and Hage (1968) recommend counting joint activities rather than basic contacts. In international educational collaborations, joint conference presentations, joint research studies, and joint publications are important as exchange processes and products. In some exchanges, other shared projects may be launched, such as cosponsored conferences; a cosponsored study program, which might range from a study tour to a summer institute; or, more rarely, a field or service project involving personnel from both partner institutions. The process of arranging and overseeing field placements of students from the partner institution is also legitimately classified as a joint activity. Examples of these activities are well-represented among the case study partnerships in this text.

As noted earlier, achievement of interdependence is viewed by some as a measure of the exchange relationship's success. Organizations that recognize their interdependence are more likely to undertake joint efforts (Gray, 1985). However, the point at which an exchange relationship moves to interdependence is difficult to measure with precision. Any assessment would include measures of the extent to which the exchange partner is routinely included and identified as a significant stakeholder in organizational functioning. These measures can range from counting distributions of key information (Is the partner on all key mailing lists?) to assessment of inclusion or exclusion in organizational strategic planning processes.

Measuring Institutionalization

The sustainability and the institutionalization of exchange relationships are closely linked. Institutionalization is fostered through the following means: ensuring that the international collaboration is tied to the goals and priorities of the partner institutions; assigning responsibility for maintaining the exchange relationship to an identified structure within each institution—a committee, faculty unit, or administrative office; and involving a critical mass of personnel from each institution in collaboration activities and plans. Together, these strategies ensure that an international collaboration belongs to the social work program, rather than to one or two individual faculty members. Without institutional ownership of the collaboration, such programs will not survive the departure of initiating personnel. Involvement of a critical mass of individuals also diminishes resentment of and competition for the resources that are allocated to the international exchange. In assessing the models presented in the following chapters and in implementing international collaboration programs, it is important to pay attention to strengthening goal relevance, assigning structural and procedural responsibility for exchanges, and developing strategies to encourage participation. Each of these items is an element to be assessed in evaluating success and impact.

The Role of Conflict

Collaborations develop with the partners in agreement on goals and processes. Research shows, however, that in any long-term collaboration, conflict or disagreements are likely and can be a sign of a healthy, dynamic relationship. According to one recent review article, "collaboration without conflict may indicate that parties are not communicating openly or that some key interests have not been included" (Taylor-Powell et al., 1998, p. 12). What is essential is that the partners have sufficient trust and commitment to address any areas of conflict.

SOCIAL WORK EDUCATION AND EXCHANGE

Legacy of the Export Model

A major focus for interorganizational theory is the examination of factors that encourage mutuality and equality in exchange relationships because these qualities lead to both productivity and sustainability. In social work, considerable attention has been paid to the damaging effects of unequal or one-way exchange: "At times in the history of social work, inequality of opportunity and inequality in access to resources among the countries of the world have led to negative patterns in professional communication and exchange" (Healy, 2001, p. 262). Such unequal exchange has been commonly labeled the "export model" of collaboration because it usually has involved the one-way transfer of curriculum models and content from one country to another. In the 1950s and 1960s, the transfer was primarily from the United States and the United Kingdom to the developing countries in Asia and Africa. A more recent wave of curriculum transfer has occurred from Western Europe and the United States to the newly independent states of the former Soviet Union and the countries of Eastern Europe where social work was suppressed or unknown prior to the late 1980s.

There have been numerous harsh critiques of the export model, as the following quotations illustrate:

> Despite its abiding humanitarian concerns, the current conception of professional social work. . . is generally irrelevant and sometimes dysfunctional to the resolution of the major issues that beset the poor nations. (Khinduka, 1971, p. 71)

We are beginning to see the tremendous weaknesses of our western systems of education as they are now functioning within many of the developing countries. (deJongh, 1969, p. 50)

The outcry was so voluminous that the journal, *International Social Work*, took the unusual step of declaring that no more articles on the topic would be accepted: "We have had quite a spate of contributions lately deploring the influence of American models of social work. . . that this theme is now worn threadbare, and no further articles on it will be welcome" (Irvine, 1972, p. 1).

Imperialism or Altruism?

The 1981 book by James Midgley, *Professional Imperialism: Social Work in the Third World*, continued and intensified the debate over one-way exchange by attaching the inflammatory label of "imperialism" to the efforts to spread social work throughout the world by sharing the experiences and curricula of developed nations—usually at the request of recipient institutions. He charges that "Western social workers exerted a powerful influence over their Third World colleagues and, claiming that social work has a universally relevant methodology and an international professional identity, they imposed alien theories and techniques on developing countries, which were unsuited to their cultures and development needs" (Midgley, 1981, p. xiii).

An alternative interpretation by Wagner (1992) suggests that rather than manifesting imperialistic motivations, it is likely that social work educators from nations with advanced social work educational systems were engaging in a process of "gift-giving." As explained above, exchange is essentially an economic concept. Wagner points out that social workers are often uncomfortable with economic concepts and market terminology and are therefore unlikely to characterize their international exchange relationships in terms of value transactions. When relationships are established between social work programs in countries with well-established professional education and institutions in countries that are only recently exploring the field, such as in the cases on Russia and Lithuania in this volume, a largely one-way transfer of resources is the most probable pattern: "It is unlikely that in an early phase of contact between unequal partners, transactions will be exchange-dominated" (Wagner, 1992, p. 125). Interestingly, these relationships are probably most characterized by altruistic intent on the part of those from the

more developed programs, a motivation more acceptable to social work than the purely rational weighing of costs and benefits. As Wagner states, "social workers and social work educators probably have more affinity with the concept of unilateral transfer than with the concept of exchange, because it is based on altruism rather than economic utility and self-interest" (p. 126).

This interpretation does not absolve social work of the responsibility to move beyond one-way transfer. In fact, unilateral transfers, even if altruistically motivated, still have often led to the transplantation of social welfare education and pedagogical models poorly suited to their new environments; further, the introduction of these models may impede the development of locally relevant forms of social work. Altruistic but unequal exchange may spread social work internationally, but it does little to advance the development of international social work.

CONCLUSION: MUTUALITY AS THE CORNERSTONE OF COLLABORATION

Within recent decades, numerous models of international collaboration in social work education have been developed. Increasingly, international collaborations embody two-way exchange, even if they are not perfectly symmetrical in their exchange of benefits. International exchange is viewed both as a means of enhancing the educational programs of the participants and as a force in contributing to the development of international social work. Indeed, Reilly (2001) asserts that collaboration builds social capital: "Continued interaction and discourse translated into shared understandings and mutual trust which created relational resources that could be called upon at future times. This building of relationships created social capital" (p. 70). In reading the case studies that follow, it is hoped that the reader will find evidence of the creation of social capital to further social work education, both locally and internationally.

These outcomes are achieved through a type of sharing that encourages diversity, not homogenization. Cross-fertilization is replacing export as the dominant concept in international collaboration. As summarized by Midgley (1992), "the development of authentic international collaboration in social work requires the emergence of reciprocal exchanges that are based on mutual respect for uniqueness and diversity within the profession" (p. 19). In their practical manual on collaboration, Mattessich and Monsey (1992) recommend that participants work to "make it very clear what member organizations stand to gain from the collaboration, and build those expectations into the goals so they remain visible throughout the life of the collaborative effort" (p. 21). Given a history of unequal exchange, mutuality in social work collaborations will require this level of careful and deliberate attention in order to be achieved.

The synopsis of relevant interorganizational theory presented in this chapter suggests that social work exchanges will be increasingly successful as the principle of mutuality is operationalized in program conceptualization and implementation. This will be further demonstrated in the wide variety of successful international educational collaborations described in the following case study chapters.

REFERENCES

Aiken, M., Dewar, R., DiTomaso, N., Hage, J., & Zeitz, G. (1975). *Coordinating human services.* San Francisco: Jossey Bass.

Aiken, M., & Hage, J. (1968). Organizational interdependence and intraorganizational structure. *American Sociological Review, 33,* 912-930.

Altbach, P. G., & Lewis, L. S. (1998). Internationalism and insularity: American faculty and the world. *Change, 30*(1), 1-4. Retrieved from the InfoTrac database, July 21, 2002.

Beatrice, D. (1990). Inter-agency coordination: A practitioner's guide to a strategy for effective social policy. *Administration in Social Work, 14*(4), 45-59.

deJongh, J. F. (1969). Western social work and the Afro-Asian world. *Social Service Review, 43*(1), 50-58.

Gray, B. (1985). Conditions facilitating interorganizational collaboration. *Human Relations, 38*(10), 911-936.

Halpert, B. (1982). Antecedents. In D. L. Rogers, D. A. Whetten, & Associates, (Eds.), *Interorganizational coordination: Theory, research and implementation* (pp. 54-72). Ames, IA: Iowa State University Press.

Healy, L. M. (2001). *International social work: Professional action in an interdependent world.* New York: Oxford University Press.

Hofstede, G. (1980). Motivation, leadership, and organization: Do American theories apply abroad? *Organizational Dynamics, 9*(1), 42-63.

Hofstede, G. (1993). Cultural constraints in management theories. *Academy of Management Executive, 7*(1), 81-94.

Irvine, E. E. (1972). Editorial. *International Social Work, XV*(4), 1-3.

Khinduka, S. (1971). Social work and the Third World. *Social Service Review, 45*(1), 62-73.

Levine, L., & White, P. E. (1961). Exchange as a conceptual framework for the study of interorganizational relationships. *Administrative Science Quarterly, 5,* 583-601.

Mattessich, P. W., & Monsey, B. R. (1992). *Collaboration: What makes it work? A review of research literature on factors influencing successful collaboration.* St. Paul, MN: Amherst H. Wilder Foundation.

Maxwell, J. (1994, July). *Educating social workers for interorganizational coordination.* Paper presented at the 27th Congress of the International Association of Schools of Social Work, Amsterdam, Netherlands.

Maxwell, J. (1995, March). *Factors influencing the process of interagency coordination* [International Centre Lecture]. Presented at the National Institute of Social Work, London, United Kingdom.

Midgley, J. (1981). *Professional imperialism: Social work in the Third World.* London: Heinemann.

Midgley, J. (1992). The challenge of international social work. In Hokenstad, M. C., Khinduka, S., & Midgley, J. (Eds.), *Profiles in international social work* (pp. 13-27). Washington, DC: NASW Press.

Padilla, Y. C., & Daigle, L. E. (1996). Social and economic interdependence in the U.S.-Mexico border region: Critical implications for social welfare. *New Global Development: Journal of International and Comparative Social Welfare, 12,* 65-77.

Padilla, Y. C., & Daigle, L. E. (1998). Inter-agency collaboration in an international setting. *Administration in Social Work, 22*(1), 65-81.

Reid, W. J. (1969). Interorganization coordination in social welfare: A theoretical approach to analysis and intervention. In R. Kramer & H. Specht, (Eds.), *Readings in community organization practice* (pp. 176-188). Englewood Cliffs, NJ: Prentice-Hall.

Reilly, T. (2001). Collaboration in action: An uncertain process. *Administration in Social Work, 25*(1), 53-74.

Rogers, D., & Molnar, J. (1975). *Interorganizational relations among development organizations: Empirical assessment and implications for interorganization coordination* (CARD Report 62). Ames, IA: Iowa State University Press.

Schmidt, S. M., & Kochan, T. A. (1977). Interorganizational relationships: Patterns and motivations. *Administrative Science Quarterly, 22,* 220-234.

Taylor-Powell, E., Rossing, B., & Geran, J. (1998). *Evaluating collaboratives: Reaching the potential.* Madison, WI: University of Wisconsin-Extension.

Wagner, A. (1992). Social work education in an integrated Europe: Plea for a global perspective. *Journal of Teaching in Social Work, 6*(2), 115-130.

Wimpfheimer, R., Bloom, M., & Kramer, M. (1990). Inter-agency collaboration: Some working principles. *Administration in Social Work, 14*(4), 89-102.

THREE

Learning Together Through Faculty and Student Exchange: Augsburg College and the University of Ljubljana, Slovenia

Rosemary J. Link and Gabi Čačinovič Vogrinčič

In July, 1998, social work students from the United States and Slovenia gathered at a picnic in Koper, on the Adriatic coast of Slovenia, for an evening of music, feasting, life stories, and learning. At a conference of educators the following year, one of the students, Victoria Hanson, made a presentation on the work she had done in Koper and described the evening as one she would never forget (Hanson, 1999). One of the indelible aspects of the experience for the U.S. group was the welcome extended by the families and seniors hosting the picnic. In some parts of the world, these families would be identified as "clients," whereas in this setting, they were hosts inviting guests to learn about a cross-generational project that was using seniors as mentors for families with members recovering from drug addiction. This informal yet powerful sharing of ideas is one example of the many projects that were realized during our collaboration program.

The Department of Social Work at Augsburg College, in Minneapolis, Minnesota, and the School of Social Work at the University of Ljubljana, Slovenia, have been developing student and faculty exchanges since 1996. Strong commitment from both academic institutions has facilitated and made sustainable this fruitful social work collaboration within the context of a broader interdisciplinary linkage. The dean of the School of Social Work in Ljubljana and the academic dean of Augsburg met in 1996 and saw the potential for the social workers from each school to build on their common interests and established record of internationalizing their respective curricula (Ramanathan & Link, 1999; Čačinovič Vogrinčič, 2000). The program they initiated is interdisciplinary, with colleagues in education, business, philosophy, and social work currently involved. This interaction across departments, schools, and the university has helped build strong relationships and offers insights into what makes an exchange work. In fact, the first point of contact for the exchange was through curriculum dialogue and class presentations between our business and social work majors concerning international trade and development. It is also very helpful to have at Augsburg an academic liaison for the project who speaks Croatian and has expertise in the economics and history of the area encompassing the former Yugoslavia. More will be said about these relationships as the history, goals, implementation, and evaluation of this program are discussed.

Although the ongoing work of organizing visits, developing curriculum, encouraging community liaison, hosting faculty, organizing, lobbying for budget allocation, and recruiting students involves a lot of faculty time, this work also leads to new perspectives for learning about social work internationally and unforgettable expanded experiences for students, field agency colleagues, and faculty. Reading back over the first exchange of letters has reminded the authors of how effective the newly developed relationships have become:

1997

Dear Dr. Vogrinčič:

I was very pleased to receive your letter enclosing articles. It came the week I met with Dean Marie McNeff and Professor Magda Paleczny to hear about their conversations with you and to discuss plans for the future. Our Department of Social Work has long been interested in developing international curriculum and we welcome global connections and learning.

Your plaidoyer [monograph] speaks clearly to issues of empowerment and your phrase "the family's right to reality is the basis for change" jumped off the page as I read. . . Dean McNeff tells me that you have made preliminary plans for the continued exchange of faculty and a future summer school and I look forward to hearing more about this and to contributing ideas from our Department. We have had exchanges in the past with Bristol University, England, the Lutheran College of Japan, and the National University of Mexico and we particularly welcome the opportunity to widen student and faculty knowledge of Slovenia and Central Europe.

This letter and others tell of the distance we have traveled in our understanding of reciprocity, mutual respect for political and social arrangements, and the profound learning that occurs whenever we encounter cultural differences. Such differences range from everyday activities to rituals and common expectations. For example, the first day in Slovenia, U.S. students were introduced to the bus system and found that buses run every few minutes to many destinations. They also discovered that few people rely on private cars for work and even fewer have more than one car in their family. This contrasted with the students' experience of two cars or more per U.S. family and the general wariness of public transportation in the Midwest. Similarly, students from the United States are used to eating three meals a day, plus snacks, but in Ljubljana the group usually had only two meals a day. Few people in Slovenia, excluding refugees, are unemployed, and Slovenian students visiting Minneapolis were surprised to see people begging for food and shelter in a country they perceived as richly endowed.

In the past there has been a tendency for people in well-resourced Western nations to export their expertise as consultants rather than as equals (Midgley, 1997). Although Slovenia's socialist state did not experience the same oppression as some of its formerly communist neighbors, Vaclav Havel's speech to the U.S. Congress still portrayed the nature of reciprocity we seek in this educational collaboration:

> The communist type of totalitarian system has left both our nations, Czechs and Slovaks, as it has all the nations of the Soviet Union and the other countries [of Eastern Europe], a legacy of countless dead. . . . It has also given us some-

thing positive, a special capacity to look from time to time somewhat further than someone who has not undergone this bitter experience. . . . What I'm trying to say is this: we must all learn many things from you [Americans], but it doesn't have to be merely assistance from the powerful and wealthy to someone who has less. We too can offer something to you: our experience and the knowledge that has come from it. The specific experience I'm talking about has given me one certainty: consciousness precedes being, and not the other way around. (Havel, 1990, pp. 14-15)

In this spirit of reciprocity, the following pages trace our work through a brief history of this exchange and the countries involved; a review of the components of the institutional agreement; an analysis of faculty visits and course development; an exploration of the evaluations from student exchanges; a discussion of unexpected developments; and a final summary incorporating lessons learned and future plans.

BRIEF HISTORY AND BACKGROUND OF THE EXCHANGE AND THE COUNTRIES

It is difficult to find more different environments than Minneapolis, Minnesota, and Ljubljana, Slovenia. The former, part of the Midwest region of the United States, is a metropolis set in sprawling urban stone with an ever-expanding suburban and ex-urban community. Minneapolis is surrounded by flat prairies to the south and west, fields, woods, and bluffs to the southeast, and spectacular terrain to the north, along the shores of Lake Superior and the Canadian border. Ljubljana is an ancient medieval town poised between Western and Eastern Europe with a variety of cultural influences in its architecture, including Roman mosaics and bath houses, Catholic churches, Muslim mosques, and an Austrian castle. The city lies in a basin surrounded by the Julian Alps and rushing glacial streams to the north and west and the forests of the Croatian border to the south and east.

Slovenia gained its independence from the former Yugoslavia in 1991 and is fast emerging as a mixed capitalist economy that welcomes foreign investment while keeping some basic human rights as a contemporary social state (e.g., universal access to housing, education, and health coverage). Homelessness is rare and politics are more often on the front page of newspapers than crime. As an emblem of its economic independence, Slovenia is in the process of joining the Euro-pean Union and has expanded its trade with Italy, France, Austria, and Hungary. Ljubljana seems to be thriving, and in the evening people typically prom-enade along the ancient cobbled streets above the Ljubljanica river or go to concerts. The town is full of narrow alleys, street vendors, open-air cafes, and musicians, and many lanes offer views of the Tivoli woods and castle. Slovenia's prime minister, Dr. Janez Drnovsek, recently stated that despite its natural beauty, or "blossoms," the country is in a precarious, or "thorny," economic situation with the denationalization of its major industries. Nevertheless, the general outlook of Slovenia is that of a country proud to be finding its way independent of the former Yugoslavia.

In contrast to the rapid changes of Central Europe, Minnesota is part of the settled United States, with an established market economy and a wide range of income and human needs. Minneapolis was founded in 1886 on the banks of the Mississippi river. The city is full of modern skyscrapers in its commercial downtown, but its citizens are leaving the city to live in spacious suburban areas, which means that the city center is more active for daytime business than as a place for families to live. Modern European American life flourishes in this land of lakes and rivers, long inhabited by Native American tribes, including the Dakota and the Objibwe, and their traditions live on. Minnesota is still described as a farming and logging economy, but it is also well known for its information technology industry and its tradition of democratic ideals.

Both Ljubljana and Minneapolis are beautiful in their own ways, and both have very different social, political, and economic traditions from which students can learn.

The forces that brought together Augsuburg College and the University of Ljubljana included a professor from Eastern Europe, who is an expert in economic change and who has lectured internationally, including at Augsburg College, for many years; a dean in Minneapolis interested in Eastern Europe and a counterpart in Ljubljana interested in the United States; a tradition of international exchange at both institu-tions, including the Kellogg funded Center for Global Education at Augsburg College and the United States of Europe funded ERASMUS scheme between Barcelona, Maastricht, and Ljubljana; a commitment to mutual learning rather than the superior-inferior situation that sometimes occurs if an exchange focuses on exporting "consulting skills" or "expertise;" and enthusiastic faculty, staff, and students.

The basic goals at the beginning of the program were as follows:

1. Faculty exchange to understand each other's approach to identified disciplines (education, business, philosophy, and social work) and to expand each institution's pedagogical resources.
2. Short student exchange courses (e.g., summer school) to broaden their understanding of differing approaches to politics, community, and social life as global citizens.
3. Reciprocal recruitment of students to spend at least a year at the Augsburg or Ljubljana campus as part of the institutional "international program."
4. Faculty and institutional development opportuni-ties, for example, presentations at scholarship fairs and conferences to contribute their learning to wider audiences.

As the Department of Social Work at Augsburg College and the School of Social Work at the Univer-sity of Ljubljana picked up the opportunity to join in this exchange, additional goals and objectives were developed that are identified later in this chapter.

COMPONENTS OF THE INSTITUTIONAL AGREEMENT

The University of Ljubljana and Augsburg College have cooperated in the exchange of faculty since the early 1990s. This relationship became more formal when the first Institutional Agreement was signed in 1997. This document was renewed in 2000 by Dr. William Frame, president of Augsburg College, and by Dr. Joze Mencinger, rector of the University of Ljubljana. The two administrations continue to encourage the exchange of students and faculty and have agreed to review their agreement every 3 years. This decision supports the academic departments in future planning and is a basic foundation for sustaining the relationship.

The Institutional Agreement contains six articles. The first confirms the commitment to joint learning: "Both institutions are guided by mutual interest to contribute towards the future development of academic cultural cooperation." Article 3 addresses the details of reciprocity and arrangements for visits and terms of accommodation, stipend, transport, and expenses. Article 4 commits the institutions to cooperation between libraries, Article 5 ensures the future of the project, and Article 6 concen-trates on language. It is Article 2 that contains the detailed guidance for the individual departments.

In Article 2 it is agreed that the institutions will exchange students and professors for "various lengths of time" and will attempt to balance the activity equally. In the Department of Social Work at Augsburg College, we have simply taken turns sending and receiving students and faculty (these visits are detailed in the next section of this chapter). Article 2 further helps the individual departments by laying down the following broad goals:

1. Joint research in the fields of mutual interest
2. Reciprocal visits by lecturers for the purposes of teaching, studying and the exchange of research experience
3. Participation in scientific conferences, symposia and seminars on the invitation of the Institution which organizes the meetings
4. Exchange of experience and information on the syllabi, the methodology of teaching and the techniques applied to didactic process
5. Exchange of academic publications
6. Support of contacts between students and student organizations within projected cultural and scientific exchange.

The act of reviewing and signing this document every 3 years has been especially important in keeping new rectors, presidents, deans, and administrators involved and supportive of the exchange. The danger of an ongoing agreement without review dates is that the document lies untouched in a cabinet or on a computer disk and later participants become less engaged in the unfolding history and development of the various departments' work. The document has been an important reminder for colleagues to keep each other up-to-date on developments and to negotiate budgets and practical arrangements early in each phase. For example, student accommodation needs to be reserved 2 or more years ahead of time, and detailed plans must be laid down for the exchange to continue to run smoothly. In essence, the Institutional Agreement has been key to the formal support, recognition, and progress of the exchange.

FACULTY VISITS AND COURSE DEVELOPMENT

Between 1997 and 2002, Augsburg College has had two faculty members visit from the University of Ljubljana, and two instructors from Augsburg have visited Slovenia. The second cycle of student exchange has just been completed as a group of U.S. students visited Slovenia in June 2001 and Augsburg College received students from Ljubljana in the summer of 2002. The previous cycle of student exchange took place in 1998 and 1999. The next cycle will include faculty exchange for curriculum development and joint research.

One of the earliest and most fruitful challenges to this collaboration was conceptual. Our colleagues from Ljubljana requested changes to our U.S. syllabus wherever we referred to Slovenia as a "former communist state." Although McCormick's text on Europe identifies the former Yugoslavia as a communist state under President Tito, colleagues from Slovenia explained the subtle and important difference (McCormick, 2000). Their country was a "socialist" state, rather than one of the totalitarian regimes of the former USSR. Yugoslavia was independent from the former Soviet Union, and developed its own model of socialism with self-government as a basic concept. Slovenians therefore prefer to have their openness to change acknowledged in the term "socialist" rather than "communist." This correction sparked an eruption of dialogue and learning for us as faculty at Augsburg College and for our students. For example, as we prepared for our first visit, none of the U.S. students could identify the countries bordering Slovenia or the date of its momentous independence from the former Yugoslavian Republic. Creating a set of orientation materials was therefore one of the first tasks we gave ourselves in developing the exchange. These data became the basis for a faculty development presentation for the wider U.S. college community (see Table 1). Similar faculty orientation took place in Ljubljana.

As the faculty partnership developed, the exchange of materials expanded to include scholarly work and social work articles from both schools. We realized that faculty visits to each other's institution would be the best preparation for exchanging students and would also be an effective way to develop curricula and syllabi. Because both institutions benefited from administrative support and early budget planning with the chair and deans of their departments, the steps in our exchange have included the following:

i.   Exchange of letters and social work articles, including those authored by the professors involved in the collaboration.
ii. Lecture visits by the professors to experience teaching and research in the other country and also to develop syllabi.
iii. Development of an oversight committee of faculty and outreach to community agencies to host foreign students.

TABLE 1. Learning from Countries in Transition: Slovenia, "Land of Blossoms and Thorns"

Introduction and Background

Area: 20,256 km sq.
Population: 2+ million
Capital: Ljubljana
Borders: Italy (west), Austria (northwest), Hungary (east), Croatia (south)
Gross domestic product: $9,352.00 per capita (1995)
Location: East Central Europe
Slovenia is a hidden country of great beauty. Hidden, that is, from Western eyes but quietly organized and open to trade and international relations since its independence from the former Yugoslavia in 1991. This is a new country politically, but it is ancient in its culture, language, traditions, philosophy, and community networks.

Striking Social Factors

- Wide middle class
- Close attention to basic needs: housing, health, education, and unemployment
- Increased tensions: expanding open market and diminishing social budgets on the Western capitalist model

Current Expectations

- Everyone be housed
- Parents paid maternity (12 months) or paternity leave (45 days)
- Universal health services
- Efficient public transport and fewer private vehicles
- Tolls on major roads

Conditions Which May Seem Restrictive to Westerners

- All families with children going through divorce meet with a social worker who is primarily responsible for custody recommendations and helping the family plan for the future.
- Noncitizens may not purchase land (except corporations)
- State has been slow to de-institutionalize
- Relatively small living spaces (offset by commitment to universal housing)

Economic Adjustments

- Loss of major trading relationships with the states of former Yugoslavia
- Economy in transition
- Increasing unemployment (employment rate was highest in Eastern Europe)
- Pressure to become more efficient and to review traditional labor agreements and working hours

Recently Accomplished Goals

- Secured foreign investment
- Increased tourism
- Signed association agreement with the European Union
- Decreased inflation
- Stabilized currency (the *tolar*)

Political System

- Since 1991, Slovenia is a democratic republic and a legal and social state
- Recognized by the United Nations since 1991
- Division of power: legislative, judiciary, and executive branches
- National Council of 90 elected members
- Advisory State Council of 40 members
- The Liberal Democratic Party is in power; there are several minority parties
- The prime minister is Dr. Janez Drnovsek; leads a 15-member government
- The president represents Slovenia's interests abroad and is commander-in-chief of the armed forces

Human Services and Social Work: Community Organization

- "Pridobivanje moci:" empowerment
- Community responsibility
- Right to reality: "people have the right to be listened to, to be heard, and to be taken seriously."
- Actionable knowledge
- Systemic connectivity
- Systemic function over dysfunction (not blaming individuals)
- Networking with people (clients)

Method of Organization

- Public service bureaucracy
- Coordination of services for health, education, housing, income, and social service
- Delivery through "Social Work Centres" and institutions
- Interdisciplinary
- Networking and outreach, both urban and rural (e.g., through the mental health network and the Rural Farm Women's Association)

Future Directions & Research

- Increased networking for empowerment and working together
- "We have a lot of theory and need to expand our skills"
- De-institutionalization
- Increased exchange with other countries
- Increased support to families in transition: divorce and suicide
- Refugee counseling
- Advocacy as service levels change
- Mixed public and private (nonprofit) services on the Western model

iv. Creation of orientation materials to be exchanged by mail for both sets of students.

v. Two 3-week visits of students with a faculty leader for coursework, agency visits, and evaluation.

vi. Ongoing planning and public relations work.

vii. Publication of articles and scholarly papers, including references to Slovenia and quotes from Slovenian colleagues in a book on international social work (Ramanathan & Link, 1999).

viii. Workshop and conference presentations involving both faculty and students.

Although the Institutional Agreement prompted a number of these activities, the department added its own ideas, for example, the social work community connection, using students as hosts, and the oversight committee. Several of the agencies that provided internships to BSW and MSW students in Minnesota and the surrounding area (Wisconsin, North Dakota, South Dakota, Iowa—the recruitment area for weekend college) offered to host some of our exchange students for 3 days of observation and learning, and others invited the whole group for a training or welcoming event. Allowing students to act as hosts was an early innovation from Ljubljana. One of the most welcoming aspects of our first visit to Slovenia was the way that each U.S. student had at least one partner to show her or him around and to organize social events. The U.S. students learned from this experience and later volunteered to be part of an organizing group for the return visit of the Slovenian students, which was especially valuable in arranging the visiting students' field internship experience and excursions. On reflection, the faculty oversight committee or "International Committee" of the Department of Social Work at Augsburg College has been another key element for brainstorming ideas, planning budgets early, tracking policies, and giving encouragement to the faculty responsible for leading the exchange and related courses. Certainly U.S. and Slovenian colleagues have been crucial in critiquing and making suggestions as the syllabus for the exchange course was developed (the syllabus is available upon request from the first author of this chapter).

The course began as an introductory program for undergraduate social workers and was expanded to be an underlying structure for international courses for both BSW and MSW students. The policy frameworks and assignments were expanded for graduate study and an experiential component was added in terms of the homestay and the agency visits.

There is a difference between the two schools in expectation for the amount of detail contained in a syllabus. Augsburg College's syllabus may be a little lengthy but it did help in recording the various steps—both pedagogical and practical—which the group undertook. Also, the initial course outline provided the groundwork for the return course, when the Slovenian students came to Augsburg College, and the second phase of student exchanges, which occurred in 2001 and 2002. There was some tension among the students about the crowded schedule and the time available to complete assignments. Generally the student feedback was very positive in relation to the range of experience and dialogue and less positive in terms of the extent of assignments and other demands on their time.

Faculty and students discussed this use of time in our debriefing and several recommendations were made and confirmed in later written evaluation, for example

- In future, have the student complete an initial policy analysis assignment before leaving their own country

- Translate all agency and syllabus materials in advance and do not assume common understanding of social work concepts such as "empowerment," "right to reality," or "transparency"

Students were placed with human service agencies in both countries, and while this offered rich opportunities for learning, it was clear that we needed to increase our level of preparation. Also, at times the U.S. faculty and agencies underestimated the strain of communicating in a second language. Although all the Slovenian students spoke English, the range of fluency was considerable. In one instance, the faculty leader was alarmed to find a message that one of the students had "blown-up" in her field agency; the leader had visions of an international incident until the translation was amended to "thrown-up." Certainly it was humbling for the U.S. faculty and students to visit Slovenia and find so many people speaking English, when their Slovenian was limited to greetings and basic social requirements. It may be argued that U.S. students are more likely to speak Spanish or French as a second language, given their Mexican and French-Canadian neighbors, but even that would be optimistic. Several faculty and students have recognized the need to expand their language skills to become true members of the global community.

STUDENT EXPERIENCE OF THE EXCHANGES

In their evaluations and feedback it was clear that the students had benefited from the exchanges at several levels. They greatly increased their knowledge of each other's countries, continents, approach to human service, and current place in the world. They reviewed and refined many of their values, particularly in relation to stereotypes (e.g., their views of communism or the political complexity in Eastern Europe and the Balkans), and they expanded their skills in the way they observed and communicated in their field placements.

Evaluation took place in several ways, including group dialogue at the end of the exchanges, students and administrator meetings, assignments, completion of individual evaluation sheets, personal and professional review through conference and workshop presentations, and through scholarly writing. In her presentation to the Minnesota Conference on Social Work Education, in the fall of 1998 at the Koinenea retreat center, former student Victoria Hanson shared her evaluation of the experience (Hanson, 1999). She remembered suddenly realizing alternatives to the ways of offering service that she took for granted as "normal" or "the only way" in the United States. Ms. Hanson had stayed for two nights with a family where the father received long-term disability support and she reported that the family appeared to experience no stigma from their community. Similarly, all families in Slovenia receive health services, regardless of income, and expect to use family-center facilities. She described a multigenerational center at Koper and several students were struck by the "one-stop" approach to human service that has been long established in Slovenia but is seen as an innovation in Minneapolis. Another student wrote vividly of her experience at the center for families with members recovering from drug addiction mentioned in the opening paragraph of this chapter. The U.S. students were struck by the involvement of seniors in supporting and mentoring these families, who offer transport and share weekly meals in return. All of the students spent an evening with these families, hearing their stories and witnessing the skills of the social work leaders as they drew everyone into profound sharing and pride in taking charge of their lives.

As with any course, the exchanges of U.S. and Slovenian students had a number of successful elements as well as areas for growth. Of the successes, the fresh look at one's own place in the world provided by visiting and meeting with colleagues in another country stood out in assignments, presentations, and feedback. Similarly, the idea of combining class lectures, discussions, and presentations with 3 days visiting agencies worked well in both Minneapolis and Ljubljana. One agency, Lutheran Social Service in Minneapolis, included its clients in planning and presenting a luncheon and a discussion relating to immigration. The focus of this dialogue included examining our values concerning inclusion and exclusion in communities and how we value our heritage and the heritage of others. In another field visit, students explored a more holistic approach to health at the new St. John's hospital in St. Paul.

The Slovenian students also noted successes in their evaluation report:

> What do we remember the most? The feeling of welcome, we were well accepted everywhere, the willingness of the professionals to answer our questions in a professional and self-confident way, willingness to cooperate with foreigners, visit to the Lutheran Social Service and life story of a Somalian woman. . . kindness in the Lindell Library, availability of literature, ambient visits for free, book-lending, computer and internet use. . . well planned summer school, encompassing many different fields of social work.

In Slovenia, the U.S. students and faculty participated in a picnic and dance at the Koper family center and heard the testimony of volunteers at a family center in Ljubljana. Students also took on expanded roles as hosts and teachers at their home institutions, and facilitators of faculty development in the case of Victoria Hanson. The students talked about their respective countries and gained basic knowledge of European and American borders and politics. U.S. students received a serious geography lesson when they planned a 3-day postcourse trip and expected to visit several countries. They were urged by their Slovenian hosts to be less ambitious and examine the map, not to mention the elevation.

In addition to the excessive amount of work discussed in the previous section, several aspects of the exchange were criticized constructively by both the Slovenian and the U.S. students and are the focus of attention for the next cycle of courses. They include the following:

i.   Too much class time combined with the visits. In our eagerness to do and see as much as possible, we had some days that proved too long for the group visiting Minneapolis. In retrospect, it may be more fruitful to see fewer agencies and sites and be able to absorb them rather than to try to do so much.

ii. More time needed for debriefing after presentations and visits. The syllabus for both parts of the exchange was full and in future it would be helpful to have a community meeting for the class and the hosts every day.

iii. Expand planning materials. Although the orientation was well received by the U.S. students, the Slovenian students would have liked more preparation papers in advance in both English and Slovenian.

iv. Gather questions from visiting students in advance, so that the hosts can prepare. Below is one example from the Slovenian students' evaluation report:

Our students should better prepare for the questions of the Americans as regards certain current issues (in our case this was the war in Kosovo), economic, political, social circumstances in Slovenia, the position of a family in Slovenia today.

v. Continue to seek funds to support the cost of travel for students.

The following items are important to the students, and have proved successful, but still need some streamlining to be sustainable over changes of faculty leaders and administration:

vi. Reciprocal accommodation and services. It is a crucial element of this exchange that the transfer of dollars and tolare are kept to a minimum through reciprocal arrangements for accommodation, most ground transport, and food. This is an advantage for all the students and increases equitable access to funds. Currently, we charge outgoing Slovenian students a small fee for their accommodation, which in effect becomes the funding for the incoming students the following year. Similarly, U.S. students are accommodated at "no charge" in Ljubljana.

vii. Advance budget planning over a 2-year cycle. We continue to work on institutionalizing the 2-year phase of student and faculty exchange, despite the traditional year-to-year administration of courses. Similarly, the administrations have approved an early accommodation "voucher" system to secure accommodation and services early in the planning

cycle. This worked well in 1999-2000 and we hope it will be repeated.

All the feedback has been constructive and has contributed to our developing expertise. The students and the faculty leaders have shared an ongoing sense of enjoyment and expanded learning through the exchange. As noted above, however, there were some practical and pedagogical elements that we will continue to work on and learn from.

UNEXPECTED DEVELOPMENTS

A number of outcomes for this exchange were not anticipated and have been welcome additions. A number of these unexpected benefits are listed below:

i.   Public relations for the institutions
ii. Ongoing student friendships through email
iii. Student and faculty joint conference presentations
iv. Joint authorship between faculty
v.   The prime minister of Slovenia's visit to Augsburg College and Minnesota
vi. Expanded dialogue among faculty concerning our role as global citizens
vii. Long-term change from the in-depth experience of collaboration between professors and students (i.e., sharing ideas, planning, and implementing the project together)

Table 2 is an example of a press release for the local Minneapolis paper, field agencies, and our internal communications. Traditionally, the Department of Social Work at Augsburg College has not been active in public relations and in external publicity about its activities. This exchange caught the attention of our colleagues and a local journalist from Slovenia, which encouraged us to be more aware of public interest and of the opportunity to let other people know of our programs.

The ongoing friendships and communication of students who have participated in the exchange is a welcome outcome and very important for sustaining the exchange. These students become our alumni and can be recruited as future hosts and organizers of agency hospitality. Also important for sustaining the program is the ongoing interest of faculty who have participated. One key to this project has been its transition from the personal investment of two interested individuals to an institutionalized exchange that can operate independently of any particular individual.

One of the exciting and unexpected aspects of the exchange was Prime Minister Drnovsek's visit to the Augsburg College campus. He was in the United States with a trade and fact-finding delegation and through the efforts of Augsburg's European faculty, Dr. Magda Paleczny, and in cooperation with the University of Minnesota and international students from Slovenia, Serbia, and Croatia, he agreed to visit. Prime Minister Drnovsek's presentation and dialogue gave a renewed sense of purpose and global connection to all involved.

SUMMARY AND FUTURE

In writing this chapter we realize that this exchange has generated many unexpected benefits in terms of lasting friendships between students and faculty. The more anticipated outcomes are the widened horizons, the expanded view of the world, the new syllabi and case studies, and the increased knowledge of social work practice that we have all gained. We have concrete evidence of our work and we also have a sense of new relationships and opportunities for understanding. We no longer stereotype the Balkans as an international "hot spot," but strain to understand what is happening and to be informed as the prime minister we had the honor of meeting struggles to keep his place.

In the last century, the United States became used to holding a position of economic and political leadership in the world. As a result of this collaboration we have come to understand new dimensions in terms of global relationships, respect, and reciprocity. The rapid changes evolving in the United States of Europe, as Europe extends its union and includes newer states such as Slovakia and Slovenia, are harbingers of global change and shifting patterns of migration that our students can welcome or ignore at their peril (Archer & Butler, 1996). As a result of the personal relationships they created, our students reach confidently for new understandings of their role as global citizens and of the potential for social work partnerships and shared learning. These relationships are the intangibles, and they represent lifelong insights and gifts of friendship, professional resilience, and creativity. We have areas of the exchange that need to be developed, including the pace of student activities, the number of assignments, the previsit orientation, the translation of agency documents, ongoing reciprocal arrangements for accommodation and budgets, and faculty transitions. However, the successes of this project far outweigh the problems. We recommend similar exchanges by colleagues and welcome requests for information and consultation.

As a conclusion to this chapter, we reprint here the closing letter from the first professor from Ljubljana to visit Minneapolis, Dr. Gabi Čačinovič Vogrinčič, as we pass the torch to the new faculty taking up this exchange:

Dear Dr. Rosemary Link,

It is the last day of your visit to Ljubljana, we have to finish our discussions, review our cooperation during your lectures for our students which considered theory and practice in social work, evaluate the exchanges, our

TABLE 2. Augsburg College and the University of Ljubljana, Slovenia: Summer School 1998 and 1999

Exploring Family and Child Welfare Services in the US & Slovenia: Learning from International Comparisons
INFORMATION FOR PRESS RELEASE

Ten Slovenian students and their faculty leader, Professor Lea Sugman Bohinc arrived in Minneapolis Tuesday 1st June, 1999 for two weeks, hosted by Augsburg College and the Department of Social Work. Their visit is part of an institutional exchange between Augsburg College and the University of Ljubljana. Students will participate in classes on campus and will visit human service agencies, including Lutheran Social Service, The Bridge, HealthEast, Freeport West, the Center for Victims of Torture and Southside Family Nurturing Center.

This set of exchange courses provides both in depth study of Slovenian and US approaches to social policy and social wellbeing for families and children and an opportunity to observe and meet with Slovenian and US Social Workers in their practice settings. It helps students learn about different regions of the world and expand their response to social issues. Students participating in the exchange course spend time in orientation with the social work faculty and visiting Slovenian Professors at Augsburg and then joined the University of Ljubljana faculty in 1998 and the faculty of Augsburg in 1999 to concentrate on child welfare services at social work centers, with issues of domestic violence, refugees, mental health and poverty. Participants work with a group of Slovenian and US students, faculty and community practitioners and the exchange is expected to be ongoing.

Summer Schools, plan ahead. So it is a good time to write a summary—farewell letter to end a period of excellent cooperation—and to start a new one, involving new teachers, new students.

First of all and without any doubt it was a good experience for all of us. I am happy—and proud—that we have been able to co-create and realise it. Our exchange is a success. Concerning the Summer School there are three main results we have achieved.

The first was the ongoing vivid and creative conversation between US and Slovenian students and teachers: there was discovering, explaining, translating concepts, exchanging knowledge and experiences, confronting and comparing. Many subjects were treated—history, socialist and capitalist systems, language and culture, social policy and human rights, students issues, sports and recreation, love and friendship. . . . We all could enjoy the widening of horizons, mutual acceptance, surprises and connections. The way the Summer School was organized offered much time and space for dialogical process. It was possible to challenge, to check, to look twice.

Our students and I, we would like to say it again, we returned home with respect and admiration for the way social work is taught and practiced. It was a very personal discovery of the US and Slovenia, but the personal linked to global issues of social policy, human rights and human well-being.

The second important issue was the practice in "talking social work." By this I mean using social work concepts, theoretical and practical knowledge in describing, exploring or discussing institutions, problem solving projects or helping processes. In those two weeks I witnessed a growing confidence in the use of professional language, both in Slovene and in English, a practice in specific social work actionable knowledge. Sometimes the discussions in the workshops or during visits looked like exercises in professional identity and in discovering the impact of social work. For the Slovenian students there was an important new insight in global issues.

The third important result was the experience of a serious and creative cooperation between students and teachers. For all of us there was new understanding and what is more—the use of new understanding in redefining our relationships, responsibilities and tasks. The share of the students in all the activities planned was much bigger and varied than expected. We all agreed that this was the best opportunity we ever had for good, deep, professional conversation between student and teacher!

An important element in our model is the institution of visiting professors, making it possible to exchange lectures between Augsburg College and Ljubljana. You and me dear friend, we have had the experience and we have enjoyed it very much. Your lectures on "Ethical Decision-Making: Local and International Perspectives" opened to our students a new and challenging global perspective. They are still discussing your statement, that studying social work is a privilege.

I have enjoyed very much the open and positive atmosphere in the courses of Augsburg, the interest of the students, their eagerness to know about Slovenia and social work concepts, their readiness to discuss. And I have learned in the wonderful Lindell Library discovering new books, unknown journals and research, discovering new perspectives in discussions with colleagues. My book on Family Social Work [Čačinovič Vogrinčič, 2000] is much better as a result. I felt at home in Augsburg College and its campus. I have met dear friends and I hope for many years of cooperation and friendship. Thank you.
Yours sincerely
Professor Dr. Gabi Čačinovič Vogrinčič

REFERENCES

Archer, C., & Butler, F. (1996). *The European Union: Structure & process.* New York: St. Martin's Press.

Čačinovič Vogrinčič, G. (2000). *Family social work.* Ljubljana, Slovenia: The University Press.

Hanson, V. (1999, October). *My experiences in Slovenia.* Presentation made to the Minnesota Conference on Social Work Education, Koinenea, Minnesota.

Havel, V. (1990, March 5). The revolution has just begun. *Time,* 14-15.

McCormick, J. (2000). *The European Union: Politics and policies.* Bolder, CO: Westview Press.

Midgley, J. (1997). *Social welfare in global context.* Thousand Oaks, CA: Sage.

Ramanathan, C., & Link, R. (1999). *All our futures: Principles and resources for social work practice in a global era.* Pacific Grove, CA: Brooks/Cole.

FOUR

East—West Exchange in Social Work Education: The Sino-American Collaboration Between Tunghai University, Taiwan, and San Jose State University

Peter C. Y. Lee

There is a growing awareness in international social work that the complexity of global socioeconomic, political, environmental, and technology-generated problems will require the collaboration of different regions and nations if we are to effectively address the crisis we now face (Johnson & Kramer, 1998; World Bank, 2000; Healy, 2001). To remain viable as an international profession, social work must significantly increase the extent to which its interventions and practices are based on the conscientious, explicit, and judicious use of current best evidence across national boundaries. Social work educators have a central role to play in designing and conducting the necessary research and in collaborating with colleagues both cross-culturally and cross-nationally.

This case study describes an international collaborative project between Tunghai University in Taichung, Taiwan, and San Jose State University in California. The major objectives of this collaboration are to learn more about each other's social work education, to compare social policies and trends, and to exchange social work faculty and students. Specifically, the principal players are administrators, faculty, and students of the schools of social work in both universities who are collaborating across international boundaries to promote sustainable exchange and development of social work practice and education.

It is hoped that the practical issues discussed in this case study will stimulate further thinking, experimentation, and research regarding international collaboration. This study may also be a useful resource for teachers, students, and practitioners in international social work.

THE BACKGROUND AND GOALS OF THE SINO-AMERICAN COLLABORATION

Any effort for international collaboration in social work must recognize the challenges inherent in the very terms *social welfare* and *social work*, the subject of many debates cross-nationally. The main theme for these challenges is the relation of values to these terms. In international exchange and collaboration, a question may arise as to whether there are different value orientations in Western and Eastern cultures. Does one place greater emphasis on individualism, while the other is more accustomed to what might be called "group values?" Are there universally recognized social work-related values to be found in all cultures, and does the profession derive its values from them? What is essential, however, is to recognize that social welfare and social work, as we know them, could not exist without different values in different societies. Therefore, what is attempted, or even achieved, by Western social welfare programs and Western professional social work, may be accomplished by different means or professions in other societies that disclaim any need for professional social work. In a world that is increasingly interrelated, it is evident that international collaboration for social work has to be viewed in the context of interdependence because we can no longer solve problems that transcend national and cultural boundaries independently (Sanders & Pedersen, 1984; Lee, 1992, 1998; Healy, 2001). In this time of rapidly accelerating globalization, it is imperative for U.S. institutions of higher learning to better understand the cultures, history, economics, and politics of other nations and to enhance scholarly exchanges; moreover, it is important to understand social work education from an Asian-Pacific context on which this case study is based.

Given the Asian-Pacific region's diversity, there are several themes evident within the context of social work that are worthy of comment:

- Known as the major player of the so-called "culture of chopsticks," Taiwan has an overwhelming majority of ethnically Chinese people and shares common historical circumstances, language, cultural heritage, physical attributes, and even strategies of development with China, Hong Kong, and Singapore (Lee, 1996). With the exception of China, the cultural setting of Hong Kong, Singapore, and Taiwan has been considerably impacted by the adoption of Western capitalism along with the acceptance of Confucianism as the essence of their major culture.

- Chinese culture does not value an individualized perspective as definitive of human behavior. Instead, the emphasis is on an individual's appropriate role and relationship to others in the larger society. Therefore, there is a greater acceptance of dependence among intrafamily relationships, even as adults. The goal of maturity has been considered, by societies ranging from India, China, Japan, and to many Pacific Islands, as continuous and satisfying dependency within the family and society.

- Increasingly in many Asian-Pacific Schools of Social Work in the last decade or so, there appears to be a shift in perception and curriculum design toward a social development perspective rather than the remedial nature of traditional social work practice (Kwan, 1987; Cox, 1991; Sewell & Kelly, 1991; Lee, 1992; Kulkarni & Nanavatty, 1997).

The conceptualization of this international collaboration between Taiwan and the United States began many years prior to the formation of the first Sino-American Conference on Social Welfare Development in 1981. To the social work education establishment in Taiwan, the 1970s and early 1980s were periods of intense consultation, transplantation, and borrowing of Western models of social work (Lee, 1995). Many Asian countries received consultative assistance for setting up social work training and academic programs. Taiwan was no exception and, for instance, established its first Graduate School of Social Work Program at Tunghai University in the early 1970s with a grant from the Asian Foundation that supported the school through its first 2 years (Lee, 1995). This collaborative project between Taiwan and the United States is intended to search for new ways of professional social work training in a manner that is socioculturally relevant.

It should be noted that the major theme running through this case study is the international perspective on the relation of the values of social work—its principles as related to practice and methods—to its societal function. From a cultural competency point of view, many critical issues in social work education—the policy and organizational characteristics, the roles and functions of social work, the philosophical and sociocultural values—in Asian-Pacific societies are profoundly different from their Western counterparts. This case study is unique in that it reports on an actual exchange in this cross-cultural setting. The wide range of collaborative activities presented here address these challenges of mutual understanding and learning in social work. The international exchange between Tunghai and San Jose State provides insight into the difficulties and possibilities of such collaborations. The following section is organized to describe the major functions carried out by both parties since the early 1980s.

PROJECT OBJECTIVES AND PROGRAM ACTIVITIES: LINKAGE BETWEEN CULTURES

The Contract

In order for the bilateral exchange agreement to be operational, a fully documented contract and a program plan were prepared. Known as "the Agreement of Academic Cooperation," the contract was agreed upon and signed on January 9, 1981 by President Gail Fullerton of San Jose State University and President Ko-wang Mei of Tunghai University. The agreement provided the following to clarify several areas of mutual concern: a summary of the program concept, a listing of information on the faculty and staff involved, a description of the facilities and support required, and a brief curriculum plan. This agreement became effective upon signature by both presidents and is subject to revision and extension by mutual consent. It can also be cut short by either party through written notification at least 12 months prior to the termination date. Even though both President Mei of Tunghai and President Fullerton of San Jose State are no longer in their respective offices, the agreement between the two universities is still in force today and the original contract language remains intact since it took effect in 1981.

Project Objectives

San Jose State University and Tunghai University sought to establish a formal affiliation for the purpose of faculty exchange, student exchange, joint research, and any other programs, including the cosponsorship of conferences, which would be considered mutually beneficial. In order to fulfill the terms of the agreement, both universities seek to realize the following objectives:

- To identify and define curricular needs associated with social work education in both countries
- To seek means to implement the mutual exchange of social work faculty members and students
- To plan and conduct joint research programs relevant to mutual concerns
- To plan, develop, and provide human services consultation and technical assistance to both universities and their surrounding communities
- To bring together U.S. and Chinese social welfare administrators and educators to discuss effective ways to address social welfare issues relevant to both cultures and societies.

Project Resources

Funding is provided by both sides to make these cooperative activities possible. These resources can be separated into two components:

a. Funding for the academic exchange and the professional training.

    The Tunghai University share of this component is funded by both government (social welfare departments at the county, provincial, and central government levels) and private sources (the Chinese Fund for Children and Families, the Taiwan Regional Development Institute, and the Social Psychiatric Institute in Taiwan). The San Jose State portion is provided by the College of Social Work and the Center for Human Services Research and Development. In general, each country provides international travel for its own participants and pays the expenses for the visiting delegations. According to the agreement between the two schools, remuneration of exchange professors in terms of their salaries and associated benefits shall continue to be the responsibility of the home institution.

b. Funding for conferences.

    Conferences were primarily sponsored by Tunghai University and San Jose State Univer-

sity, with cosponsorship from the Council on Social Work Education (CSWE) and the Inter-University Consortium for International Social Development (IUCISD). The presidents of Tunghai and San Jose State were leading forces in bringing the conferences to fruition. The major funding was provided by a consortium of various organizations including both universities, the Taiwanese government, and private foundations in Taiwan such as the Pacific-Cultural Foundation and the Foundation for Scholarly Exchange.

Program Activities

A major objective of this collaboration is to bring social welfare issues to the forefront in the Chinese communities in Taiwan and to advocate, influence, and initiate change through educational programs and training projects. A further objective is to help Taiwan find more sustainable and effective alternatives to the U.S. social welfare system and to avoid the same mistakes these U.S. systems have already made. Accordingly, collaborative activities directed toward achieving these solutions began in 1981. What follows is a brief description of the activities that have been completed to date:

a. Faculty and student exchange.

    In 1982, soon after the agreement was signed, social work faculty exchange started and continued until 1996. (Between 1996 and 2001, faculty exchanges took place in three other departments—economics, art & design, and English—between Tunghai University and San Jose State University. Both universities continue to work together as sister institutions, but unfortunately, the social work faculty exchange stopped due to a lack of funding on both sides.) Under the agreement, faculty members were nominated for exchange by their home institution. Faculty members were then further approved by the host institution based on criteria established internally. According to the agreement, the maximum number of faculty members to be exchanged from each institution was two per academic year. The period of each exchange was limited to a year, although that period could be extended for an additional year with the consent of both parties. Teaching workload and assignments were distributed in accordance with the established rules and practices of the host institution, although other conditions could be applied at the discretion of that institution. Between 1982 and 1996, a total of eight faculty members were involved in the exchange program (four from Tunghai and four from San Jose State).

Although the agreement places no limit on the number of exchange students, nominees must first meet the admission requirements of the social work department in the host institution. Once admitted, exchange students are entitled to a waiver of tuition and of other institutional fees while attending the host institution. They can take coursework for credit, which can be applied toward a degree; or, they can work on a joint research project between two institutions, performing noncredit work and remaining entitled to the tuition waiver. According to the contract, any exchange student who fails to meet the academic requirements of the host institution may be placed on probation for a period up to 6 months. If the student has not met the requirements at the end of this probation, her or his participation in the exchange is terminated. Students return to their home institution at the conclusion of their exchange period.

Between 1982 and 1996, a total of five graduate students from Tunghai attended the MSW program at San Jose State. Unfortunately, none of the students from San Jose State went to Tunghai during this period.

b. Training programs.

A comprehensive plan for professional social work training was developed during the fall of 1987, with activities beginning in the spring of 1988. San Jose State's Center for Human Services Research and Development, Kai-Suan Psychiatric Hospital and Institute in Taiwan, and Tunghai's Social Psychiatric Institute of the Graduate School of Social Work formed the Joint Training Implementation Committee that designs and oversees the cooperative initiatives of this program. In further collabora-

tion with the Santa Clara County Mental Health Bureau, the 3-month training program known as the "Transcultural Mental Health Training Project" was initiated in Santa Clara. Various other psychiatric and community mental health programs also participated. This training program was specifically relevant to the implementation of community mental health programs in Taiwan, which were mandated by the Chinese Mental Health Act in 1988 (Lee, 1995).

The Transcultural Mental Health Training Project was designed with two major objectives in mind: (a) to provide educational opportunities for current psychiatric professionals to raise their level of competence and to broaden their expertise in community mental health; and (b) to improve current psychiatric programs in Taiwan to better prepare community mental health professionals and to support experimentation with culturally appropriate methods of interventions. As of spring 1999, 12 social workers and other allied mental health professionals from Taiwan had completed their work in the Transcultural Mental Health Training Project.

Under the agreement, the Center for Human Services Research and Development at San Jose State also collaborated with the School of Social Work at Tunghai and the Chinese Fund for Children and Families in Taiwan to conduct child abuse and neglect prevention training sessions between 1989 and 1992. More than 60 child welfare professionals and administrators from Taiwan came to the San Jose State campus and received this training, which included visits to various child welfare agencies in Santa Clara County.

It is essential in the context of this agreement that San Jose State faculty members and students and human service practitioners in Santa Clara County develop international and cross-cultural perspectives. The arrangement of holding public forums, presented by visiting professionals from Taiwan at the end of their training, has broadened the horizons of the U.S. faculty, students, and practitioners. These individuals are now more aware of other cultures, socioeconomic and political systems, and diverse approaches to social problems.

Activities like these training programs were discontinued in 1999 because the very high cost of living near San Jose State University, which is located in Silicon Valley, became a major barrier for Chinese participation. However, there has been renewed interest in resuming the collaborative effort between the two institutions. In the spring of 2002, the Chinese Ministry of Education invited a delegation from San Jose State University to visit Taiwan. The delegation, led by the president and the provost, held a joint meeting with Tunghai University leadership and the participants agreed to refocus their collaboration by addressing social welfare issues or other problems of mutual interest. While it is too early to make definitive conclusions, both Tunghai and San Jose State are currently working with the Salzburg Seminar and the Foundation for European Cultural Exchange on a proposal to hold an international conference on comparative welfare states, scheduled to take place in Salzburg, Austria in the spring of 2003.

c. Consultation and technical support.

The consultation and technical support program was designed to provide short-term consultation and training that could contribute significantly to the planning, development, and implementation of child abuse and neglect prevention programs in Taiwan. In keeping with the spirit of the agreement, two faculty members from San Jose State served as child welfare consultants and made four trips to Taiwan. They provided consultations to the Chinese Fund for Children and Families and conducted child abuse and neglect prevention workshops for over 200 child welfare workers.

d. Conferences.

Cosponsored by the two collaborating institutions and CSWE, the first Sino-American Conference on Social Welfare Development

was held in Taipei, Taiwan from December 29, 1980 to January 3, 1981. This conference marked the beginning of the cross-national collaboration between San Jose State University and Tunghai University and provided an international forum for the discussion of social welfare issues, such as child welfare, health and mental health, gerontology, housing, and social policies and programs. Over 200 people were in attendance, with the majority representing Asian countries (Brown, Lee, & Quadros, 1985). Of the 43 participants from the United States, representing institutions from California to New York, 9 held positions in the U.S. government (Ambassador Charles Cross of the American Institute in Taiwan and representatives of the National Institute of Mental Health), 9 were deans of schools of social work or senior administrators from U.S. universities, 4 were from private organizations (including Robert Hill of the National Urban League and representatives from the Council of International Programs), and the rest were professors of social work, sociology, economics, or law (Lee, Li, Kiang, & Bai, 1981). In addition, the executive director of CSWE attended as a cosponsor.

The significance of this conference for the Taiwanese government was reflected by the presence of high-level government officials and policymakers (Interior Minister Chuang-Huan Chiu; Yien-si Tsiang, secretary-general of the ruling party Kuomintang; and Mayor Teng-hui Lee, who later became the president of the Republic of China in Taiwan), as well as educational and nonprofit organizational leaders. Many of the participants from other Asian countries, including Japan, Hong Kong, Australia, and the Philippines, were well established and highly regarded in the social welfare communities of their own countries and on the international stage (Brown, Lee, & Quadros, 1985).

Tunghai University, San Jose State University, IUCISD, and CSWE jointly sponsored the second Sino-American Conference on Social Welfare Development. Held in San Jose, from August 12-15, 1984, its theme was "An

Intercultural Exploration: Changing Family Needs and Services in the 1980s." Building on the goals of the first Sino-American Conference, this second meeting provided a forum for the continued examination and evaluation of the critical issues facing Chinese and U.S. family systems.

The third cross-national conference on social welfare took place 6 years later in Taipei: the 1990 Sino-American-British Conference on Social Policy. From July 22-28, official representatives and scholars from three countries—the United States, the United Kingdom, and Taiwan—participated in this weeklong exchange of views on social welfare needs and strategies. In addition to specific social policy recommendations, the conference participants unanimously adopted a resolution stating that "If the nations of the Asian-Pacific are to achieve significant social development gains, then, effective programs of regional self help, mutual aid, cooperation, and technical assistance will have to come into being and effective social policy and programs have a vital role to play in national development."

Unfortunately, there have not been any conferences held between the two institutions in the last decade. The collapse of supporting resources, especially the declining budgets of California state universities in the early to middle 1990s, dealt a serious blow to the joint sponsorship of such meetings.

OUTCOME MEASURES AND PROGRAM ASSESSMENT

Based on our experience and observations during this collaboration, the interest and involvement in international activities of faculty, programs, and students in U.S. institutions of higher education is likely to continue. Several reasons exist for this long-term participation: the extensive history of U.S. involvement in the international arena, expanded global economics and corresponding research and entrepreneurial opportunities, the changing role of the United States in this global economy, decreased state funding, the increasingly diverse student populations in the United States, and the continued commitment to the education

of students as global citizens. How important international cooperation and collaboration is to U.S. institutions really depends on the particulars of their missions and future aspirations in international social work. The social work profession has had a long history of international action and collaboration ever since its inception (Healy, 2001). As social workers continue to consider international exchanges and collaborative work, it is important to assess the experiences learned from this Sino-American project, which was initiated two decades ago.

International and cross-cultural perspectives permeate the entire cooperative project between Tunghai University and San Jose State University, especially the faculty exchange, training programs, and joint sponsorship of international conferences. Most noteworthy is that both countries are collaborating as equal partners in an endeavor, which has benefited and will continue to benefit both on a long-term basis. As a result, both institutions share ownership of the program and are respectful of the participating cultures while promoting socioculturally appropriate social work knowledge and skills, including in the design of their curricula.

Another important outcome of this collaboration is the strengthening of the national relevance of social work education in Taiwan as a whole. The continued consultation and support from sponsoring institutions, especially IUCISD, has led to the founding of the social work doctoral program at Tunghai University in 1990, the first social work PhD program to be established in Taiwan.

The project has not been without problems, especially the faculty exchange program. With the exception of one senior social work faculty member from San Jose State University, who is originally from Taiwan, language presents a barrier to effective communication for most U.S. and Chinese faculty under exchange. A second obstacle is gaining the cooperation of those to be involved in the training projects. Many professionals in the U.S. setting consider themselves competent in dealing with different cultures without realizing how little they understand about Chinese culture and people. The two major aspects of the educational design—experiential field learning with a weekly field seminar and an integration seminar at the end—were regarded as interactive and essential parts of the whole experience for both trainees and trainers. This arrangement reflected the project's purpose of broadening perceptions and provided an opportunity for acquiring experiential cultural learning from one another. A third problem is cost. Given the financial constraints of the sponsoring agencies, placing foreign professionals in optimal learning experiences on a short-term basis posed a serious but not insurmountable difficulty. In fact, many human services agencies in Santa Clara County donated their staff's time and resources to cosponsor the training programs for the professionals from Taiwan.

The impact of this collaboration is empowering at multiple levels. Given the historical diversity between Chinese and U.S. societies, each has a great deal to learn from the other through the sharing of knowledge and skills while collectively addressing common issues in social welfare. The principal organizers of this collaboration are those who have had the longest tenure in international networking and cross-cultural involvement. At the micro level, individual participants on both sides of the Pacific have expressed their appreciation for the opportunities this program has provided for traveling and learning from one another. At the macro-societal level, and even the global level, this program offers the hope that social work knowledge and skills should and will be increasingly relevant to the important global concerns in the 21st century.

This collaborative program, especially the training project, is particularly relevant and useful because community mental health and child protection were two mutually agreed upon focuses. These issues fulfilled an urgent need, as expressed by Taiwanese participants, to provide child welfare workers in Taiwan with working knowledge of mental health theories and intervention strategies in the community. The requisite skills also proved useful for working with children and their families in the United States. Activities included short-term training of psychiatric and child welfare professionals from Taiwan in community mental health programs and child protection intervention strategies. In turn, this training project opened the door for many faculty and local practitioners who have since engaged in a variety of related opportunities in consultation and research.

Continued support and cosponsorship by CSWE and IUCISD for many of the exchange activities is another significant aspect of this collaborative project. In helping to bring together an international forum for the sharing of social welfare knowledge, the involvement of these two major international organizations was an unqualified success.

Perhaps one of the most significant events in the Tunghai–San Jose State collaboration was the first Sino-American Conference in Social Welfare Development, held in 1981, which is viewed as a landmark event in Asian-Pacific social welfare (Brown, Lee, & Quadros, 1985). The various follow-up conferences, organized and held under the auspices of the agreement signed by the two participating institutions, continue to bring together government officials, social welfare scholars, nongovernmental organization (NGO) representatives, and practitioners from both countries. It is clear that most participants leave these conferences with the important realizations that developing countries like Taiwan need to give priority to social welfare and that social welfare training must prepare professional social workers for carrying out developmental roles. There is also a clearly emergent mutual identification of interests and concerns when participants discover how much can be learned from one another, irrespective of which countries they represent. These conferences serve as a bridge by linking cultures and by bringing into existence a forum in which social issues can be discussed and means for addressing them explored.

Based on the information and knowledge shared through these jointly sponsored conferences, it is clear that several main sectors (government policymakers, social welfare educators and scholars, and NGO representatives from Taiwan) will be shaping Taiwan. Broad social development and social welfare policies will be defined and implemented, especially family welfare, aging, and child welfare. For example, some of the issues confronting the Chinese participants were perhaps more serious than they were willing to admit at the conferences, particularly in the area of gender equity and child welfare (specifically, abortion, unwed mothers, wife and child abuse, and juvenile delinquency; Lee et al., 1981; Lee, 1988).

Considerable efforts have been made by both sides to arrange study tours to coincide with these joint conferences. Participating faculty from San Jose State were exposed to the full spectrum of the unique social welfare needs of Taiwan and other Asian countries through these well-organized tours. In turn, these U.S. faculty, who are already teaching comparative welfare courses, often serve as resources for their colleagues interested in comparative social welfare and international social work education.

CONCLUSION AND IMPLICATIONS FOR CROSS-NATIONAL COLLABORATION

International exchange projects and programs, as Healy (2001) points out, have been prominent in the development of social work as a global profession. This chapter is an attempt to present the Tunghai-San Jose State collaborative experience as an international phenomenon and to articulate elements of a challenge that should concern social work educators and practitioners: providing opportunities for people of different nations to collectively work toward common goals through cross-national collaborations, thus making social work a powerful force in furthering social development in the global community. The networking and exchange experiences between the two institutions from markedly different countries are examined in a cross-national context and certain goals and priorities are espoused: realistic curriculum designs, reassessment of societal needs and professional objectives, and synthesis of values and reality. Overall, this collaboration provides an excellent example of an international action to improve human well-being through the use of curricular and educational exchanges. What is unique about the Sino-American experience presented here is that the exchanges between the two institutions involved many levels. These include the ongoing exchanges of information and social welfare policies at professional conferences involving policymakers, practitioners, and social welfare and social work scholars and educators; consultation and technological support; organized projects of training between social work professional agencies and organizations; and faculty and student exchanges between the two universities. In addition, the importance of contributions and expertise from two internationally known organizations—CSWE and IUCISD—is recognized.

It is clear from this case study that a program of international collaboration that focuses on social work education, practice, and research is essential and possible, even with limited resources. Such programs provide valuable opportunities for examining diverse ways for dealing with social welfare issues and for testing social work approaches in varying cultural and socioeconomic contexts. In a very real sense, the key to sustaining the link between these two collaborating institutions for nearly two decades lies in the effective response of the faculty involved.

The many forms of human predicament—poverty, inhumanity, injustice, and oppression—require a much more cooperative arrangement in our global village.

There is likely to be increasing collaboration between nations regarding social welfare concerns. Increasingly, the preparation of future social work practitioners will involve an acknowledgement of the reality of global conflicts at varying levels and will incorporate the development of the relevant and necessary competence to address these conflict situations. It is, therefore, our hope that, individually and collectively as social work professionals, we will resolve to stimulate further thinking, experimentation, and research regarding the potential of the cross-national collaboration.

REFERENCES

Brown, J., Lee, P., & Quadros, O. A. (1985). Reflections on the first Sino-American Conference on Social Welfare Development in the 1980s. In B. Mohan (Ed.), *Toward comparative social welfare* (pp. 47-56). Cambridge, MA: Schenkman.

Cox, D. (1991). Social work education in the Asian-Pacific region. *Asian Pacific Journal of Social Work, 1,* 6-14.

Healy, L. M. (2001). *International social work: Professional action in an interdependent world.* New York: Oxford University Press.

Johnson, C. D., & Kramer, J. M., (1998). Canadian-Chinese collaboration on sustainable development: Initiatives for social and technological change. *Social Development Issues, 20*(1), 33-45.

Kulkarni, P., & Nanavatty, M. (1997). *Social issues in development.* New Delhi, India: Uppal Publishing House.

Kwan, A. (1987). *Social welfare services in Hong Kong* [in Chinese]. Hong Kong: Ji-Suan.

Lee, P., Li, J., Kiang, Y., & Bai, H. (Eds.). (1981). *Proceedings of the Sino-American Conference on Social Welfare Development in the 1980s.* Taichung, Taiwan: Tunghai University Press.

Lee, P. (Ed.). (1988). *Dimensions of social welfare transition: Sino-British perspective.* Taipei, Taiwan: Chu Liu Book Company.

Lee, P. (1992). Social work in Hong Kong, Singapore, South Korea, and Taiwan: Asia's four little dragons. In M. Hokenstad, S. Khinduka, & J. Midgley (Eds.), *Profiles in international social work* (pp. 99-114). Washington, DC: NASW Press.

Lee, P. (1995). *Social policy analysis: Theory and practice* [in Chinese]. Taipei, Taiwan: Chu Liu Book Company.

Lee, P. (1996). Social welfare of Hong Kong, Singapore, and Taiwan: Progress and challenge. *American Journal of Chinese Studies, 2*(3), 225-233.

Lee, P. (1998). A critical review of the social security system from a social development perspective [in Chinese]. *Journal of Modernization Research, 14,* 28-37.

Sanders, D., & Pedersen, P. (Eds.). (1984). *Education for international social welfare.* Honolulu, HI: School of Social Work, University of Hawaii.

Sewell, S., & Kelly, A. (1991). *Social problems in the Asia Pacific region.* Brisbane, Australia: Boolarong Publications.

World Bank. (2000). *Entering the 21st century: World development report 1999-2000.* New York: Oxford University Press.

FIVE

Collaboration in an Era of Social Transition: The Eotvos Lorand University, Hungary— Case Western Reserve University Connection

M. C. "Terry" Hokenstad

Massive social change, both good and bad, marked the final decade of the 20th century. Some referred to this period as the "end of history." More specifically, it witnessed the end of the Cold War—an ideological conflict that separated the world into two armed camps—and the beginning of a new era in which many countries were starting to incorporate democracy into their political systems and the free market into their economies. Greater political freedom and increased opportunity for economic growth were coupled with increasing unemployment, poverty, and resultant social problems in these countries—including the transitional societies of Central and Eastern Europe.

This new era has also led to increased opportunity for collaboration in many different arenas. Increasing political and economic interaction has been accompanied by an environment conducive to increased international contacts in the arts, the sciences, and the professions. University-based exchanges, although in existence during the Cold War era, have now expanded exponentially, both between Western and Eastern Europe and between the United States and the former Soviet bloc countries. Collaboration in education and research is high on the list of potential benefits resulting from the growing number of these exchange programs.

The social problems facing the transitional societies of Central and Eastern Europe make social welfare a logical and appropriate arena for East-West exchange and alliance. Growing poverty and unemployment are evident in these societies as the free market economy means increased economic opportunity, but also less security. Attention to social policy, which determines the social safety net in free market societies, is equally important in Hungary and the United States. Problems such as homelessness, drug use, and crime require individual services and community development, as

well as enlightened social policy. Thus, the need for professionally educated social workers and social policy analysts is evident in these transitional societies.

International contacts and collaboration in social work and social policy existed before the end of the Cold War. Social work had a limited existence in some Central and Eastern European countries and it was beginning to emerge in others for the first time since the Second World War. A few social workers from the communist bloc visited the United States as part of the Cleveland International Program and similar exchanges. The International Association of Schools of Social Work (IASSW) in the middle to late 1980s provided consultation and a venue for interaction with Western colleagues. However, these contacts were sporadic and limited. The social transition ushering in the 1990s gave both opportunity and urgency for the exchange of people and ideas in social welfare.

OVERVIEW OF THE COLLABORATION

It is against this background that the Eotvos Lorand University (in Budapest, Hungary) and Case Western Reserve University (in Cleveland, Ohio) connection was made in social work and social policy. Planning for the linkage was initiated in February of 1990 and ongoing collaboration continued through August of 1996. The principal agent of this program's implementation was the exchange of educators between the Social Policy and Social Work Department of Eotvos Lorand University (ELTE) and the Mandel School of Applied Social Sciences at Case Western Reserve University (CWRU). Exchange faculty contributed teaching, program consultation, and collaborative scholarship. Although the major linkage was between the faculty of the two universities, the program's benefits extended considerably beyond the institutional affiliation. This was primarily because ELTE's Department of Social Policy and Social Work provided national leadership for the establishment of the social professions in Hungary during this period.

The ELTE–CWRU connection was funded by a University Affiliations Program grant from the United States Information Agency (USIA). This grant provided the financial base for faculty exchange over a 5-year period. The funding enabled nine faculty members from the two universities (five from ELTE and four from CWRU) to make 12 exchange visits from November of 1991 through April of 1996. The primary purpose of this project was to strengthen educational programs in both universities through this faculty exchange. The secondary purpose was to help build social work education throughout Hungary.

The specific objectives were as follows:

- To provide international teaching expertise at both universities in social policy, human development, and research.
- To support ELTE, and through ELTE other educational programs in Hungary, in the development of the social work curriculum and field education for social work students.
- To offer consultation in educational program development for both universities.
- For ELTE: consultation for the development of PhD-level education for social policy and social work.
- For CWRU: consultation for the expansion and enrichment of its international curriculum.
- To promote joint scholarship in international and comparative social policy and social work.

While this faculty exchange project has been the hub activity of the collaboration, it must be placed in the context of related cooperation prior, during, and after the project.

BACKGROUND OF THE COLLABORATION

Hungarian social work and social work education started to receive attention in the middle 1980s as part of a gradual liberalization of that society prior to the more pronounced transition at the end of the decade. Contacts with the IASSW led to Hungarian participation in IASSW conferences and in consultation by social work educators attached to the nearby IASSW headquarters in Vienna. A few social work educators

from the United States were in Hungary on Fulbright Scholarships during this period and worked with Hungarian colleagues in the establishment of part-time programs. Terry Hokenstad, chair of the PhD program in social welfare at CWRU and a member of the IASSW board of directors, had the opportunity to become acquainted with colleagues from Hungary during these conferences, and in particular, during a Central and Eastern European workshop in Vienna in the summer of 1988.

In February of 1990, at the request of IASSW, Professor Hokenstad traveled to Budapest to consult with Hungarian colleagues about ways in which U.S. social work education could be supportive during the period of Hungarian social transition, which was then just underway. He found a group of highly competent educators and scholars already engaged in institution building for social work education. The national leadership for these activities was clearly located at ELTE with Professor Zsuzsa Ferge, chair of the Department of Social Policy, and faculty members Kinga Goncz, Gabor Hegesyi, and Katlin Talyigas. They were working with educators from other Hungarian universities and colleges in the development of a uniform social work curriculum and had formed an association of faculty members with social work program commitments, which was headed by Professor Ferge.

It was obvious that strong leadership and considerable talent and expertise had been assembled. At the same time, the social work background of this group was very limited. The participating educators represented disciplines as diverse as sociology, law, psychology, social administration, and psychiatry. There was considerable knowledge of policy and theory, but little of social work practice and the acquisition of knowledge and skills needed for that practice. The group was particularly deficient in the area of the field practicum and the instruction of students in practice settings. Thus, while there was a solid foundation for the full time programs of social work education that were being planned, there was also the need for support in program development and implementation.

During the remainder of 1990, ongoing communication and a brief visit to CWRU by Gabor Hegesyi continued the initial dialogue about cooperation and consultation. At the same time, discussions with the Cleveland International Program (CIP) led to plans for bringing a group of Hungarian social work educators to the United States for intensive learning about U.S. social work education. Then, in December of that same year, Professor Hokenstad, along with Dean Richard Edwards of CWRU, went to ELTE to work with their Hungarian colleagues in planning a long-term collaboration. Following that visit, three program proposals were successfully submitted to funding agencies. CWRU cooperated with CIP and its national organization, the Council of International Programs, in sending a proposal to the Soros Foundation for short-term training of Hungarian educators in the United States. A year-long project designed to help Hungary build national associations of social professions and social services, entitled Promote Associations Through Hungary (PATH), was funded by USIA. Finally, the joint proposal from CWRU and ELTE was submitted to the University Affiliation Program of USIA for support of exchange and collaboration between the two universities in the fields of social policy and social work. The grant was approved for a 3-year period (later extended to 5 years), assuring long-term cooperation.

Brief mention should be made here of the short-term training and the building of national association projects. In addition to being important in their own right, these projects provided both context and reinforcement for the ELTE–CWRU collaboration. Nine Hungarian educators arrived at CWRU in April of 1991 for the beginning of a 3-month program. They were selected from colleges and universities throughout Hungary and included Kinga Goncz and Katalin Talyigas from the ELTE social work faculty. Their first 2 weeks in the United States featured a seminar on social work education taught by Professor Hokenstad and colloquia on various components of the social work curriculum given by the other members of the CWRU faculty. The Hungarian educators also visited local social agencies and met with social work practitioners. Following this initial period in Cleveland, the nine visitors dispersed to various schools of social work throughout the United States for 2-3 month internships arranged by CIP. When the participants in this program returned to their homeland, they provided decade-long leadership to the development of social work education throughout Hungary.

The PATH project accomplished its objective of building national associations in social work, social work education, social policy, and family services through exchange visits, consultation, and technical assistance. The Hungarian leadership for these groups made several trips to the United States in 1992 to visit U.S. associations and to attend national and international conferences. Several CWRU faculty went to Hungary to consult on association functions and structure and to give technical assistance on operational details.

After the completion of the PATH project in 1992, faculty connected to the faculty exchange continued their involvement with the development of these national associations. They explored the possibility of an umbrella organization uniting the four associations and provided some funds for this initiative. Beginning in 1994, this development was supported by funding from PHARE (the main channel for the European Union's financial and technical cooperation with the countries of Central and Eastern Europe). By the end of 1995, the four associations had formed and incorporated a uniting organization known as the Association of Social Professions and elected Professor Ferge as its first president. Professor Hokenstad had the privilege of addressing the assembly of delegates for this new organization in a visit to Budapest in 1996.

COLLABORATION THROUGH UNIVERSITY AFFILIATION: ACTIVITIES AND ACCOMPLISHMENTS

Central to this collaborative project was the faculty exchange which was funded by the USIA University Affiliations Program. Over the 5-year period of program implementation, there were 12 exchange visits by nine faculty (five from ELTE and four from CWRU). These visits provided the structure in which the process of collaboration took place and the program objectives were attained. Individually, the visits involved classroom lectures, training workshops, colloquia on topics of current importance, community speaking engagements, consultation on program development, and cooperation on joint scholarly publications. Collectively, the visits contributed to the development of both classroom and field practicum components of social work education in Hungary and the now-operationalized PhD program in social policy and social work at ELTE.

Program accomplishments resulted from trips both ways across the Atlantic. ELTE faculty contributed to the CWRU education program through classroom teaching in social policy and human development, their areas of scholarly expertise, and through community colloquia and lectures about the social transitions in Central and Eastern Europe. They consulted with CWRU faculty about international and comparative content for policy and human development courses, while also using their visits for information gathering and dialogue about the content and methodology of U.S. social policy and social work education. In addition to their important contributions to CWRU, the Hungarian visitors gave colloquia for the Sociology Department and had interaction with CWRU faculty from the departments of economics, history, and sociology, as well as the School of Nursing. Their presence certainly enriched the International Program at CWRU.

Faculty visitors to Hungary from the United States spent as much time providing program consultations and training workshops as teaching in classrooms. Two of the exchange faculty had experience as chairs of the PhD program in social welfare at CWRU and thus gave considerable attention to consultation about the design and the details of the social policy and social work PhD program at ELTE. Other U.S. visitors gave workshops on generalist social work methods and nonprofit management for faculty and community agency leaders. All of the CWRU faculty spent time in workshops and in consultation with field practicum coordinators and instructors. These discussions also extended beyond ELTE to meetings with the social work and social policy faculty at other universities in Hungary: KLTE Szociolgiai Tanszek in Debrecen, Vitez Janos Tanit Okepzo Foiskola in Esztergom, Szote Egeszeg Ugyi FoiskolaiSzak in Seged, Illyes Gyula Pedegogiai Foiskola in Szekszard, and Barczi Gueztav Gyopypedagogiai Tanarkepso Foiskota in Budapest. Their classroom lectures and seminar participation included sharing expertise in administration, child welfare policy, pension and social security policy, poverty and homelessness, mental health and family therapy, social work methods, and social service evaluation. These visits were directed to both program development and classroom learning.

Tangible contributions of the affiliation are clearly defined. The PhD program at ELTE matriculated its first students for the 1995-1996 academic year. It was the first program of its kind in Central or Eastern Europe and its existence is a tribute to the leadership of Professor Ferge and her faculty at ELTE. Both Hungarian and U.S. faculty participants in the collaboration project made a variety of contributions to the planning and implementation of this program. Three of the nine students in the first class are social work educators who participated in the April 1991 seminar at CWRU. The ELTE–CWRU collaboration was one of the sources of energy and ideas behind this major accomplishment.

An equally important result was the project's contribution to the continued development and strengthening of professional social work education in Hungary. While some social work educators became students in the ELTE PhD program, many other faculty and field instructors benefited from workshops and consultation given as part of the faculty exchanges. In addition to these workshops and meetings, the project resulted in ongoing communication and sharing of journal articles and other written material on curriculum building and educational methodology. The ripple effect of this exchange over a 5-year period impacted all of the colleges and universities offering social work education in Hungary.

Some scholarly collaboration also resulted from the project. Members of the ELTE faculty contributed a chapter on Hungary in *Profiles in International Social Work* coedited by Professor Hokenstad (Talyigas & Hegyesi, 1992). Also, a special issue of the journal *Ageing International* entitled "The Forgotten Generations of Central and Eastern Europe" was coedited by Hokenstad and Dr. Zsuzsa Szeman, a gerontologist with the Hungarian Academy of Sciences and a part-time teacher at ELTE (Hokenstad & Szeman, 1994). Although scholarly productivity was not the primary purpose of this project, it was a logical corollary to the faculty's collaboration.

Other outcomes are more difficult to measure. CWRU students and faculty certainly gained greater knowledge and understanding of the social transition in Central and Eastern Europe. Presentations by ELTE faculty, coupled with informal dialogue, had a cumulative impact over the 5 years of interaction. During this period, there was an increase in international course content and student interest in global and cross-national issues at CWRU. Study tours and field placements for CWRU students were arranged in Central and Eastern Europe. This increased international emphasis was due to a number of forces, but the ongoing presence of the ELTE–CWRU collaboration was an important influence.

The opportunity for continued cooperation, due to both institutional and personal interaction, is another less tangible but still-evident result. Cross-Atlantic communication among faculty continues to include the exchange of curriculum materials, scholarly publications, and research project findings. Professional colleagueship resulting from the collaboration has produced both ideas for joint scholarship and joint conference presentations. Finally, friendships that grew out of the project have led to exchange visits by faculty not directly involved in the official collaboration. Such spin-offs clearly point to the ripple effect of this project.

Finally, the collaboration provided a base for the building of an 18-country training and program development project from 1997-1999. This home- and community-based care program was funded by the Open Society Institute and conducted by CWRU in cooperation with several Hungarian organizations. Multidisciplinary teams from 18 countries in Central and Eastern Europe and the Newly Independent States of the former Soviet Union participated in the training and developed programs for older people throughout the region. Former participants of this collaboration from both sides of the Atlantic worked together in planning and providing leadership for this larger and more recent project.

THE COLLABORATIVE MODEL: LESSONS LEARNED

The ELTE–CWRU affiliation was an international collaboration that produced both tangible and intangible results. Curriculum building, program development, field instructor training, and enriched student education are documentable outcomes. Professional and cultural enrichment through international travel, increased knowledge of global issues, and opportunities for the exchange of ideas and information are more qualitative outcomes. On a larger scale, the collaboration contributed directly to the building of an educational and social service infrastructure for Hungary and indirectly for other Central and Eastern European countries during this time of social transitions. This new infrastructure is vital to the welfare of the larger society as these transitions have created and exacerbated social problems at the same time as providing political freedom and economic opportunity.

Principles of Collaboration

Certain principles that contributed to the success of the project can be identified and used as guidelines for building a collaborative model.

The length of the process, in terms of both planning and implementation, is the first important factor. The long-term nature of the project (February 1990–August 1996) enabled seeds of cooperation to be planted, roots of interaction to grow, and fruits of collaboration to be harvested. The ripple effect of the project was reinforced by new exchange visits and new program activities each year. Clearly, the length of time available for project implementation strengthened the collaboration and made the accomplishment of the project objectives more feasible. Spreading out the funds for this relatively low-cost project over a period of years created the opportunity for feedback and for more effective use of project faculty, which enhances the likelihood of permanent impact.

Networking is the second collaborative principle that was evident in this project. The ELTE–CWRU affiliation benefited by connections with prior and parallel projects sponsored by USIA and the Soros Foundation, which provided a foundation for the collaboration and mutual reinforcement. Faculty participants in this collaboration established the linkages with these other training and association-building projects. More recently, programs to establish quality standards in Hungarian social services and to develop home- and community-based care in Central and Eastern Europe have drawn on the expertise and knowledge that resulted from this affiliation project. The network of social work and social policy educators to which this project has contributed and from which it benefited has heightened its value.

Reciprocity has been another key to project success. Both partners contributed to and gained from the collaboration. According to the Hungarian faculty participants, this reciprocity was particularly valued and often missed in other international projects. Tangible results, such as the new PhD program, the strong field component in the social work education program, and the establishment of the Association of Social Professions, are evident at ELTE and in Hungary. At the same time, the project has been an important influence for the new international course content and the increased number of students with international interests at CWRU. Students from both universities gained from the shared expertise, both in increased knowledge, and for some, in career focus. Faculty interaction impacted not only those nine educators directly involved in the exchange, but also their colleagues who cotaught courses or shared ideas and materials with the project participants. Additionally, social work administrators and practitioners outside of the university benefited from the collaboration, either through attendance at colloquia (in the United States) or through participation in training workshops (in Hungary).

Institutionalization of project results is the final principle of collaboration that has been evident in the ELTE–CWRU exchange. The collaboration took place through individual involvement, but the key to achieving ongoing impact was the influence on the institutions and their programs, which is evident in a number of ways. In Hungary, ELTE is providing national leadership both in the preparation of social policy analysts and social work practitioners, and now in the preparation of PhD-educated researchers and teachers for the social welfare field. This impact extends beyond Hungary's national borders because this is the only PhD program of its kind in Central or Eastern Europe. In the United States, CWRU has expanded its international curriculum and has started an International Social Work emphasis in its graduate program, which enables students to add a global dimension to their understanding of social welfare policies and programs. It provides students with the capacity for analyzing international issues and their implications for social work practice nationally and internationally. It also offers the opportunity for students to experience social work programs and practice outside of the United States. Thus, the collaboration contributed to the establishment of new programs in both universities, as well as enriching the current curricula. This is a prominent and permanent outcome of the ELTE–CWRU connection.

REPLICATION OF A COLLABORATION: CLOSING THOUGHTS

Each university collaboration project is unique. The context, the timeframe, and the available resources all impact the structure and content of the exchange. The ELTE–CWRU collaboration was shaped by the opportunity and the needs resulting from the social transitions in Central and Eastern Europe at the start of the 1990s. It was built on prior interaction through the programs of IASSW and it was made possible, and its structure was determined, by a grant from the University Affiliations Program of the USIA. The unique combination of these underlying factors makes it impossible to replicate this particular collaboration.

Yet some insights resulting from the project may be helpful for thinking about similar collaborations in the future. Certainly prior interaction and careful planning, especially over a period of years, provides a solid foundation upon which to build a successful exchange program. Although planning meetings are important, prior personal interaction is essential to establish working relationships and to insure cooperation during the exchange. The planning process also should produce project objectives that emphasize the benefits for both universities. If the exchange is to be truly collaborative, it must be seen as reciprocal, not just in the exchange visits but also in the planned outcomes.

This project focused on faculty exchange as the vehicle for collaboration. The lack of student exchange directly connected to the project was in some ways a limitation. Students benefited from the faculty visits but certainly would have benefited more from visiting the partner country. However, the project objectives were focused on program building and enrichment, and the outcomes of the collaboration reflected this targeted approach. This type of collaboration is best accomplished with clear objectives and a focused agenda.

Finally, international collaboration does not necessarily require large amounts of funding, but it does need an adequate funding base to insure continuity and stability. If the universities themselves cannot provide base support, grant funds must be located. Both governmental and foundation support are available, although it is usually highly sought after, often by many different disciplines. Systematic efforts to identify and apply for such funds during the planning stages is a key step in the preparatory process.

REFERENCES

Hokenstad, T., & Szeman, Z. (Eds.). (1994). The forgotten generations of Central and Eastern Europe [Special issue]. *Ageing International, 21*(3).

Talyigas, K., & Hegyesi, G. (1992). Social work in Hungary: New opportunities in a changing society. In M. C. Hokenstad, S. Khinduka, & J. Midgley (Eds.), *Profiles in international social work* (pp. 59-70). New York: NASW Press.

SIX

Mutual Assistance Through an Ongoing United States—Caribbean Partnership: University of Connecticut and University of the West Indies in Jamaica

John A. Maxwell and Lynne M. Healy

The ongoing link between the Department of Sociology and Social Work at the University of the West Indies, Mona Campus in Kingston, Jamaica, and the University of Connecticut School of Social Work in West Hartford has been characterized by a mutual interest in West Indian migration and by a confluence of facilitating factors. Both of these elements have led to a long-term exchange featuring mutuality and varied and sustained activity. The facilitating factors include elements of each program's mission that could be addressed through exchange activities and the concomitant founding of a new regional social work education association that involved personnel from the two institutions (Healy, Maxwell, & Pine, 1999).

BACKGROUND

Program Contexts

The University of the West Indies (UWI) is a regional university, serving Belize and 16 island states in the English-speaking Caribbean. There are three campuses, located at Mona, in Kingston, Jamaica, at Cave Hill, Barbados, and at St. Augustine, Trinidad. Social work education began at Mona in 1961 and became a full baccalaureate degree in 1969 within the Department of Sociology and Social Work (in 2002, this name changed to the Department of Sociology, Psychology, and Social Work). Initially, Mona served as the social work education center for the region; undergraduate social work education was subsequently introduced to the University of Guyana in 1970; to the College of the Bahamas in 1980; UWI at Cave Hill, Barbados in 1988; UWI at St. Augustine, Trinidad in 1990; and, most recently, to the University of Belize in 1995. An MSW program was opened at Mona in 1993.

UWI at Mona now offers a BSc Social Work and an MSW with alternating concentrations in Direct Service and in Management through the Department of Sociology and Social Work, a unit of the Faculty of Social Sciences.

Jamaica is classified by the United Nations Development Program (UNDP) as a developing country in the "medium human development" category; while it has achieved acceptable standards in literacy and child mortality, it has high rates of poverty, low economic growth rates, and the associated problems of street children, squatter settlements, and high crime levels (UNDP, 2000). These have been exacerbated in the past 2 decades by international debt. As will be discussed later, Jamaica continues to experience high rates of outward migration, mostly to the United States.

The University of Connecticut (UConn) School of Social Work is a large graduate program, located in the greater Hartford area of Connecticut. The MSW program requires a method concentration and offers elective subspecializations in substantive areas, including international issues. A doctoral program was recently initiated. Although part of the graduate school of the larger university, the School of Social Work functions autonomously in curriculum decision making and is also autonomous in day-to-day programmatic decisions, including expenditure issues.

The UConn School of Social Work is located in the suburbs of Hartford, one of the 10 poorest cities in the United States, despite being located in Connecticut, which has the highest per capita income of any state in the country. Social workers in Connecticut therefore deal regularly with the social problems of both poverty and affluence. Of particular significance to the collaboration, the greater Hartford area is home to a large population of immigrants from the West Indies, primarily Jamaica; it is estimated to be the third largest settlement of West Indians in the United States.

Instigating Factors

The link began with West Indian migration identified as an important area of interest to faculty members at both schools. Recognition of an area of common interest helped legitimize the collaboration. In addition, it complemented two other linkage goals: mutual interest in increased publications and research, and UConn's goal of increasing outreach to the Caribbean American population in Connecticut.

At the initiation of linkage discussions, in 1992, UWI was preparing to launch the first MSW program in the English-speaking Caribbean. The Department of Sociology and Social Work was looking for assistance in this venture and this support was the primary reason for the program's interest in an international linkage. The introduction of the MSW degree at Mona had been under active consideration for several years and UWI was in discussion with the McGill University School of Social Work (in Montreal, Canada) regarding a linkage and consultation project. A proposal to the Canadian International Development Agency (CIDA) was submitted in 1992; if accepted, the grant would have provided assistance to UWI by funding lecturers and consultants from McGill to assist in the development of the graduate program. Late in 1992, the schools learned that the proposal would not be funded, as CIDA determined that UWI was already the beneficiary of sufficient CIDA grants in other areas. An additional factor was the increasing pressure for publication by UWI faculty, which led to a search for research opportunities and access to avenues of publication.

In 1992-1993, the School of Social Work at UConn was in the process of formalizing the Center for International Social Work Studies in order to intensify the school's focus on international perspectives. Having had several experiences with cross-national collaborations, the school was looking for a new opportunity to link with an institution with shared interests. High priority was placed on developing a Caribbean linkage, because, as noted above, the Hartford area is heavily populated with immigrants from the West Indies. The school's mission statement clearly expresses its intention to expand its international efforts: "Recognizing the growing impact of international events on human need and the reality of global interdependence, the School embraces an international perspective in its teaching, research and outreach activities, with particular emphasis on applying international knowledge to domestic social work practice and policy" (UConn, 1994). The emphasis on the domestic applicability of these cross-national efforts was highlighted by calling for awareness of the needs of immigrant groups and for "special attention to meeting the needs of . . . people of color, especially those who are African American, Caribbean American and Puerto Rican" (UConn, 1994). Thus, the mission statement gave institution-wide credibility to the link with UWI. As in most universities in the United States, increased opportunities for research and publication remain important priorities; thus, UConn also welcomed a project with a research and publication goal.

Other facilitating factors included geography—the relative ease of travel from Hartford to Kingston, in terms of time and cost, and the proximity of Hartford to New York City, an area frequently visited by faculty from UWI—and the simultaneous founding of the North American and Caribbean regional association of the International Association of Schools of Social Work (IASSW).

In February, 1992, a meeting was convened in Jamaica to discuss the reformulation of the North American regional association of IASSW, which was then comprised of only U.S. and Canadian educators. Representatives from the social work education associations in these two countries met with representatives of the English-speaking programs in the Caribbean and agreed to form a North American and Caribbean regional association (later named the North American and Caribbean Association of Schools of Social Work, NACASSW). The plans for the reconstituted association were ratified at a regional general meeting held at the IASSW Biennial Congress in Washington, DC in July, 1992.

The formation of NACASSW facilitated the UWI-UConn link in two ways. First, the director of the UConn Center for International Social Work Studies, Lynne Healy, was a delegate to the February 1992 meeting at Mona, where she first proposed the link to the head of the UWI social work program, John Maxwell. Dr. Healy was also program chair for the Washington, DC congress of IASSW, and she used the opportunity to invite Dr. Maxwell to participate in the congress as a presenter. Both were named to the executive board of the newly formed NACASSW, with Dr. Maxwell selected as the first president of NACASSW and Dr. Healy as the first secretary. This connection provided additional opportunities for contact and collaboration.

One of the primary goals of NACASSW is to facilitate linkages among schools in the region. Migration and the Caribbean Diaspora in North America were identified as key areas of interest. The confluence of these goals with those of the UWI-UConn linkage was fortuitous and considerably aided the project.

Goals of the Collaboration

As stated in the Memorandum of Agreement signed in 1995, the purpose of the linkage between the UWI and UConn social work programs is to achieve a "collaborative relationship for the mutual benefit of both parties." More specifically, the goals are for collaboration in four major areas: (1) faculty exchange for the purposes of enhancing the UWI MSW program and UConn's capacity to address West Indian issues in its curriculum and programs; (2) sharing and provision of curriculum materials, including outlines, bibliographies, videotapes, and other teaching resources for the same purposes as the faculty exchange; (3) student exchange; and (4) research. As elaborated in the agreement, "both parties wish to stimulate collaborative research, culminating in publications, on a range of cross national and comparative issues of mutual interest, including the one that first brought the parties together, West Indian migration."

Areas of Mutual Interest

As briefly noted in the description of the programs, West Indian migration has a significant impact on both Jamaica and the Greater Hartford area. Recent figures indicate that Hartford has the third largest percentage of West Indians by city in the United States; as of 2000, immigrants from the West Indies made up 8.3% of the city's population, with even more immigrants living in the suburbs (Swift, 2002). More than 53,000 Connecticut residents have at least one parent born in the West Indies, and every year about 1,000 new immigrants come from Jamaica alone (Swift, 2002). Recently, the typical pattern of migration for families from the Caribbean is for one (most often the mother) or both parents to migrate first. Children are left in the care of grandparents, other relatives, neighbors, or older children. When the parents have saved adequate funds and have stabilized their immigration status, the children are sent for and the family is reunited. This pattern has permitted many families to migrate successfully and has aided the economic advancement of these immigrants. It is also fraught with potential social and adjustment problems for both the children and the parents. Periods of separation can extend to 5 or more years; children left as preschoolers may be reunited as young adolescents with parents they hardly know, and sometimes with families that include an unfamiliar stepparent. Children waiting to migrate may suffer from a lack of motivation in school or from a sense of abandonment (Allen, 1995; Crawford-Brown & Rattray, 2001; Glasgow & Gouse-Sheese, 1995; Gopaul-McNicol, 1993; Sewell-Coker, Hamilton, Collins, & Fein, 1985).

Migration from Jamaica is so significant that it has a substantial macro-level impact. Remittances—money sent from migrants back to their families—are now the second largest source of foreign exchange for Jamaica (Planning Institute of Jamaica, 1999). While migration involves the loss of productive members of the population, the money they send back is critical to the struggling economy. In Hartford, macro policy issues are also involved, especially since the 1996 changes to immigration law that have put some West Indian immigrants at risk of deportation and have made family reunifications more difficult, thereby compounding the previously mentioned social problems. Voluntary return migration involves smaller numbers, but it is significant enough that Jamaica has adopted policies to address the needs of returnees. Thus, migration is a topic of significant interest to social work, and faculty members at both UWI and UConn identify migration as a key area of research, scholarship, and advocacy interest.

Although migration was initially identified as the main area of mutual interest, participants in linkage activities have also pursued and developed other areas for joint work. Among these are child welfare and children's rights, youth and violence, human service management, and community organization. There have already been joint conference presentations on human service management and on youth and violence, and a number of joint publications are underway in these areas.

IMPLEMENTATION: ACTIVITIES AND ISSUES

Exchange of Personnel, Students, Materials, and Other Resources

Over almost a decade of activity, many resources have been exchanged between the collaborating schools. These include materials, faculty, and students, as well as less tangible resources such as access and expertise. Each program has provided the other with course syllabi, bibliographies, books, and videotapes.

While more material resources have flowed from UConn to UWI, the exchange has been two-way. As detailed in Table 1, three instructors from each program have taught courses at the partner university, while there have also been numerous short-term faculty visits. Four UWI MSW students have completed field placements in Connecticut and one UConn student has been placed in Jamaica; additional placements are planned for the near future. Other student exchange experiences have occurred through a study tour and through student participation in the jointly sponsored conference described below.

Access to information and to opportunities for conference presentations has been an important element in the exchange. As a result, a number of UWI faculty have presented at Council on Social Work Education (CSWE) conferences in the United States, and several UConn faculty have become regular participants in the biennial Caribbean social work educators conferences. Conference access has been enhanced because linkage participants have held positions within national and regional professional organizations.

In 1998, the linkage moved from exchange to collaboration when the partners agreed to cosponsor a major international conference, the 4th Biennial Conference of Caribbean and International Social Work Educators, which was held on the UWI campus in June of 1999. Referred to as Mona99, planning and

---

TABLE 1. Exchange Activities and Accomplishments:
Department of Sociology and Social Work UWI and University of Connecticut School of Social Work

From UWI to UConn

- 3 UWI faculty have taught at UConn: a year-long visiting professor appointment: a semester-long visiting faculty; and a 2-year appointment
  - taught a range of required courses in UConn program (fall, 1994; 1998–99; 2001; 2002)
  - guest lectures in other classes and special seminars
- 8 short-term UWI faculty visits to UConn
  - conducted seminars and workshops for students and area practitioners, including: a half-day seminar on transracial adoption for all adoption professionals in CT; a 4-session workshop on working with West Indian families for state child welfare supervisors: and many more
  - outreach to Hartford West Indian social workers and community
- during visits and through other exchange activities, UWI faculty conducted library and field research in CT
- shared course outlines and teaching materials and videos in social work methods and Caribbean issues
- department head traveled to UConn and participated in UConn-SSW strategic planning retreat as an invited key stakeholder
- 4 UWI MSW students went to UConn for final field placement in CT
- provided access for UConn faculty to Caribbean conference presentation opportunities
- case presentations and web-based discussion between a UWI lecturer and a UConn class

From UConn to UWI

- 3 UConn faculty have taught at UWI (2 twice) through full-year sabbatical stay (1997–98) and 4 short-term visits (1994 and 1995)
  - helped to develop and did initial teaching of two courses in new MSW program
  - presentations to social work practitioner groups
- 6 short-term UConn faculty visits to UWI
- 12 UConn faculty and deans traveled to Jamaica to participate in the 1999 Caribbean Conference
- 1 UConn student went to UWI for final field placement in Jamaica
- 10–12 UConn MSW students participated in the 1999 Caribbean Conference as student assistants and presenters
- curriculum materials, books, and journals were provided to the UWI program
- UConn faculty conducted research in Jamaica for publications and presentation on topics such as AIDS, social work history, migration, violence, and sickle cell
- provided access for UWI faculty to CSWE presentation opportunities and to publication information
- developed and delivered seminars on training field instructors to UWI field coordinator and 2 field supervisors at UConn for a 10-day study visit (2001) and in Jamaica (2002) for a larger group

Joint Efforts

- planning, promoting, and implementing the 4th Biennial Conference of Caribbean and International Social Work Educators, held June 1999
- joint publications, including a case book on Caribbean social work; an article in *Social Development Issues*, a book underway of papers from the Caribbean conference, and other articles in progress
- joint conference presentations at the CSWE Annual Program Meeting, IASSW Congress, NASW, and biennial Caribbean conferences
- a for-credit study tour to Jamaica for UConn students (June, 1999)
- work on the launch of *Caribbean Journal of Social Work*, 2001 to present (with ACSWE), first volume issued March, 2002

implementing the conference was a fully collaborative process, involving cost sharing, bilateral committees, and "shared glory." The collaboration continues with work on a postconference book. The conference greatly aided the institutionalization of the linkage, as it required considerable administrative involvement on both sides. It also created many opportunities for participation by faculty, students, and area practitioners.

Other evidence of collaboration is the small but growing number of publications resulting from the link, including jointly authored or edited books and journal articles and joint conference presentations. UConn has also been contributing funding and editorial board participation to the launching of the *Caribbean Journal of Social Work*, a venture led by the Association of Caribbean Social Work Educators.

Administration and Institutional Issues

The Memorandum of Agreement was signed by the two programs in 1995. Because the linkage did not have a stable funding source, the letter of agreement was drafted to be flexible. It committed the two units to a partnership and outlined activities to be pursued to the extent they were feasible. This wording satisfied the administrators involved that they were not committing resources that might not be available. Another aspect of flexibility was that the agreement was between the School of Social Work at UConn and the Department of Sociology and Social Work at UWI. This permitted decision makers at these programs to agree to a set of activities without involving higher bureaucratic levels. At least on the UConn side, university-level linkages are rarely entered into unless external funding has been secured. Although this might appear to be a weak agreement, its flexibility allowed the partnership to move forward while granting the added legitimacy of the signed document.

It should be noted that there is a great disparity between the two partners in degrees of autonomy in decision making. The operational link is between an autonomous school of a social work and a unit of a department within a faculty, as illustrated in Figure 1. The UWI social work unit has no separate budget, instead depending upon a department that has two other, larger constituencies (sociology and now psychology). The department is accountable to the Faculty of Social Sciences, which is the principal budget holder. Thus, this social work program depends upon two higher levels of support to function in a meaningful reciprocal relationship with the UConn School of Social Work.

It is interesting to note that the linkage has survived three UConn School of Social Work administrations. The project was initiated under one dean, the Memorandum of Agreement was signed under a second dean, and the linkage has flourished, including the Mona99 conference, under a third dean. The UWI program has also undergone changes in leadership in the Faculty of Social Sciences and at the departmental level. Some of these changes were fortuitous: the former head of the social work program became the department head for 5 years and is now Deputy Dean of the Faculty; the former department head, who was directly familiar with the linkage, became Dean of the Faculty. Whether the linkage can survive without its two originators, both of whom remain with their institutions, has yet to be tested.

FIGURE 1. Structure and Autonomy of Participating Programs

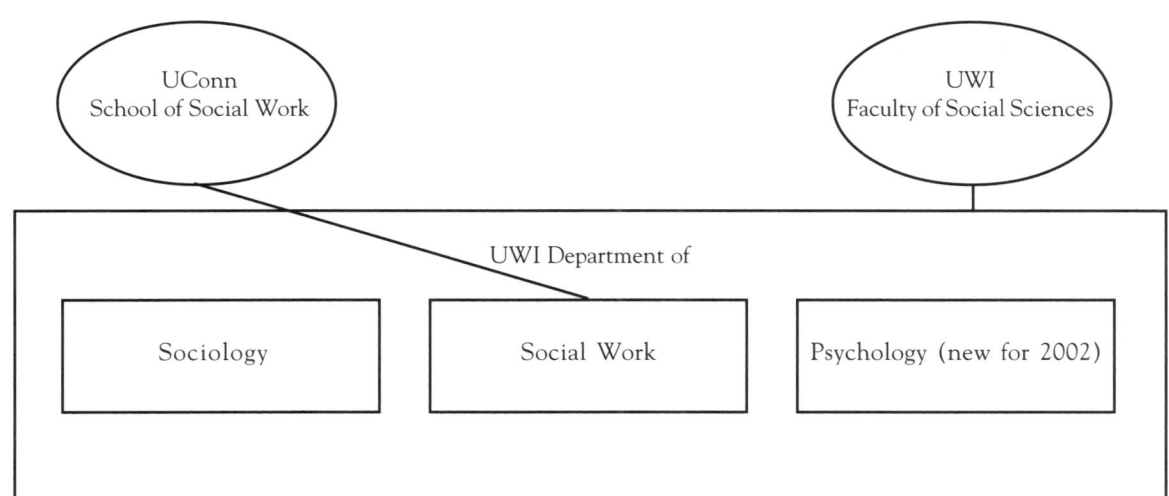

Funding

This long-term linkage has functioned largely without external funding. Initially, it was hoped that a university-affiliation grant could be secured under the United States Information Agency (USIA) program. During the period of the project, however, Jamaica has not been an eligible country. However, four small grants were received early in the link. The United States Agency for International Development (USAID) gave individual study grants that allowed two faculty members from UWI to make 2-week visits to UConn in 1994. In 1994 and 1995, two UConn faculty received academic specialist grants from USIA that permitted short-term travel to UWI. Otherwise, funding for the exchange activities has come from the budgets of the two programs and from in-kind contributions by individual staff members for hosting and accommodation.

Although the lack of stable external funding may have impeded some of the goals of the project, in other ways it has had beneficial effects. External funding can be a "box" that restricts a linkage, in terms of both time and activities. Many thriving linkages end when their external grant expires. The UWI–UConn partnership has existed with no preconceived time limits. The lack of grant funding means that there was never a scramble to replace a terminating grant. The regulations of some funding sources also impede mutuality. U.S. government grants for educational linkages often presume, and in fact require, that the U.S. school function in a consultant or expert role and that participants from other nations, especially developing countries, function as learners. Thus, the small grants that UWI faculty received from USAID specified that they should come to UConn on short-term study programs. In reality, they spent more than half of their time delivering lectures and training to community practitioners. Reports to USAID had to emphasize how they took advantage of consultations with the UConn faculty to learn, rather than to exchange expertise or plan for collaborative research.

Both partners for this project have learned to live without external funding. Nevertheless, they would welcome the opportunity for a grant to support linkage activities in the future. Also, it is probably advantageous that the small external grants were secured early in the partnership, before each institution was thoroughly convinced of the value of the exchange. Once the schools saw the benefits of these programs, the spending of institutional resources for exchange-related travel was easier to justify.

RESULTS: BENEFITS OF THE LINKAGE

Benefits to UWI

Over the 9 academic years in which there have been active programs of collaboration, the Department of Sociology and Social Work at UWI in Mona and UWI as a whole have benefited from UConn's contributions of resources and faculty service and through enhanced experiences for its faculty and students through participation in the project. Visits by UConn faculty members to the Jamaican campus have resulted in the development and the initial instruction of two courses for the MSW program: one in Program Planning, Monitoring, and Evaluation and one in Evaluation of Social Work Practice. The exchange of course curricula and materials provided resources that were incorporated into other MSW courses. Additionally, the field practicum program was enhanced through presentations to practitioners and UConn personnel contributed to the review and ongoing planning of the MSW program. Although these efforts were targeted at the MSW program, the undergraduate program also benefited, as all UWI educators teach at the undergraduate level. The recent trip to UConn by UWI's social work practicum coordinator and two agency field supervisors, as well as the follow-up visit to Jamaica by a member of UConn's field education staff, were particularly advantageous to the much larger undergraduate program.

Through their short-term visits to UConn, UWI faculty and agency field supervisors have had opportunities to observe and participate in programs in their areas of expertise, to utilize library facilities, and to make presentations to faculty, students, and local practitioners. Enhanced experiences were provided through a semester-long sabbatical visit for one faculty member, a year-long appointment as a visiting professor for another, and a 2-year visiting appointment for a third UWI educator. Through mutual collaboration, UWI faculty have gained increased access to opportunities for publications and conference presentations. Thus, there have been considerable occasions for academic and professional development for UWI faculty through the link with UConn. Additionally, four UWI MSW students gained exposure to U.S. social service systems through practicum placements in the greater Hartford area, with three more to arrive soon.

Funding and other forms of support from UConn assisted UWI in implementing the 4th Biennial Conference of Caribbean and International Social Work Educators (also called Mona99). With a total of more than 200 registered participants from 12 Caribbean and Central American countries, large numbers of attendees from the United States and Canada, and a few from the United Kingdom and Europe, this conference was the largest social work assembly ever held in the English-speaking Caribbean. The staging of this conference, which launched a new journal and will produce a textbook, should be noted as providing a great deal of credit and respect for the UWI social work program and the university as a whole.

Finally, it should be mentioned that in the context of a university in which social work is only a unit within a department, and a region without well-established professional associations, the need for the promotion and recognition of social work education is especially important. The UWI-UConn partnership has unquestionably made a meaningful contribution.

Benefits to UConn

This project has also brought many advantages to the University of Connecticut. Institutional benefits include curriculum enrichment, enhanced reputation in the West Indian community (especially among West Indian social workers), increased national and regional visibility within social work education as an international participant, and improved faculty productivity in the form of joint conference presentations and publications. The visits of faculty from UWI have also enabled UConn to offer numerous seminars and workshops to area practitioners and agencies.

Individual faculty have benefited in various ways. For some, the link has provided the occasion for their first international involvement. For others, it has presented an opportunity for participation in an international project that extends their expertise in migration, Caribbean issues, or the comparative study of other topics. The Mona99 conference provided an opportunity for newer, untenured faculty to present at an international conference and to participate in the linkage project. Some of these educators may be able to build on this experience for future research partnerships.

Additionally, a comparative view is often helpful in assessing one's own program. For example, the involvement of UConn's social work management faculty in consultation with UWI on the development of its new program shed light on UConn's own program. The UWI program heavily emphasized theory, perhaps to the neglect of practical managerial skills. When the UConn faculty introduced a highly skill-focused course on program planning into the UWI curriculum, they

realized the need to reconsider the role of theory in their own management curriculum. Similarly, as the UConn faculty recommended that UWI extend the length of their major practicum, they discovered that UWI had developed an evaluation tool for field placements that is much more specific and outcome focused than the tool used at UConn. Mutual learning is a revealing process.

Although the link was initiated because of an area of strong mutual interest, the two programs have also benefited from sharing different interests and focuses. Living in a developing country with significant external debt, Jamaican social work educators are concerned with structural adjustment policies and their impact on social welfare. This was a largely unfamiliar concept to the UConn faculty; UWI provided UConn with an excellent videotape, and supplementary instructional materials, on debt and structural adjustment. These resources have been useful in the international issues class at UConn. Likewise, the UWI educators have commented on the extent to which U.S. social work curricula cover areas of human oppression and recognized that content on homophobia and gay rights is noticeably missing from the curriculum in Jamaica.

Web-based joint work was first experimented with in 2001. The technology consultant at UConn's School of Social Work gave a workshop for Caribbean educators in web-based distance learning at the 2001 Conference of Caribbean and International Social Work Educators. In the fall of 2001, instructors from UConn and UWI collaborated to bring a Jamaican case presentation and subsequent web-based discussion into a UConn course. In the spring of 2002, this collaborative effort spread to the UWI program in Trinidad, with a link between a course on computer applications at UConn and a course in Trinidad's social work program. Plans are underway to expand the technology-based components of this exchange.

UConn students who have been taught by visiting UWI faculty have gained from the different perspectives of these instructors. A recent 2-year teaching engagement by a UWI educator who was completing her doctoral research provided significant contact with UConn students and faculty, as the long-term stay meant she was involved in field advising and committees as well as classroom teaching. About a dozen UConn students participated in the Mona99 conference, mostly acting as assistants together with a group of students from UWI. The experience of working and living with their Caribbean counterparts during the conference was very rewarding. It suggests that efforts to build more joint student projects into the linkage would be valuable.

ASSESSMENT OF LIMITATIONS

The above discussion of results has described the many successful features and outcomes of the UWI-UConn linkage. While the project has exceeded the expectations of the two partners in most ways, several aspects have been less fruitful than initially hoped.

Student Involvement and the Field Placement Exchange

Students from both institutions, especially those from UConn, have benefited from this exchange through opportunities to learn from visiting faculty or to hear special presentations. However, only one UConn student has traveled to Jamaica for a field placement, while four students from UWI have completed placements in Connecticut. It was expected that UConn students would be eager to take advantage of international placements in Jamaica, but few have expressed interest. Difficulties in course scheduling and commitments to families and jobs may be partly responsible.

Fear of violence may also impede U.S. student and faculty interest in travel to Kingston, as Jamaica's crime problems are widely publicized in the media. Two months before the Mona99 conference, there was an outbreak of protests against fuel price increases in Jamaica that sparked road blockades and several violent incidents. Several faculty members considered withdrawing from the conference and the student assistant cancelled his wife's reservation. This situation was resolved when, at a faculty meeting, several members expressed their concerns and asked a visiting lecturer from Jamaica to comment. She told the faculty that while the violence had been localized and had abated, she could understand their concern. Continuing, she said that on her recent trip home to Kingston, she had had to explain to friends and relatives there why she enrolled her children in a U.S. public school where incidents such as the Columbine massacre had occurred. Her comments had quite an impact. No one withdrew from the conference and the graduate student rebooked his wife's flight. Nonetheless, Kingston's violent reputation has probably dampened some enthusiasm for exchange experiences and security remains a major concern in efforts to arrange student placements there.

Another obstacle for student involvement has been the lack of housing for students visiting Hartford. The School of Social Work at UConn is a nonresidential campus and there are no facilities for student housing. This situation has complicated the accommodation of Jamaican and other international students. These students need low-cost housing accessible to public transportation, which is a very rare commodity in the Hartford area. This shortage is exacerbated by economic disparities between Jamaica and the United States, especially the continued erosion of the Jamaican dollar's value. To date, UConn has not been able to overcome this barrier to international exchange.

Community Involvement

The involvement of the greater Hartford Caribbean American community was one of UConn's goals for this project. This objective has proven to be challenging at times and has been only partially realized. The enthusiasm of UConn graduates of Jamaican heritage has been very positive for the linkage; they have been a ready audience for programs with visiting UWI speakers and some were involved in the planning for Mona99 and attended the conference. Additional programs included a day-long conference on serving the West Indian community in January, 1995 that was cosponsored by UConn's School of Social Work and a committee of local West Indian social workers. A Caribbean night with speakers, food, and entertainment was held for the school community in the spring of 1999, again with local participation in planning and implementation. The wider social welfare community (i.e., non-West Indian) has also been interested in programs associated with this project because of the desire to learn more about serving the West Indian population. Therefore, agencies have been glad to host visits by UWI faculty in exchange for informal presentations and discussions with the staff. For instance, the Connecticut Department of Children and Families sponsored a four-session training course for their supervisory staff that was presented by a UWI faculty member.

Nevertheless, the degree of success desired for community involvement has not been realized. No significant fundraising has been achieved. Individuals have provided some support for the linkage: one alumna donated and delivered a computer to UWI early in the project and others have sent textbooks and assisted with housing and hosting visitors from UWI. Initially, UWI staff had hoped that Hartford-area Jamaicans would provide financial support and made a specific request for donations of video equipment. This request was not met. Fairly early in the link, a newspaper article that could have been positive for the program turned negative as some community leaders perceived the university's actions as an attempt to dictate to the community or to define its problems. This misunderstanding was never fully resolved, as the local West Indian newspaper refused to print letters from either UWI or UConn staff in response to the criticism of the project. This incident suggests the need to concentrate on efforts to consult with local leaders in projects with a desired community component.

Additional Evaluative Questions

If a more formal evaluation were to be conducted, an assessment of the relative effectiveness of this project's exchange strategies could assist in defining priorities for the future. These would include the following: (1) an assessment of the relative benefits to individuals and their institutions of short (2-4 weeks) versus long (entire semester) faculty exchange visits; (2) an examination of the validity of placement exchanges for students' professional development and future practice; (3) an examination of whether the promotion of UWI faculty publication should emphasize access to opportunities, joint authorship, or both; and (4) an assessment of the impact of curriculum materials exchange on UWI's reliance on North American literature and implications for promoting culturally relevant indigenous literature from the Caribbean.

More immediate programmatic directions for the future have also been suggested. The partner schools will expand their use of video and electronic exchange mechanisms, especially web-based instruction. The common interest in migration has generated a number of ideas that have not yet been implemented, including a jointly sponsored international working conference on Caribbean migration and service projects to help families address migration separation and reunification. To carry out these and other ideas, the past successes of the linkage should be used to seek funding for expanding its impact.

LESSONS LEARNED: POSSIBILITIES FOR REPLICATION

The high level of activity sustained in the UWI-UConn partnership has been aided by factors that may be difficult to replicate, such as the involvement of personnel from both schools in the regional association of the IASSW. However, other characteristics, such as flexibility and success in functioning without major funding, suggest that the lessons learned from this project may be useful to other programs. The following

are elements of this partnership that contributed to its success and should be considered by other programs.

The selection of the exchange partners was based on the identification of a common area of interest and the presence of an immigrant population linking the two regions. The mutual area of interest has been important in justifying and continuing the linkage by providing an easy answer to the question: Why a link with Jamaica/ Connecticut? This initial mutuality has continued to be important, even as other areas of shared interest have been discovered.

While shared interests can focus on aspects of social work practice or commonly experienced social problems, the presence of an immigrant community may be a particularly potent factor for strengthening a collaboration. As discussed throughout this chapter, the ongoing migration of Jamaicans to the Hartford area, along with some return migration, has provided a common issue for research and education and has ensured student and practitioner interest in the collaborative activities of the two programs. In some cases, an immigrant community may provide financial support for a collaboration, as has been the case in another social work project that linked UConn and Yerevan State University, in Armenia. Therefore, in developing such a project, schools of social work might examine the local population to determine the feasibility of building on the presence of significant immigrant populations in their community.

Other considerations in purposeful selection of an exchange partner are geography and the costs and ease of travel and communication. Low travel costs and relatively short distance have definitely helped maintain a high degree of contact between UWI and UConn. In fact, this article even understates the contact between the partners. Former students from exchange-taught classes have maintained professional contacts with their instructors and faculty members have met in many different conference settings.

The goals of the linkage have supported and contributed to the mission and goals of the participating institutions. The presence of a large West Indian community meant that UConn's project addressed CSWE accreditation standards that require schools' curricula to be relevant to its community. Thus, activities of the exchange project can be extensions of the curriculum or normal program activities. In part, the timing for this link was favorable as UWI was beginning a new MSW program and UConn was expanding its international focus. In addition, personnel involved in the collaboration were conscious of the need to fit the project within their institutions' priorities.

The exchange partners have been relatively successful in achieving wide participation in the linkage activities. This has been particularly true for UWI, where most members of the social work faculty have participated in some way, either through visits to UConn or through co-authorships. Although UConn has not achieved total involvement, more than half of the faculty have participated at some level. While only three have taught at UWI, 12 faculty members attended Mona99 and participated in a joint luncheon and planning session with the UWI social work faculty. Three additional faculty members who did not attend served as abstract reviewers for the conference. At least three UConn faculty members have served as external reviewers for UWI courses, and at least four are involved in joint publication projects. Needless to say, broad-based participation contributes to support for the project and to the likelihood that it can survive without its founders.

Less tangible resources for exchange, including access, reputation, and expertise, were discovered to be important factors. Access has proven particularly valuable, as conference information and opportunities for publication have been shared and, occasionally, directly provided. These are noncost items that depend only on truly viewing your collaborators as partners and remembering to pass on information and invitations.

Most importantly, the linkage has been characterized by mutuality. As documented above, the exchange of benefits has been two-way. Although this project is between a developing country institution and a North American university, it was not conceived of or implemented as a North-South consultation project. Expertise has flowed in both directions, which has helped achieve mutuality throughout the exchange.

Mutuality was also aided by the attitudes, values, and communication styles of the personnel involved in the exchange. Conscious efforts to develop a cosmopolitan ethos—i.e., an open-mindedness and belief in the value of diverse cultures and experiences—and facility in cross-cultural and cross-national communication among faculty are important strategies for developing and maintaining mutually beneficial exchange relationships (Maxwell, 1994).

In summary, the social work collaboration between the University of the West Indies, Mona Campus, and the University of Connecticut has been sustained for almost a decade with only minimal external funding. It has yielded several publications with more in process, a jointly sponsored international conference, and many other accomplishments. In addition, a number of very significant friendships have developed. It is expected that the institutional collaboration will continue; certainly the personal connections will endure.

REFERENCES

Allen, J. A. (1995). African-Americans: Caribbean. In R. Edwards (Ed.), *Encyclopedia of social work* (19th ed., pp. 121-129). Washington, DC: NASW Press.

Crawford-Brown, C., & Rattray, M. (2001). Parent-Child relationships in Caribbean families. In N. B. Webb (Ed.), *Culturally diverse parent-child and family relationships* (pp. 107-132). New York: Columbia University Press.

Glasgow, G. F., & Gouse-Sheese, J. (1995). Themes of rejection and abandonment in group work with Caribbean adolescents. *Social Work With Groups, 17*(4), 3-27.

Gopaul-McNicol, S. (1993). *Working with West Indian families.* New York: Guilford Publications.

Healy, L. M., Maxwell, J. A., & Pine, B. A. (1999). Exchanges that work: Mutuality and sustainability in a Caribbean/USA academic partnership. *Social Development Issues, 21*(3), 14-21.

Maxwell, J. A. (1994, July). *Educating social workers for interorganizational coordination.* Paper presented at the 27th Congress of the International Association of Schools of Social Work, Amsterdam, the Netherlands.

Planning Institute of Jamaica. (1999). Balance of payments. In *Economic and social survey of Jamaica 1998.* Kingston, Jamaica: Author.

Sewell-Coker, B., Hamilton-Collins, J., & Fein, E. (1985). Social work practice with West Indian immigrants. *Social Casework: The Journal of Contemporary Social Work, 66,* 563-568.

Swift, M. (2002, July 24). West Indians feel pull of change. *The Hartford Courant,* A1, A5.

United Nations Development Program. (2000). *Human development report 2000.* New York: Oxford University Press.

University of Connecticut School of Social Work. (1994). *Mission statement.*

SEVEN

Collaboration Between Two Universities in Industrialized Countries: The National Danish School of
Social Work, Aarhus, and Boston University

Terry Saunders Lane, Ole Langsted, and Lee H. Staples

This case study describes a 14-year (1989-present) international collaboration between the National Danish School of Social Work in Aarhus, Denmark and the Boston University School of Social Work in Boston, Massachusetts (BUSSW). The study demonstrates how social work educators and students from two wealthy countries can learn from different perspectives regarding social care, social work practice, and social work education. It also illustrates the collaboration that is possible when schools have the financial and institutional capacity to regularly support some of the expenses associated with mutual exchanges for their students and faculty. The exchanges in this project include regular week-long study programs for students and faculty, lectures by visiting faculty at the partner schools, and field placements for Danish students in Boston human service agencies.

INITIATION OF THE COLLABORATION

Two members of the BUSSW faculty initiated this collaboration in order to expand and strengthen the international opportunities for MSW students and faculty. This approach grew out of these educators' personal interests and shared commitment to international education. With encouragement from the dean of the BUSSW, they wrote letters of inquiry to several schools of social work in countries that would be relatively easy to reach and were appropriate for the proposed project. These considerations included travel costs and the ability to take U.S. students with limited foreign language proficiency into situations where English would be readily available.

The dean of the National Danish School of Social Work in Aarhus responded enthusiastically. This school already had established connections with a variety of programs in Europe, and the dean was interested in

developing a new link to a school in the United States. The letter from BUSSW came at a time of emerging awareness for the importance of international cooperation in social work education (and in education in general). This contact was the starting point of a trend that led the school in Aarhus to develop a specialization in international social work.

These three founders, the two BUSSW educators and the dean of the National Danish School of Social Work, planned and implemented the initial program. In the second year, a new faculty member took over the management of the Danish portion of the collaboration, and he has continued in this role ever since. Additional participants joined the BUSSW team after 5 years so that they could maintain the project when the originators went on to other activities.

GOALS OF THE COLLABORATION

The partner schools have common goals for their participation in this collaboration. The goals can be split into three categories: knowledge, attitudes, and skills. (Sanders, 1977; Sanders & Pedersen, 1984; Healy, 1988; Asamoah, Healy, & Mayadas, 1997; Mizio & Lugar, 1997). First, both institutions hope that participants will gain knowledge in several specific areas:

- The role of the United States and Denmark in the global community
- Social welfare issues in different countries and the distinct types of welfare policy responses
- The roles and functions of the social work profession in different societies
- The cultural values that shape the social work profession
- Ethical dilemmas in social work practice

The attitude goals of this project include the awareness of one's own values through comparison to other cultures, as well as cross-cultural sensitivity and understanding. For the skills goals, it is hoped that expanded knowledge and the exploration of attitudes can be transformed into skills that enable participants to validate cultural differences and carry out social work practice in a culturally competent manner—either in international or domestic settings.

WHY DENMARK AND THE UNITED STATES?

This exchange program enables students and faculty from both schools to learn about different approaches to social welfare and to social work practice. For example, many U.S. social workers view Denmark with envy because social and economic indicators place it as one of the most prosperous countries in the world, and all of its citizens benefit from its wealth. The poverty rate is quite low—at less than 5% of the population (Ministry of Social Affairs, 1995) compared to 13.3% in the United States (U.S. Bureau of the Census, 1997). Infant mortality rates are lower (5 deaths per 1,000 births in the first year of life) compared to an overall rate of 7 per 1,000 in the United States, which also has large discrepancies between White infants and African American children (U.S. Bureau of the Census, 1997). The Danish social welfare system provides many of the economic, health, and social supports that are only distant visions in the United States. Child care, health and unemployment benefits, and educational programs for all ages are virtually universal. Danish programs embody the institutional approach to social welfare as the state plays a central role in promoting the well-being of all citizens through comprehensive and long-term coverage in this small (5.3 million people) nation with an overwhelmingly homogeneous ethnic and religious (Lutheran) population. In contrast, social policy in the United States leans toward the residual model, in which government services are available only to those in need. Emphasis is placed on limited government intervention and reliance on personal responsibility, family and private care, and the free market system (Titmuss, 1974). These distinct approaches to social welfare are supported by great differences in public taxation. Danish citizens accept a high taxation rate (47% of their gross domestic product compared to 29% in the United States) and a high proportion of their gross domestic product devoted to public expenditures:

58% in Denmark versus 36% in the United States (Mogensen, 1995).

The values that undergird contemporary life, social policies, and the social work profession in Denmark are quite different from those in the United States. The primary philosophical tradition for Danish culture is social solidarity, rather than U.S. society's emphasis on individualism. This collective ideal stresses the responsibility of the society for the welfare of all. In Denmark, social solidarity is shaped by a tenet of the Lutheran religion that stresses care for others in this world as a prerequisite for salvation in the afterlife. Following the doctrines of the 19th-century philosopher N. F. S. Grundtvig, great value is also placed on literacy in all aspects of life, as evidenced by "folk high schools" that are supported with public funds and attended by citizens of all ages to learn about their cultural heritage (Carlsen & Borgaa, 1993). Danish life is further marked by humility, modesty, and self-deprecation, but also persistence and a nonauthoritarian ethos (Hofstede, 1997). It is considered most appropriate to "fit in" to the group, and to follow the premise of *jante*—to think of oneself as "no better than anyone else." This attitude is in contrast to the mainsteam U.S. notion that every individual is "as good as anyone else." Within the general framework of seeing an individual as an integral part of society, the Danes also value tolerance and the lack of interference in personal lifestyle choices.

Visiting U.S. social workers are generally impressed that a wealthy society can provide for the basic needs of its citizens, but they are also surprised about the relatively limited roles that most social workers fill. Danish social workers focus on care giving—through case management, by assisting clients to obtain the resources to which they are entitled, and in helping them to function independently once the array of state-supported resources are in place. Typically, they are not involved in psychotherapy with individuals, families, or groups, community organizing, advocacy, or empowerment work. Most social workers are employed by public agencies that deliver social welfare and health services, and usually they are members of a trade union. (Holst & Ito, 1982; National Danish School of Social Work in Aarhus, 1996). This role for social workers reflects the values that underpin Danish society. It emerges out of an assumption that the society can provide a "good life" for its members if people understand societal norms and expectations, participate in and support the community, and access the available resources. Thus, the social worker is an expert guide who navigates through the state-run bureaucracies on behalf of clients, intervenes for them, and provides solutions (Vincenti, 1997).

When Danish social workers come to the United States, they are surprised at the depth of individualism that informs social welfare policy and social work practice. Social work in the United States always has been marked by a persistent struggle between the amelioration of individual suffering versus social change to address the structural flaws in the culture that fosters the varied ills that individuals experience (Lee, 1937; Reamer, 1990). This tension derives from competing views about the purpose of charity. On the one hand, the United States is founded on the tenets of individualism, including the opportunities for individuals to reap the benefits of their own initiative and personal freedom. These opportunities are combined with expectations for personal self-reliance and responsibility. The United States has a modest commitment to universal benefits and programmatic assistance for the needy. On the other hand, there is a tradition of duty to provide aid to vulnerable people, initially expressed as a religious duty to care for those in need (Hutchinson, 1992; Reamer 1990).

Several social work themes emerge out of these strands of philosophical conflict: client self-determination, clients' rights to privacy and confidentiality, and the right of freedom from interference by others (Hutchinson, 1992). Other themes include respect for diversity of ethnicity, race, and ideas; building on client and community strengths; and empowerment. It can be argued that the long-standing presence of oppression in U.S. history has set the stage for struggle and advocacy in the pursuit of social justice, as witnessed by a host of social movements, including organized labor, civil rights, women's suffrage, gay rights, anti-war, Native Americans, and disability rights. The profession still pursues ongoing efforts to determine what these concepts mean in everyday practice (Council on Social Work Education [CSWE], 2001; National Association of Social Workers [NASW], 1997).

Additionally, Danish visitors often notice the visibility and discussion of empowerment and advocacy on behalf of individuals and communities in U.S. social work practice. Some Danes point out that empowerment is imbued in their everyday life, and it is therefore not necessary to highlight it as a special part of social work. Others feel that this concept has not been recognized sufficiently and that new strategies should be incorporated into Danish social work practice. For example, Vincenti (1997) argues that social workers should

abandon their positions as professional technicians and concentrate more on the promotion of self-determination. Uggerhoej (1996) supplements these ideas with a plea for strengthened relationships between workers and clients that are marked by respect, involvement, and engagement, in addition to knowledge of the system's benefits.

WHAT HAS BEEN EXCHANGED DURING THE RELATIONSHIP?

The relationship between the partner schools contains three components:

- Week-long student and faculty study-travel exchanges to both countries, consisting of lectures, site visits to human service agencies, lodging with host families, and tourism
- Field placements in Boston for Danish social work students
- Visiting faculty lectures

Study-Travel Exchanges

The study-travel programs have taken place steadily throughout the past decade. Between 1989 and 2000, seven U.S. groups traveled from Boston to Aarhus, and six groups of Danish students visited Boston. Close to 150 U.S. participants have traveled to Aarhus in groups of 20-25, and about 100 Danes participated in groups of 9-31.

These study-travel programs address the special interests of the visitors. For example, the BUSSW participants are primarily MSW students who are enrolled in a semester-long course. A few faculty members and professional social workers have also joined each group. Most trips have been linked to a required advanced course on ethics in social work practice; a few were part of a course on international social policy. The ethics course is one section of a required advanced elective. It examines social work values, as well as ethical and legal issues, in the United States and considers the similarities and differences to ethical matters in Denmark. The strategy of discussing U.S. social work values and ethics in comparison to similar issues in other countries is quite unusual (Hoefer, 1996). Most U.S. schools of social work infuse information on ethics and values throughout their curricula without offering a separate required course, and most schools integrate the discussion of international issues into courses on comparative social welfare policy (Healy, 1988, 1991; Estes, 1992; Tracy, 1992; Hoefer, 1996).

The goals of the ethics course are consonant with the values and ethics guidelines in the CSWE Educational Policy and Accreditation Standards (CSWE, 2001). The course first assists students in developing an awareness of their own values within the context of U.S. society. It then discusses the values of the U.S. social work profession and explores how this profession has developed historically. The course requires students to confront how they will make decisions and seek practical solutions when several values conflict. The course also stresses that values and ethical dilemmas vary in different cultures. It considers the implications of different value traditions (e.g., community solidarity versus individualism) on the development of different social welfare systems and social work practice models. It then explores the extent to which such differences shape discussions about ethical dilemmas and decision making.

When students travel to Denmark, they learn about the ways that the profession has developed there and about the ethical issues that arise in fields of practice such as child welfare, mental health, family service, and work with refugees and immigrants. They also stay with host families—typically Danish social work students. These visits provide regular opportunities to discuss differences and similarities in informal settings.

In contrast, the Danish participants visit Boston to attend an Institute on Group Work and Empowerment that is designed specifically for them by BUSSW. This program is not connected to any specific course in the Danish curriculum. The topic was chosen because it provides a perspective on U.S. culture as well as information about a subject that is not emphasized in Danish social work education. The program includes lectures by professors from BUSSW and site visits to agencies that can demonstrate group work or empowerment strategies. The program also includes "open classes" where Danish students can join ongoing class sessions with BUSSW students. An orientation to Boston enables students to explore the city during their free time. Many participants stay with host families, preferably social work students, with whom they can discuss the teaching and cultural differences that they experience. Before or after their week in Boston, the group spends 3-4 days in New York City as tourists. Student evaluations reveal that participants are enthusiastic about the trip and the program. Some have said that they learned more in a week in Boston than they learned in a whole semester at home.

Danish participants include students from all levels of the educational program, based on personal interest and the ability to pay for the trip (U.S. $600-700). Whereas the European Union funds exchange programs between European countries, no sponsor has been found for this Denmark–United States exchange. Thus, every student has to pay for the trip—which is very unusual in a country where education is free. Consequently, even if there is enormous interest among the student body, actual attendance is unpredictable. Often about 10-15 students are able to attend, but some years have inadequate enrollment to support the program, while others have a surplus, such as the fall of 2000, when 27 students participated.

Field Placements in Boston for Danish Social Work Students

Between 1995 and 2002, 13 Danish students completed 5-month field internships at community-based organizations in Greater Boston that engage in macro social work practice, including organization, advocacy, collective empowerment, and community development. Experienced staff members who have an MSW degree (the Danish program requires supervisors to have an MSW) have acted as practice placement supervisors. BUSSW faculty serve as institutional supervisors, which are analogous to faculty advisors at many U.S. schools of social work. Students' field work assignments have included home visits, door-to-door recruitment, leadership development, action research, campaign planning, staffing task groups, developing written materials, agenda planning, working with local news media, helping plan training programs, and evaluation activities. Many of these types of experiences are not available in most Danish social work field internships.

To date, the outcomes of these field placements have been positive for all concerned. Danish students have been exposed to a wide variety of macro practice knowledge, methods, and skills in these community-based organizations. All of the students have informally attended BUSSW courses concurrent with their internships. This academic material has provided a conceptual underpinning for their work in the field, as faculty can explicate the links between theory and practice. Typically, the students have been enthusiastic about their newfound expertise and have expressed great interest in future practical applications—with appropriate modifications—in Denmark. Agency supervisors have been very pleased by the performance of the Danish interns. The continuous placements mean that students are consistently available for large blocks of time. This feature has enabled supervisors to design work assignments containing a good measure of student independence and responsibility. The requirement for fluency in English has not been a significant problem for any students. Thus far, all Danish students have received high marks on their field evaluations, with U.S. supervisors frequently lauding qualities such as work ethic, interpersonal skills, flexibility, follow-through, and the capacity to be a "quick study."

Faculty Lectures at Host Schools

The third component of the exchange has been the provision of lectures by visiting faculty members. BUSSW group work and community organization educators have traveled to Aarhus, where they deliver lectures and workshops to students, faculty, practicing social workers, and pedagogues. The National Danish School of Social Work pays each lecturer an honorarium and provides accommodations. One BUSSW faculty member delivered a series of lectures and workshops on the theory and practice of empowerment, contributed a paper on this topic to the National Danish School's 40th anniversary celebration publication (Staples, 1997), and helped to stimulate the formation of "the Empowerment Group," a working task force composed of both academics and practitioners. Three members of this task force recently published a book about empowerment in the Danish context (Andersen, Brok, & Mathiasen, 2000). At BUSSW, Danish faculty have discussed the history and components of social welfare in Denmark and the role of center-based childcare in the everyday life of most young Danish children. These lectures have inspired dialogue and debate in a variety of welfare policy and human behavior courses at BUSSW.

ISSUES OF COMMON INTEREST

The development of cultural competence (the ability to be aware of cultural differences and to engage in a sensitive and effective manner with members of diverse groups) is a common goal for social work educators and practitioners throughout the world. This exchange project's experiential learning process immerses students and faculty from both institutions in different cultural settings. Participants are forced to question basic assumptions about the nature of their own welfare states, about the role of social work in their local social welfare context, and about the efficacy of particular social work methods. Through lectures and site visits, the students are exposed to very different models of social work practice and practitioner roles. Engagement with faculty, students, social workers, and community members from the "other" society serves to challenge preconceptions and stereotypes. Visiting students and faculty call additional assumptions about social work into question and begin to grapple with these difficult issues. Discussions within the visiting groups often lead to fresh insights and an increased appreciation for cultural differences. The entire program contributes to first-hand knowledge about a different culture, to attitudinal changes born of direct experience, and to new skills developed through a process of active learning.

Cultural competence has added relevance for both U.S. and Danish social workers, because both countries are currently struggling with the integration of newcomer populations. The phenomenon is not new in the United States, a nation that historically has alternately welcomed and rebuffed—but always had to deal with—immigrants and refugees. As noted earlier, Denmark is a relatively homogeneous society with a high level of cultural consensus. Nevertheless, a combination of "guest workers," who have remained long after labor shortages have disappeared, and recent refugees from a variety of international disaster areas has served to introduce an unprecedented level of cultural diversity into Danish society. Although the United States often struggles with anti-immigrant backlash—frequently born of racism and classism—"multiculturalism" is a concept with growing currency. Despite "English only" campaigns and punitive legislation in many parts of the country, the old "melting pot" model of assimilation is gradually giving way to a "tossed salad" metaphor, whereby newcomers become integrated into mainstream U.S. society without losing their distinct cultural identity. For the most part, Danes have eschewed a mean-spirited backlash but have been slow to replace assimilation with a multicultural paradigm. The collective attitude toward newcomers often seems to be, "Welcome! Now come and be Danish and put aside your old cultural identity." Clearly, this exchange project offers excellent learning opportunities about other cultures for both U.S. and Danish participants.

INSTITUTIONAL SUPPORT AND EFFORTS TO INSTITUTIONALIZE THE COLLABORATION

This collaboration has thrived due largely to the enthusiasm and willingness of those individuals who organize each of the elements. These educators and administrators are all committed to international study and mutual exchange and have been willing to take on the work associated with organizing the study-travel program and the field education placements. In addition, institutional support from both schools has maintained the collaboration. For example, at BUSSW, the study-travel trip must enroll enough participants (at least 10) to make it worthwhile. Because it is linked to one section of a required course that all students take, enrollment is more predictable than if it were connected to a strictly elective course. Secondly, the organizational responsibilities associated with the exchange program have been incorporated into the job of a full-time administrator who also has teaching duties. Thus, staff members from that office handle many of the program details. Finally, funds have been made available to partially support the expenses of the program coordinator's travel to Denmark and to pay for expenses associated with hosting the Danish visitors in Boston.

The school in Aarhus also supports the collaboration in several ways. International social work is part of the school's education policy, so the collaboration with Boston is an important part of an exchange program with several other, mainly European, components. Danish students in U.S. field placements receive the same level of financial assistance as those with internships in other European countries. The management of these international relations is the main job of one administrator at the school, and she takes care of planning the programs for the BUSSW visitors in collaboration with a full-time teaching professor. The trips to Boston are planned by this professor, who also joins the students on their tour. The professor receives some reduction in his teaching load, and the school pays all of his travel expenses. The school also supports the visitors from Boston by paying some smaller expenses, like transportation around Aarhus. Unfortunately, the school cannot afford to pay for the expenses of the Danish students who travel to Boston (except for a tiny amount, which pays for their transportation within Denmark). Certainly, many more students would join the trips to the United States if some of the expenses were covered.

MUTUALITY IN THE COLLABORATION

Both partners value the mutual benefits and responsibilities of the collaboration. They try to provide parallel experiences by developing programs that are tailored to the special interests of the partner school, recruiting host families, and accommodating fairly large groups of visitors. In addition, each program has been willing to respond to the special circumstances of the students. For example, BUSSW assists in setting up field internships in Boston for Danish students, but parallel arrangements have not been requested in Denmark due to language requirements there. In turn, the school in Aarhus invites (and partly pays the expenses of) a visiting professor to give lectures, providing Danish students with an opportunity to learn more about social work in Boston.

IMPACT OF THE COLLABORATION ON THE PARTICIPATING INSTITUTIONS

This partnership has generated substantial benefits for both organizations. In Boston, it laid the groundwork for the expansion of international study-travel programs to other locales (London in 1999 and Mexico in 2000). BUSSW faculty and administrators who have made the trip to Denmark have been intellectually enriched and have gained additional knowledge, case materials for teaching, and potential overseas collaborators for scholarly work—as witnesses this case study. Research and articles prepared by Professor Ole Langsted, from the National Danish School of Social Work, have been included in the Introduction to Human Behavior course at the BUSSW. Danish students provide high-quality staff assistance for service agencies in Boston and add an international perspective to these agencies' community work. The visiting students have also become valued—albeit temporary—members of the BUSSW community. Often, they team with U.S. social work students in field placements, which leads to many stimulating learning opportunities. As frequent visitors to BUSSW courses, Danish students usually become active participants in class discussions, bringing their unique insights and viewpoints to these dialogues.

In Denmark the collaboration has also had a substantial impact. Some of the Danish participants in an early Boston study-travel program were so inspired by the teaching on empowerment that they implemented the method in Denmark, and published a book on the subject (Andersen et al., 2000). In addition, the school's curriculum has incorporated a number of empowerment concepts. The field placement program in Boston has shaped the Danes' thinking about field education as well. Danish students' internships take place during their fourth semester, and the students typically had no coursework during that period. However, a "reflection group' is now utilized throughout the internship period to help integrate classroom learning and the practice experience. This approach, inspired by BUSSW's concurrency of methods courses and field education, now is referred to as the "Boston Model" in the Aarhus program.

PROSPECTS AND CHALLENGES FOR THE FUTURE

As is clear from the previous discussion, this collaboration has been marked by substantial successes. An enormous and positive impact has been realized in terms of the exchange of knowledge, the development of curricula, scholarship, and the emergence of strong friendships. In addition, because the exchanges have taken place numerous times, lessons have been learned and incorporated into subsequent trips. For example, at BUSSW protocols have been developed for exchange program components such as participant recruitment and selection, travel and financial arrangements, university liability, orientation for international travel, and management of group dynamics.

Nevertheless, challenges also have emerged. One of the best features of this exchange can also be seen as its biggest challenge—it is nurtured and maintained by a small group of deeply committed individuals. When they inevitably turn to other endeavors, the ability to continue the project may be threatened. For example, as BUSSW personnel have changed over the years, it has not always been clear who was going to handle the workload associated with the partnership.

Other challenges have included opportunities for students to join study programs visiting other countries. Because only a finite number of students have the financial resources to travel, programs can wind up competing with one another for participants. As the costs of the trips are borne by individual students in both countries, those without adequate personal resources have not been able to participate in the exchanges. Additionally, at BUSSW, the recruitment of student hosts has become increasingly difficult. In response to the rising cost of rental housing, students either live in cramped quarters or they live far from BUSSW's downtown campus and far from public

transportation. Neither situation is conducive to comfortable hosting arrangements. Thus far, language differences have posed minimal problems, for the simple reason that the Danish faculty and students have been fluent in English. Lectures and site visits in both countries have been conducted almost entirely in English. BUSSW program coordinators have pointed out the lack of mutuality in this aspect of the relationship to their U.S. students, which often generates lively discussions about the role of English-speaking nations in the international arena.

POSSIBILITIES FOR REPLICATION

This type of collaboration can be replicated if some of the key factors are put into place.

Host-Organization Commitment. An exchange program, such as the one described above, will not be possible without the enthusiasm and support of the respective host organizations. Deans, faculties, and program directors must all be on board if success is to be expected. Although these projects are not inordinately expensive, direct financial resources, the assignment of a program coordinator, faculty time, and administrative support will be required to move forward. A solid institutional commitment is essential.

Clear Goals and Objectives. Participating institutions need to be clear about what they hope to gain from such an exchange and what they are willing to do in order to make it work. The Aarhus-Boston exchange project has featured common goals with regard to knowledge, attitudes, and skills. However, there has also been room for distinct institutional objectives, such as the ethics course at BUSSW and the U.S. field placements for the Aarhus program. Flexibility within a shared programmatic framework has worked more effectively than a rigidly parallel format.

Competent Coordinators. A fundamental reason for the success of this program has been the presence of strong, knowledgeable coordinators at each school. While individual coordinators have changed over the years, their role has been a constant throughout this program's history. These individuals must be committed to institutional collaboration, international study, and mutual learning. They are responsible for program planning and implementation, recruitment, teaching, processing group dynamics with their own and visiting delegations, evaluation, and a plethora of logistical and administrative details.

Effective Communication. A relationship of collaboration and trust is built on open communication and rapport between partners. Geographic distance, cultural differences, and the potential for mistakes and confusion from nuances "missed in translation" add challenges for long-distance communication. Multiple forms for interaction can be an antidote (email especially is a great boon), and sufficient lead time should be built in to enable extra communication exchanges to take place.

Receptivity to the Needs of Partner Schools. The Aarhus-Boston exchange has been enhanced by the willingness of each partner school to listen and respond to the special requests of the other. It is important that programs enter into any collaborative relationship with a genuine spirit of mutuality and receptivity to the needs of the partner institution, rather than focusing exclusively on their own interests and agendas.

Attention to Administrative Details. Coordinators and administrative-support staff are responsible for a range of specific details, including recruiting and screening students, collecting (or accounting for) payments, curriculum content, air-travel planning and logistics, visiting student housing, program planning for lectures and site visits, managing group dynamics, policies for free-time touring, visa and health insurance issues, and evaluation materials. It is vital that these details are attended to carefully and competently. Rather than learning through trial and error, it is advisable that new exchange programs contact existing partnerships to examine already-developed protocols and to access acquired experience, knowledge, and wisdom.

CONCLUSION

This Aarhus-Boston exchange features a partnership between two advanced industrialized nations. Students are able to examine two distinct approaches to social welfare policy from countries that have reached a comparable level of development. Although the cultural values undergirding these welfare policies and programs are in stark contrast, the relative economic prosperity in both nations affords study tour participants the opportunity to make comparisons of different welfare state policies and programs that are more a function of values and ideology than economic imperatives. And this same economic affluence makes it possible for a genuine two-way relationship to exist, with significant numbers of students from each country able to afford the costs of a study-travel exchange program.

REFERENCES

Andersen, M. L., Brok, P. N., & Mathiasen, H. (2000). *Empowerment paa dansk* [Empowerment in Danish]. Frederikshavn, Denmark: Dafolo Forlag.

Asamoah, Y., Healy, L. M., & Mayadas, N. (1997). Ending the international-domestic dichotomy: New approaches to a global curriculum for the millennium. *Journal of Social Work Education, 33,* 389-401.

Carlsen, J., & Borgaa, O. (1993). *The Danish folkehoejskole.* Copenhagen, Denmark: Royal Danish Ministry of Foreign Affairs, Secretariat of Cultural Relations.

Council on Social Work Education. (2001). *Educational policy and accreditation standards.* Alexandria, VA: Author.

Estes, R. (Ed.). (1992). *Internationalizing social work education: A guide to resources for a new century.* Philadelphia, PA: University of Pennsylvania School of Social Work.

Healy, L. M. (1988). Curriculum building in international social work: Toward preparing professionals for the global age. *Journal of Social Work Education, 24,* 221-228.

Healy, L. M. (1991). *Introducing international development content in the social work curriculum.* Washington, DC: NASW Press.

Hoefer, R. (1996). A conceptual model for studying social welfare policy comparatively. *Journal of Social Work Education, 32,* 101-113.

Hofstede, G. (1997). *Cultures and organizations— Software of the mind.* New York: McGraw-Hill.

Holst, E., & Ito, H. (1982). Denmark. In M. C. Hokenstad & R. A. Ritvo (Eds.), *Linking health care and social services: International perspectives* (pp. 61-80). Thousand Oaks, CA: Sage.

Hutchinson, E. (1992). Competing moral values and use of social work authority with involuntary clients. In P. N. Reid & P. R. Popple (Eds.), *The moral purposes of social work: The character and intentions of a profession* (pp. 120-140). Chicago: Nelson-Hall.

Lee, P. R. (1937). *Social work as cause and function and other papers.* New York: Columbia University Press.

Ministry of Social Affairs [Denmark]. (1995). *Social policy in Denmark.* Copenhagen, Denmark: Author.

Mizio, E., & Lugar, R. (1997, February). *Exchange program method for providing cultural and international content: Theoretical and practice perspectives.* Paper Presented at the 43rd Annual Program Meeting of the Council on Social Work Education, Chicago.

Mogensen, G. (Ed.). (1995). *Work incentives in the Danish welfare state*. Aarhus, Denmark: Aarhus University Press.

National Association of Social Workers. (1997). *Code of ethics*. Washington, DC: Author.

National Danish School of Social Work in Aarhus. (1996). *Social work education in Denmark*. Aarhus, Denmark: Author.

Reamer, F. (1990). *Ethical dilemmas in social service* (2nd ed.). New York: Columbia University Press.

Sanders, D. (1977). Developing a graduate social work curriculum with an international cross-cultural perspective. *Journal of Education for Social Work, 13*(3), 76-83.

Sanders, D., & Pedersen, P. (Eds.). (1984). *Education for international social welfare*. Honolulu, HI: University of Hawaii School of Social Work and the Council on Social Work Education.

Staples, L. (1997). Toward an empowerment model of social work. In C. Christensen, S. Hansen, B. R. Jenson, V. Jonasen, B. L. Kristiansen, & U. Viskum (Eds.), *Den Sociale Hoejskole i Aarhus:1957-1997* [The National Danish School of Social Work in Aarhus: 1957-1997 Jubilee; pp. 37-49]. Aarhus, Denmark: National Danish School of Social Work in Aarhus.

Titmuss, R. (1974). *Social policy: An introduction*. London: Allen and Unwin.

Tracy, M. (1992). Cross-national social welfare policy analysis in the graduate curriculum: A comparative process model. *Journal of Social Work Education, 28*, 341-352.

Uggerhoej, L. (1996, March). *Support or dependence*. Lecture delivered at the National Danish School of Social Work, Aarhus, Denmark.

U.S. Bureau of the Census. (1997). International Data Base. Retrieved from http://factfinder.census.gov/servlet/BasicFactsServlet?_lang=en

Vincenti, G. (1997). From ethnic minority elderly to social work education—What can we as social work educators in Denmark learn? In C. Christensen, S. Hansen, B. R. Jenson, V. Jonasen, B. L. Kristiansen, & U. Viskum (Eds.), *Den Sociale Hoejskole i Aarhus:1957-1997* [The National Danish School of Social Work in Aarhus: 1957-1997 Jubilee; pp. 37-49]. Aarhus, Denmark: National Danish School of Social Work in Aarhus.

EIGHT

A Binational, Bilingual Doctoral Program in Social Work: The Collaboration of the University of Texas at Arlington and Universidad Autónoma de Nuevo León, Mexico

Doreen Elliott, Catheleen Jordan, Manuel Ribeiro Ferreira, Santos H. Hernández, and Héctor Luis Díaz

The Joint Doctoral Program in Social Work and Comparative Social Policy offered in partnership by the University of Texas at Arlington (UTA) and Universidad Autónoma de Nuevo León, Monterrey, Mexico (UANL), began with six Mexican and five U.S. students in the fall of 1997, thus establishing the first doctoral program in social work in Mexico. At the time, it was also the first doctoral program in social work in Spanish-speaking South and Central America. The doctoral program was preceded by academic collaboration between the two universities at the master's level. UTA students undertook study-abroad programs in comparative social policy in 1992 and 1993, and several professors from UTA taught at UANL as guest lecturers in the MSW program. Preliminary discussions were held between the faculties of the two schools in 1994 and the planning process for the joint doctoral program began in 1995. A total of 17 students are currently enrolled in the program: three students from the initial cohort (1997), five from a second cohort (2000), four from a third cohort (2001) and five from a the fourth cohort (2002). Two students have already graduated and three more are expected to graduate during the 2002-2003 academic year.

The University of Texas at Arlington, with an enrollment of approximately 20,000 students, is the second largest of the 15 institutions constituting the University of Texas system. It is a comprehensive teaching, research, and public-service university with about 20% of its students pursuing graduate studies. The doctoral program in the School of Social Work has been well established since the 1970s and has a student body of approximately 50.

The Universidad Autónoma de Nuevo León is a public university located in Monterrey, Mexico, a city of over three million people in the northern state of Nuevo León. UANL is one of the largest institutions of higher education in Mexico, with an enrollment of about 100,000 students. Its research facilities are equipped with the latest computer technology.

UANL's School of Social Work was founded over 27 years ago and, until recently, offered the only master's-level social work program in the country. Its faculty represent the fields of anthropology, sociology, and social work. The graduate program currently enrolls about 20 students and the undergraduate program enrolls about 2,000 students.

BRIEF DESCRIPTION OF THE JOINT DOCTORAL PROGRAM

The joint doctoral program is a 60-credit-hour dual degree in social work with a specialty in international comparative social policy. Students are awarded degrees by UTA and by UANL. The program structure is summarized in Table 1, and the organizational structure in Figure 2. The 1st-year courses are taken in Monterrey, the 2nd-year courses in Texas, and students may choose the location of study for their 3rd year, depending on their research topic. Admission requirements include a master's degree in social work, social welfare, or a related behavioral or social sciences discipline from an institution recognized by both UTA and UANL; a minimum grade point average of 3.4 in graduate courses and 3.0 in undergraduate courses; and fluency in both Spanish and English (Mexican students must score at least 550 on the Test of English as a Foreign Language [TOEFL] and U.S. students must achieve a Spanish proficiency level of "Advanced" or "Superior" in the test administered by the American Council for the Teaching of Foreign Languages). Professional experience in social work is desirable for all students. All applicants to the program must obtain acceptable scores in the graduate admissions tests used in the United States (GRE or PAEG) and in Mexico (EXANI-III). A revision of UTA's graduate admissions criteria was motivated by laws recently enacted in Texas: the graduate admissions test requirement can be waived for applicants with high master's-level grade point averages.

FACTORS MOTIVATING THE CREATION OF THE PROGRAM

For UANL, the motivation for this joint project was the desire to create a doctoral social work program. The faculty of social work at UANL wanted to develop this program to complement and build on the considerable role played by their established master's program in the growth and professionalization of social work in Mexico. An additional incentive was provided by the government of Mexico, which required that all faculty teaching in Mexican universities must have a PhD by the year 2006. Because the social work profession in Mexico is relatively young, UANL has only two faculty with doctoral degrees in social work. The other professors in the program earned their doctoral degrees in

related disciplines, such as sociology and anthropology. Consequently, it became necessary to seek the support of an institution with an established doctoral program to support the UANL initiative.

UTA's rationale for the creation of this program incorporates three areas: academics, demographic and cultural shifts in Texas, and economic and political influences.

From an academic perspective, the joint doctoral program prepares future leaders from the United States, Mexico, and other Central and South American countries to deal with complex social problems at the local, state, national, and international levels. The implications for social work of globalized economies require the understanding of different cultures as well as the development of responsible and informed leaders. These leaders must be capable of using a broad international perspective to formulate and analyze social welfare policies that are oriented toward the improvement of life conditions in diverse cultures.

UTA also established this joint program because Texas has the second largest population of Hispanic origin of all U.S. states. By the year 2025, persons of Hispanic origin will account for 44% of Texas's

TABLE 1. Structure of the Academic Program

Joint Doctoral Program in Social Work, Specialty in International Comparative Social Policy: University of Texas at Arlington (UTA) and Facultad de Trabajo Social Universidad Autónoma de Nuevo León (UANL), Monterrey, Mexico

1ST YEAR (at UANL)

1st semester	2nd semester
Introduction to Social Policy Analysis (3 hrs.)	Social Policy in Mexico (3 hrs.)
Advanced Research Methods (3 hrs.)	Seminar in Qualitative Investigation Methods (3 hrs.)
Program Planning, Evaluation, and Administration (3 hrs.)	Seminar in Applied Research (3 hrs.)
Seminar in Applied Research (3 hrs.)	*Core Comprehensive Examinations*
Diagnostic Evaluation	

2ND YEAR (at UTA)

3rd semester	4th semester
Social Policy in the United States (3 hrs.)	Elective II (Social Policy, 3 hrs.)
Intermediate Statistics (3 hrs.)*	Comparative Social Policy (3 hrs.)
Elective I (3 hrs.)	Advanced Statistics (3 hrs.)
Dissertation Seminar I (3 hrs.)	Dissertation Seminar II (3 hrs.)
	Specialty Comprehensive Examination
	Dissertation Proposal

3RD YEAR (at UTA OR UANL)

5th semester	6th semester
Dissertation Seminar III (3 hrs.)	Dissertation (9 hrs.)

Note. The 1st year of the program takes place at Universidad Autónoma de Nuevo León and the 2nd year at the University of Texas at Arlington for all students. The 3rd year, during which the dissertation is completed, may be taken at whichever location the students select, depending on their financial situation and the nature of their investigative projects.
*An introductory course in social statistics is offered for students who do not pass a qualifying exam to enter Intermediate statistics. This is regarded as a prerequisite and does not count for doctoral credit.

population growth. At that time, Texas will have a 17% share of the total U.S. population of Hispanic origin, which will still be the second largest in the United States, by state (U.S. Census Bureau 1996). Given that institutions of higher education should reflect the communities they serve, the joint doctoral program with UANL seemed to be a step toward achieving this goal.

Economic and political influences in the late 20th century also created propitious circumstances for the development of collaborative agreements between Mexican and North American universities. In January 1994, Canada, the United States, and Mexico signed the North American Free Trade Agreement (NAFTA) or Tratado de Libre Comercio. This created the world's largest free trade area, and through its goal of promoting further socioeconomic development in each country, it influenced public policy and created a climate of cooperation.

FIGURE 1. Organizational and Committee Structure for Dual Degree Track With a Specialty in Comparative Social Policy in the PhD in Social Work Program

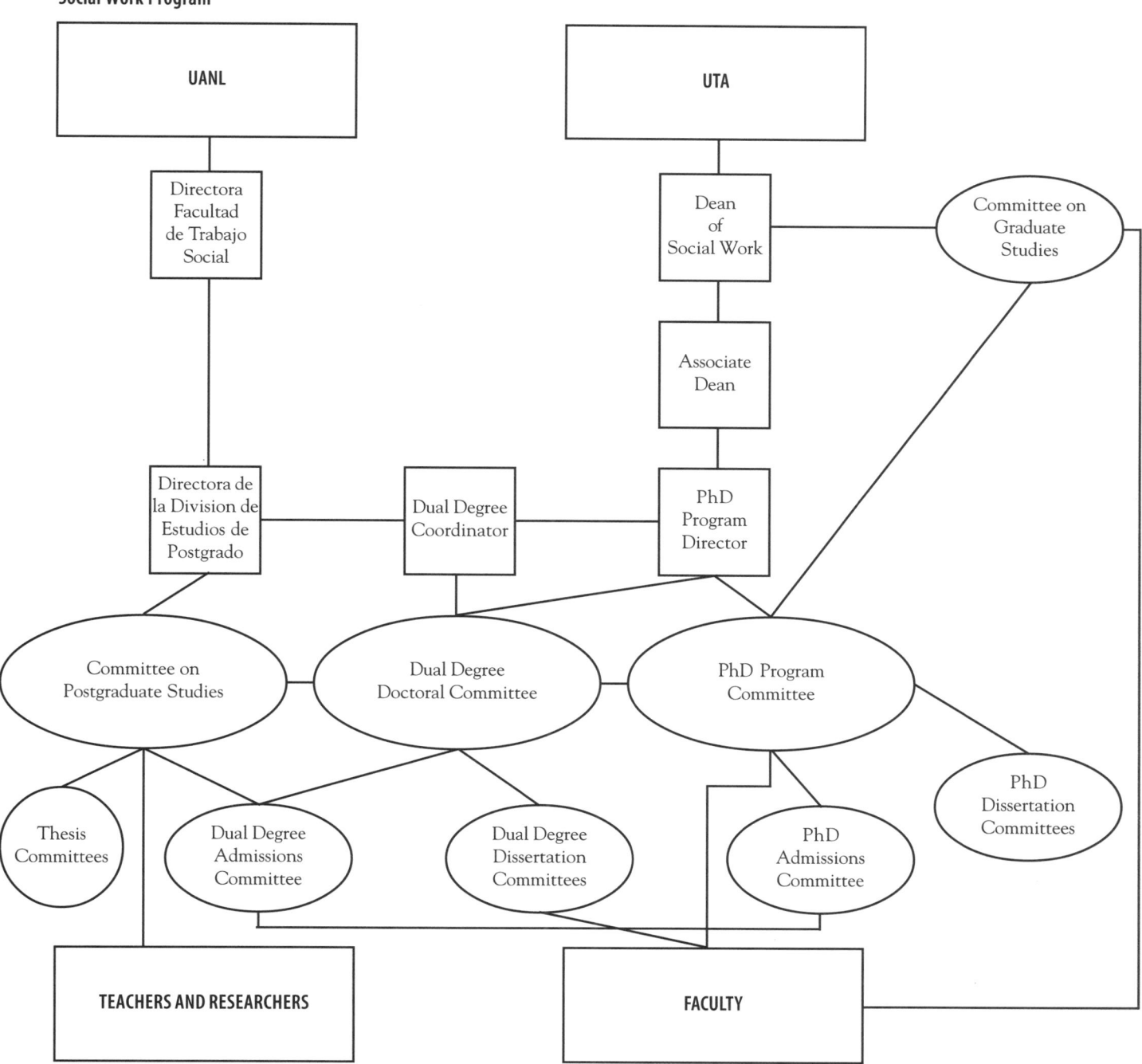

PROGRAM GOAL AND OBJECTIVES

The sociopolitical and sociocultural context described in the previous section motivated the doctoral program planning committee to formulate specific program goals and objectives. The main goal of the program is therefore to prepare doctoral students with knowledge and skills relating to the research, analysis, development, implementation, and evaluation of social welfare policies and programs designed to improve social conditions in the United States, Mexico, and other Latin American countries.

Program objectives are as follows:

- To produce scholars equipped to conduct independent quantitative and qualitative research in the development, implementation, and evaluation of social welfare policies and programs.
- To develop in students the capacity for critical analysis and the ability to propose strategies to respond to social welfare problems.
- To prepare students for leadership positions in the development, management, and implementation of social welfare policies and programs, and for leadership in academic institutions concerned with social policies and programs.

EXCHANGES

This joint doctoral program is based primarily on international recruitment and the exchange of students. Each student cohort (both U.S. and Mexican) completes its 1st year of study in Mexico at UANL. During this time, students take several courses and begin working on their doctoral dissertation proposal. Students are expected to take their qualifying examinations in Mexico upon completion of their first two semesters of study. During the 2nd year, all students move to Arlington where they take additional courses at UTA and continue working on their dissertation proposals. By the end of their 2nd year, students are expected to have completed their dissertation proposal. Following the successful defense of their proposals and after passing their specialty examinations, students are able to begin their doctoral dissertation research. During this 3rd year, they have the option of staying in either Mexico or the United States to complete their dissertation research, depending on their research interests and available resources.

The first student cohort entered the program in 1997 and was comprised of six Mexican and five U.S. students. The second cohort, which entered the program in 2000, was made up of six Mexican and one U.S. student. The third cohort started in 2001 and was comprised of four students of Latin American origin who are permanent residents or citizens of the United States. The fourth cohort, started in the fall of 2002, was made up of two Mexican, two Mexican American, and two Puerto Rican students.

The exchange of faculty has represented a greater challenge for this international program due to the fact that most faculty at UTA are not fluent in Spanish and most at UANL faculty are not fluent in English. A small number of bilingual faculty from both universities have been able to participate in seminars, conferences, and presentations held at the partner institution. This has facilitated mutual understanding and the sharing of the purpose of and approaches to social work.

INSTITUTIONAL SUPPORT

The financial and overall support of both universities for this doctoral program has been quite significant. Both institutions are committed to financially supporting this program in spite of the fact that, because of its nature, it is relatively expensive. The program requires considerable faculty input for small numbers of students and is therefore very labor intensive. Also, the distance between the two programs involves travel for planning, program administration, and teaching and involves the use of expensive technology for other forms of communication, for example, dissertation defenses.

This interinstitutional commitment has made it possible to lower the tuition costs for all students enrolled in the program. Initially, Mexican students paid tuition at UTA as if they were from Texas and U.S. students paid tuition at UANL as if they were Mexican. Currently, the new interinstitutional agreement allows UTA students to only pay tuition to UTA, even when they are taking courses in Mexico, while Mexican students are allowed to only pay tuition to UANL, even when they take courses in the United States. For the purpose of fairness to both institutions, the current arrangement requires that a balance be maintained between the number of UTA and UANL students in the program.

Each institution also contributes the necessary financial and human resources to ensure that the program functions properly. A binational doctoral faculty committee has been created and charged with the responsibility of program oversight, including management, planning, evaluation, and follow-up. This committee meets at least twice a year in either Mexico or the United States and both universities provide funding to cover the expenses associated with these meetings. The program receives administrative support from the presidents of both universities; a preliminary agreement was signed in Mexico by the presidents, followed by a final agreement that included the terms on which the program was established as a joint degree.

The administrative staff of the UTA graduate school has also been very helpful in adapting and responding to the unique and special challenges presented by this very unconventional program. For example, during the initial year special arrangements had to be made with the UTA Registrar's Office to accommodate students who were taking classes in Mexico while admitted to UTA. Another adaptation was to offer the option of a Spanish graduate admissions test as an alternative to the GRE for all applicants to the program. This change was the result of collaboration between the Doctoral Program Committee, the Committee on Graduate Studies of the School of Social Work, and the Graduate School. This alternative test, Prueba de Admisión para Estudios Graduados (PAEG), was developed and is administered by the Educational Testing Service, and its validity and reliability is equal or better than that of the GRE. This has been one of the few concessions made by the UTA administration for the joint program, and UTA has put a lot of effort into demonstrating the comparability of standards with the established PhD program.

CHALLENGES TO ACHIEVING MUTUALITY

If there was a guiding principle, albeit unwritten, for the planning process, it was mutuality. The planning committee consisted of representatives from both universities, and the organizational structure of the program ensured equal participation from other committees at each institution (see Figure 1). The negotiations began with UTA as the provider for a binational program between Mexico and the United States, but it very quickly developed into a dual-degree program. Currently, successful candidates are awarded a degree from both UTA and UANL, and the ultimate goal is to make the program Pan-American, through the involvement of the United States, Mexico, and eventually, Canada and other Latin American countries. This

Pan-American focus is motivated by both the educational goal of including a global and multicultural perspective and by the pragmatic understanding that there are funding possibilities for Pan-American programs. The planning committee meetings were held alternately in the United States and Mexico and the position of chair of the planning committee also switched between universities at each meeting. Figure 1 shows that the dual-degree admissions committee is made up of members from both universities, as are the dissertation committees. All students in the program have two dissertation advisors, one in the United States and one in Mexico, with the advisor from the student's home institution serving in the primary role. The bulk of the communication between the two universities takes place through the Internet, with telephone calls playing a lesser role. Dissertation defenses are conducted via teleconferencing, which makes it possible for the doctoral students to defend their dissertations before a binational committee, half of which is in Mexico and half of which is in the United States.

Mutuality of purpose has been strong on each side from the beginning of the planning process and it has helped the participants address the inevitable challenges associated with a collaboration between two institutions with unique organizational cultures, politics, and educational philosophies.

One of the greatest challenges in achieving mutuality was bringing together two distinctly different academic traditions in doctoral education. The Mexican approach is akin to the European tradition of few classes, independent research under supervision, and no comprehensive examinations. In contrast, the UTA doctoral program in social work has two sets of examinations: qualifying examinations at the end of the initial year, and comprehensive examinations at the end of the course work and prior to the students' admission to candidacy for the doctoral degree, when work is focused on dissertation research. The proposal for the joint program would not have achieved the agreement and the degree of support that it did from the doctoral faculty or from the Graduate Assembly at UTA (an elected body that oversees academic policies, approves new courses, and is concerned with the maintenance of academic standards) without the clear comparability of standards between the proposed and the established programs. It was therefore agreed that the joint program would follow the more structured U.S. model. Nonetheless, the UTA faculty has also made a significant deviation from this model, inspired by the Mexican tradition of ongoing and individualized mentoring in the area of research. They now view the dissertation as the central experience of doctoral education. As a result, students take a dissertation seminar each semester throughout the program.

Another challenge in mutuality was language. Planning meetings were conducted in the language of the chair, and only one or two of the participating faculty members were fluent in both languages. Several had virtually no knowledge of the other language. In the absence of resources for concurrent translation, alternative devices were used, such as pauses for translation, and written materials and charts were widely distributed to facilitate comprehension. All documents were produced in both languages.

EVALUATION

Because evaluation was seen as very important from the beginning, an evaluation plan was included in the planning process. Evaluation data were collected from the first cohort of UTA-UANL students and from seven UTA faculty members who taught in the program during the 2nd year of its operation. A questionnaire designed by the program's director and the PhD Curriculum Committee was used to collect this information. The evaluation had three parts: identification of students' status and progress in the program, ratings of student preparation for the program, and overall ratings of the joint program. Results are presented below.

Identification of Students' Status and Progress in the Program

This section of the questionnaire addressed two areas: student retention and timeliness of degree completion.

Retention. As of the fall semester 2002, a total of 23 students have been admitted into the program as part of four different cohorts. Out of these 23 students, two have already graduated, five are working on their doctoral dissertations, nine are completing coursework, and seven are no longer in the program for various reasons (two could not pass the TOEFL, four did not pass the qualifying examinations, and one had to leave because she could not afford to stop working on a full-time basis). As reflected by the previous figures, the overall program retention rate is currently 70%.

Timeliness of Degree Completion. Students admitted by UANL into this program are expected to complete all degree requirements in 3 years. This is a condition of the agency of the Mexican government that provides

scholarships to these students, CONACYT. UTA regulations, on the other hand, allow up to 4 years after passing the qualifying examinations to complete the PhD. So far, no student has been able to graduate after only 3 years. Many students are in their 4th or 5th year in the program. Although this is not in keeping with the stated completion goal for these students, their progress toward degree completion is comparable to that of students in established doctoral programs in the United States.

Students admitted into this program by UTA and who are not funded by CONACYT are also expected to complete their initial year of studies in Mexico on a full-time basis. They have the option, however, to complete their 2nd and subsequent years on a part-time basis.

Ratings of Student Preparation for the Program

Respondents to the program evaluation survey were asked about the recruitment of capable students and about the students' readiness for doctoral education. Seven of the 11 students in the initial cohort are continuing with the program, which is an indication that the students are capable of doctoral-level work. Concerns expressed by the responding faculty, however, noted the difficulty of recruiting highly qualified students from the United States for this program. This difficulty is primarily due to the lack of resources available to help them with relocation and tuition expenses, a problem exacerbated by the fact that Mexican immigration laws do not allow international students in Mexico to work at all. The first group of students from Mexico had some financial support from UANL, but such support was not provided to the second cohort. Additionally, UTA must compete for social work students with many other doctoral programs in the United States, whereas UANL has the only social work doctoral program in Mexico. Although the greatest challenge associated with recruiting U.S. students for this program is financial, the biggest problem for UANL is finding enough students who are proficient enough in English to study in the United States.

So far, the students recruited by UTA are primarily practitioners with little or no experience in academia. By contrast, the UANL students are mostly experienced faculty under a government requirement to obtain their PhD. The UANL group are perceived by UTA faculty as possessing a scholarly orientation and being well prepared for doctoral education. However, several do not have an MSW degree and this is seen as a potential limitation for the study of social policy issues in social agency arenas. An additional concern is the decision to allow students to enroll at UTA with a score of only 500 on the TOEFL and to give them the first semester in the United States to achieve the required score of 550. The students with these lower scores had a particularly difficult time in the classroom.

Overall Ratings of the Joint Program

In this section of the questionnaire, students and faculty were asked to list program strengths and weaknesses; these are enumerated below.

Program Strengths. Both UANL and UTA faculty are committed to the joint program, are well qualified to offer a program in comparative social policy, and are excited about this unique idea. University administrations in Mexico and the United States have been supportive and willing to develop the program, as new policies and procedures have had to be implemented at every stage. Students have the opportunity to experience the structure and function of social policies in both Mexico and the United States. Additionally, two Canadian universities have expressed an interest in joining this educational collaboration. Adding Canadian partners would offer even more opportunities as students and faculty would be able to learn from experiences in three countries. For now, the administrators of UTA and UANL have decided not to pursue this expansion given the complexities and challenges associated with the functioning of this program. The Canadian option, however, may be further explored in the future.

Program Issues. The unavoidable turnover of deans, coordinators, and directors of the social work doctoral program at UTA caused a gap in communication between the two schools. UANL has also experienced a change in leadership. The absence of a coordinator for this program from 1998 to 2000 caused difficulties with student recruitment and retention and overall program facilitation. These problems included a delay in developing program specificity and better documentation of program procedures. During this period, there were also challenges with interpreting the culture and educational philosophies of the partner institution.

Difficulties in assessing language proficiency in Mexico and the United States caused some problems in accurately evaluating applicants and students' academic performance. Since 2000, UTA has conducted more aggressive and widespread recruitment efforts which have, so far, resulted in a more steady flow of incoming students. Nevertheless, more financial resources are needed to help U.S. students relocate to another country for a year.

LESSONS LEARNED AND CHALLENGES TO PROGRAM DEVELOPMENT

Both universities have had to deal with several difficulties associated with program development and implementation. These problems included obtaining institutional approval for granting this joint doctoral degree, getting both universities to agree on admission requirements, defining the program structure and requirements, and establishing guidelines for completing the doctoral dissertation.

This program presented several recruitment challenges, especially the bilingual requirements, the additional financial resources needed by students living in another country, and the program's policy focus in the face of U.S. students' predominant interest in clinical practice. The language barrier in particular represents a very practical difficulty. Few students in either country possess sufficient mastery of a second language to undertake advanced graduate study.

An additional challenge is the dearth of faculty members at UTA or UANL who speak both fluent Spanish and English. Most educators, therefore, can only evaluate dissertations written in their own native language. The current agreement between the universities makes it possible for doctoral candidates to write their final dissertation in either English or Spanish. Nevertheless, drafts of this document must be provided to each dissertation committee member in his or her native language in order to enable their active participation. Doctoral defenses are conducted bilingually with the doctoral candidate alternating between English and Spanish or by means of a translator.

The program faced an additional administrative challenge which has been successfully resolved. UTA requires doctoral students to be enrolled for a minimum of nine credits during the semester in which they defend their dissertation. This represented a problem for students who were working on their dissertation research in Mexico because they also needed to graduate from UTA. In fact, this requirement was an additional tuition cost for any students who needed to be registered at both universities during their last semester in the program. This fee was not covered by student scholarships, creating a hardship for students who already had scant financial resources. This issue was solved by a UTA administrative decision that now allows students in this unique program to register for nine credit hours at either university during their last semester.

Another challenge relevant to this discussion is the difficulty of conducting comparative research projects. Students can conduct secondary analysis of data or reflect on conceptual and theoretical issues. However, conducting empirical, comparative, and international studies is problematic because of the increased cost associated with these projects. It is difficult enough for students to obtain the financial resources to collect data in one country, and performing these studies in two distant geographic locations doubles the cost. A possibility that should be considered is engaging in joint research projects between faculty and students from both universities so that the program's students can become part of existing studies.

PROSPECTS FOR THE FUTURE OF THE COLLABORATION

Prospects for the future of the collaboration look very positive. Beginning with the 2000-2001 academic year, UTA was able to hire a Spanish-speaking faculty member to coordinate the dual-degree program. This new coordinator possesses administrative experience, is fully bilingual, and has particular interest and experience in the areas of international social work, comparative social welfare policy, and social development. He has conducted research in South America and is familiar with higher education in Mexico. Efforts are also being undertaken to complement this acquisition with an increased number of bilingual support staff at the school. Both of these developments will substantially enhance the ability of the two institutions to coordinate the development of the program.

Plans at this time call for an increased effort in student recruitment and program promotion. We will maintain a more sustained recruitment effort through marketing at professional conferences, advertisement in professional journals and publications, and networking with Hispanic and other organizations that have demonstrated interest in Mexico–United States policy and human service issues.

The benefits of this collaboration will inevitably reach UTA students not enrolled in the program. UTA will establish study tours of Mexico for students enrolled in the regular campus MSW and PhD programs. Participants will study the human service system in Mexico and will compare it to the U.S. system. These courses will be more closely coordinated with UANL to take advantage of the relationship established through this collaborative venture. This will also provide the added benefit of giving greater visibility to the collaborative program and piquing interest among the students in the regular program. Faculty interaction through seminars expands the intercultural knowledge of educators in both countries. For example, to coincide with one planning visit of the UANL faculty to UTA, a faculty seminar was held in which UANL faculty presented their current research on the Mexican family. Increased faculty knowledge benefits future students, even if they do not participate in the program.

There are also plans for more frequent coordination trips between Arlington and Monterrey to maintain closer contact among faculty and students than the twice-a-year administrative coordination meetings have provided in the past. As a part of this coordination effort, the existing policies and procedures that have evolved since the program's inception will be incorporated into a revised program plan for the collaboration and into a handbook for students.

Plans are being discussed for having faculty from UTA deliver coursework at UANL while the students are in Monterrey and for UANL faculty to do likewise at UTA when students are in Arlington. This exchange will facilitate the engagement of students with faculty from the other institution and will enhance the program's ability to monitor student progress and program developments in a more timely fashion. It will also allow faculty to more effectively develop a common understanding of the educational philosophies of the two institutions.

Increased efforts are also planned to develop methods for more effectively financing student participation in the collaborative program. These efforts are generally one of three types: individual funding opportunities for UTA students studying internationally, tuition-exchange funding, and program-development support funding. UANL is anticipating difficulty continuing their level of funding for Mexican students traveling to UTA next year. To offset this, UTA is exploring the feasibility of accelerating the admissions cycle to enroll a cohort of UTA students next fall instead of the subsequent fall. These students would then begin their studies in Monterrey at the same time as the UANL students in Arlington, allowing the students to balance against each other in the existing tuition exchange program that Texas institutions have with foreign schools. This plan would require that the exchange students be matched on a one-to-one basis but would allow each student to pay tuition at their home institution while studying at the partner school. This would greatly reduce the financial strain on these students but will require an adjustment in the original program plan.

Funding possibilities also exist through NAFTA development programs. Preliminary discussions have been undertaken with a Canadian PhD program to develop a tri-national project that would build on UTA's experience with UNAL. This tri-national program is envisioned as a collaboration among two institutions in Mexico, two institutions in the United States, and two institutions in Canada. The necessity of two institutions from each country relates to the funding requirements of the NAFTA program that would fund such a project. Students would be recruited and admitted through each participating institution and enroll for courses as a cohort at the various other institutions on a rotational plan, with the dissertation completed at the student's home institution. While ambitious, such a collaboration would provide a truly comparative international educational experience to participating students.

Although there is much to be done, the lessons learned from the past few years, combined with the appointment of a dedicated program coordinator, enhance the prospects for the future development of this joint program. The potential is great for preparing a generation of professionals well versed in comparative international perspectives for the social issues confronting the human services.

REFERENCE

U.S. Census Bureau. (1996). *Population projections for states by age, sex, race, and Hispanic origin: 1995 to 2025.* Retrieved December, 2002, from http://www.census.gov/population/www/projections/ppl47.html

NINE

Home and Host Models of Collaboration for Service Learning: Grand Valley State University Programs in El Salvador and South Africa

Julia A. Guevara and Ruth S. Ylvisaker

In the early 1990s, the School of Social Work (SSW) at Grand Valley State University (GVSU), in Allendale, Michigan, took a significant step into the global arena. Through an initiative funded by the Soros Foundation and the U.S. Agency for International Development, GVSU-SSW provided support for the creation of a school of social work at the University of Tirana, Albania. Although these early efforts focused on curriculum development and a limited faculty exchange, there was little surprise when the activities spawned heightened student and faculty interest in international social work experiences. The relationship between GVSU-SSW and the University of Tirana, as well as individual faculty members' exposure to international social welfare practice, pushed the program to look beyond the West Michigan region for educational opportunities for its students and faculty.

Simultaneous to these developments, the GVSU administration elevated the position of director of the office of international affairs to that of dean. In addition, GVSU's commitment to international opportunities and study for faculty and students was included in the university's official long-range plan. The SSW quickly optimized the university's international interest by creating an SSW International Committee that developed policy governing international initiatives, encouraged faculty participation, and initiated marketing strategies.

During this period of convergent interests in international programs, GVSU-SSW developed two distinct models of study to provide undergraduate and graduate social work students and faculty with meaningful international experiences. The first model is a faculty-led or "home" model, in which SSW faculty have the responsibility for developing linkages with nongovernmental organizations (NGOs) and for directing academic learning and direct-service experience in close collaboration with nongovernmental social service agents in the host country. This model, piloted in El Salvador, requires students to engage in a comparative study of social work between countries and offers students experience with NGOs in direct-service work through grassroots practice in their field of choice. The success of the home model is highly dependent on collaborative relationships between the host country NGOs and the GVSU faculty members leading and developing the program. GVSU-SSW has replicated the home model with projects in Ireland and Albania that are built on already-established linkages between GVSU faculty and NGOs in these countries.

The second model is a "host" model, in which GVSU educators collaborate with the university directors of an established international program in a host country. In this model, social welfare policy comparisons are made between multiple countries and are illustrated through direct-service experience in the student's field of choice in the host country. This model for international study, which takes place in South Africa, was loosely modeled after the Bristol International Credit Earning Program from the United Kingdom, which has hosted U.S. students since 1990 and in which GVSU-SSW has participated. An important modification for this South Africa program was the inclusion of the service-learning component.

The development of both collaborative models was encouraged by the dean of GVSU-SSW to provide broadened educational opportunities that emphasize both social work practice and policy. Case studies of both models are presented below to demonstrate the respective differences and strengths of each model.

CASE STUDY OF THE HOME MODEL

Despite being less than a decade past a bitter and divisive civil war, the small Central American nation of El Salvador was an excellent stepping-off point for GVSU's expanded foray into international education. A SSW faculty member had recently completed an extended study of the impact of an NGO within El Salvador and had both knowledge of the country and a network of health and human service connections. Moreover, although the Salvadoran health and human service infrastructure and higher education institutions were in the process of reconstruction, there was great need for health and human service intervention and international assistance. These conditions, although hardly unique in the international arena, proved ideal for the inauguration of international service-learning opportunities for baccalaureate-level social work students at GVSU.

In the spring of 1997, 10 BSW students from GVSU-SSW traveled to El Salvador and participated in an independent study course, Social Work Practice in a Global Perspective. The following year, a formal proposal was made to the GVSU Curriculum Committee to add this course as a permanent elective in the BSW program. The course was approved and titled, SW 354: Social Work—An International Service Learning Approach: Blurring the Dichotomy. The instructor who had experience in El Salvador developed this course and has provided leadership for the service-learning program in El Salvador for the past 4 years. Specifics of the course are outlined below.

SW 354 is a 2-3 week experiential service-learning course that requires travel to a specified country, in this case El Salvador. During this 2-3 week course, students learn about the practice of social work in the context of the social-, economic-, and political-welfare structures of El Salvador through a combination of meetings with NGOs, social welfare organizations, governmental organizations, neighborhood groups, and service learning opportunities.

Students spend at least 3 days as part of a service-learning experience, working in a nongovernmental, neighborhood, or community grassroots organization either in the urban center of San Salvador or in a marginalized community in rural areas of the country. The focal point of the experience—i.e., child welfare, women's health, homelessness, etc.— reflect the student's interest and is mutually agreed upon by the student and the instructor. The student is then assigned

to an NGO that works in this specific area. A minimum of 6 hours each day with direct hands-on experience at the agency or organization is expected.

Students are also expected to document the specific frameworks and interventions used by this agency or organization, with the intention of incorporating this information into an analysis and comparison of social work practice and policy in the United States and El Salvador. At the conclusion of each day, faculty and students actively participate in daily group and individual debriefings.

A significant part of the experience includes a 3- or 4-day stay in a rural Salvadoran community along the Honduran border. Students as well as faculty live with host families.

Most of the Salvadoran program is translated for students. Therefore knowledge of Spanish, the host country's language, is not required, although completion of an entry-level Spanish course is encouraged. During the service-learning and host-family stay experiences, translation is not provided. However, every effort is made to have an English speaker available at the service-learning site. Relevant to the practice of social work is the use of nonverbal communication, which students will further develop and rely on as they encounter situations in which spoken words are not the primary mode of communication.

Rationale

The GVSU-SSW faculty seeks to integrate into the BSW experience emphases on service learning and andragogy. These emphases are discussed in this chapter, as is the importance of NGO linkages and cross-national relevance to this type of program.

Service Learning. The SSW has consistently defined service learning as an instructional method for integrating community service with academic instruction that focuses on critical, reflective thinking and civic responsibility. The incorporation of service learning into the international study experience is intended to encourage students to learn more about themselves and others, to develop a greater awareness of social issues, to learn about potential careers in the international service arena, and to build personal and professional abilities and self-esteem. Course expectations have therefore been created with a focus on commitment, advocacy, teamwork, and global responsibility.

Because of this focus, GVSU-SSW students perform work that is of value to the host community. Some of the specific tasks GVSU students have undertaken include the following:

- Assisting street children, including providing encouragement and instructions for personal hygiene and health practices, such as bathing, hair washing, and tooth brushing; removing drugs and drug paraphernalia from children's possession; helping youth find safer places to sleep and secure food; leading recreational activities; providing referrals and transportation to appointments at health clinics and other social service organizations.
- Preparing food and providing instruction in meal preparation for homeless or destitute individuals and families.
- Providing childcare services and instruction in infant care for young or inexperienced parents.
- Supporting women, children, and elderly populations in health clinic settings, including providing assistance, transportation, and encouragement for appointments at other NGOs and public service organizations.
- Participating with local groups in environmental remediation efforts, often involving youth, such as graffiti cleanup and mural painting.

In addition to service-learning experiences within the international setting, many cohorts of students have initiated projects prior to their trips abroad to collect clothing, medical supplies, food, and money to be donated to NGOs in the host country. This hands-on volunteer experience has highlighted some of the obstacles philanthropic organizations encounter, as well as methods for surmounting such obstacles, in the creation of effective international relief efforts.

This GVSU international experience consistently emphasizes the transformation of theoretical knowledge about global politics, economics, and social welfare into student behavior that provides a tangible service to benefit the individuals, families, and communities in which the international learning experience occurs.

Andragogy. The andragogical underpinnings for this international experience reflect the SSW's intent to focus on and support the principles of adult learning, including such practices as self-directed learning and critical reflection, also known as transformational learning (Knowles, 1984). As a result of this andragogical emphasis, the SSW promotes active, process-oriented learning, as opposed to learning through only lectures and written assignments. Students who participate in this exchange project are expected to take considerable responsibility for shaping their experience—including its intended

outcomes and objectives—as well as for evaluating whether the course objectives have been achieved and the outcomes reached.

NGO Linkages. Although many schools of social work have created their students' international experiences through linkages with foreign institutions of higher education, GVSU has implemented this program exclusively through connections with NGOs. GVSU's decision to use NGOs was initially based on existing faculty-NGO relationships. Moreover, higher education organizations in El Salvador were in disarray and of uneven quality in the years following the civil war, and they would not have made strong partners for GVSU.

The experience of the first 2 years of utilizing NGOs in El Salvador was overwhelmingly positive, not only from the perspective of GVSU students, faculty, and administration, but also from the perspective of the host organizations in Central America. When GVSU sought to expand its international program to Ireland and Albania, the Salvadoran NGO-based linkages were judged by GVSU faculty to be not only exceptionally productive for student learning, but also to have certain advantages that are discussed below.

First, linking the GVSU-SSW with international NGOs has consistently proved to be relatively straightforward to accomplish through informal channels. These links do not depend on highly structured legal agreements or negotiated relationships between universities, but instead on the shared interests of individuals who have already established a working relationship. In many cases, these individuals are human service professionals, which has made such linkages collegial rather than legal in character and has contributed to their flexibility as well as to their successful performance.

A second positive feature of using NGO connections is that the communication is more direct and can be focused on meeting the needs of the students as learners as well as the needs of the NGOs' clients. The NGOs utilized have had a very high level of interest in, and concern for, client well being. This helps the international learning experience achieve its service focus without sacrificing the students' needs as learners. Such balance would be much more difficult to achieve if the NGOs were not very actively involved at every stage of planning and implementation.

GVSU-SSW's direct and ongoing involvement with NGOs in host countries has the added advantage of providing an incentive for participating faculty to forge, strengthen, or extend linkages with colleagues and organizations outside of the United States. Educators are becoming increasingly aware that their own lifelong learning processes are enhanced by looking at conference or sabbatical travel abroad as an opportunity for continuing professional development that may result in relationships with practicing social workers from other nations. These relationships can result in GVSU students visiting and learning from these agencies and NGOs. This potential adds yet another dimension to professional collaborations such as research, evaluation opportunities, and comparative field studies.

There are also limitations associated with linking to NGOs rather than to universities. These include reduced contact with student peers in the host nation; limited student access to formal learning resources, such as trained faculty or university support staff, library facilities, computer laboratories (including Internet access), and other academic materials; and placement of students in settings where access to English-speaking translators or English-language instruction is minimal.

Another limitation of working directly with NGOs is that these organizations are almost always focused principally on meeting the needs of their clients, rather than on the learning needs of our students. In many underdeveloped nations, material resources are few and often inadequate for meeting client needs. These circumstances require GVSU faculty to prepare the NGO staff, as well as the students, for service in these agencies that are less focused on students' educational expectations than agencies in West Michigan. However, with appropriate attention to this reality, coupled with strong support from the faculty liaison, it is possible for students, the NGO, and the clients of the NGO to benefit from a service-learning placement.

Overall, GVSU's reliance on NGO linkages has proven to be positive, affording the SSW an opportunity to expose students to an extremely broad range of organizations: from child welfare agencies, hospitals, prisons, community-based radio stations, rural medical clinics, mental health programs, to projects focusing on urban sex workers. The NGO focus provides the SSW with a chance to develop new student experiences quickly and efficiently as international conditions change and as social services evolve to meet these new challenges and opportunities. It also allows the SSW to immediately discontinue or modify any student service-learning site that does not meet the faculty's expectations.

National Cross-Relevance. GVSU designed this international study course to be adaptable to most any nation. Although piloted and operated consistently for 5 years in rural and urban El Salvador, the course goals, expected outcomes, and objectives are not country specific; nor is the scope or grading of assignments. Students undertaking a service-learning experience in El Salvador meet the same requirements as students going to Ireland or Albania.

The Importance of Preparation

Students participating in this course often comment that nothing could have fully prepared them for the realities they encountered abroad. This is by design. The program has learned that this type of comment is not an indication of a failure to get students ready for their experience. Rather, the SSW faculty has learned over the past several years that the element of surprise is one of the most powerful features of the learning process associated with international study. Typically, GVSU students spend months intellectually preparing for this experience. They attend classes that inform them about the geography, history, culture, politics, and economic situations of their host nations. They read, discuss, and write papers about the health and human service structures and educational programs that exist. In these same ways, they also explore the status of philanthropy and the social work profession. As their journeys begin, students invariably express confidence in knowing what lies ahead and in being ready to tackle and overcome any obstacles they may encounter. And then the plane lands.

It often takes only a few hours in a strange milieu before the students' confidence is shaken and before they are confronted with conditions they never imagined. For some students, this is their first foray out of West Michigan—even their first time on an airplane. For almost all, it is the first time they have ever been immersed in a non-English-speaking environment. Moreover, for virtually all of the participants—students and faculty—the experience provides constant reminders of how advantaged their lives typically are.

There is no way to fully prepare U.S. university students for a gut-wrenching confrontation with the poverty in which many of the world's people live their daily lives—or with the health and social consequences of this poverty. Indeed, if coursework could fully prepare them for the conditions in which two thirds of the world's population live, there would be significantly less value in international travel.

Instead, the goal is to prepare students through a series of pretrip seminars, discussions, and other learning experiences to recognize their feelings of inadequacy as a crucial juncture in their learning adventure. While in El Salvador, the course provides multiple debriefing experiences during which faculty provide guidance and support for students as they learn to deliver services outside of their customary comfort zones. Upon returning to the GVSU campus, students and faculty continue to meet and reflect upon the experience in an effort to integrate the students' feelings and knowledge into their emerging identities as social work practitioners.

Discussions with program graduates who formerly participated in the international service-learning course often revolve around the theme of how much they gained from the relatively brief period spent in the other country. Their consistent message is that they learned a great deal about themselves and their own nation after they discovered how little they knew about the rest of the world.

Replicating the Home Model

The GVSU-SSW model of linking with NGOs in other nations to create powerful learning opportunities for BSW students is not universally appropriate, but it is likely to be a good fit for many social work programs across North America. Several characteristics define these potential programs, including the following:

- Baccalaureate programs within departments and universities that encourage and support innovation and faculty initiatives with funding and other resources, including release time for course planning and development.
- Programs within universities that have missions that include international service or an emphasis on service learning.
- Faculty who have established connections to international NGOs or an interest in creating and fostering such linkages.
- Programs that include significant international content in other social work courses, such as those on diversity, macro and micro practice, evaluation, and human behavior.
- A program, department, or university climate that is not risk-adverse—an environment in which penalties for failure are minimal and rewards for success widely known.
- Students with an intellectual curiosity about the world and a willingness to learn from the unfamiliar.
- Programs with one or more strong champions for international learning who are willing and able not

only to pioneer the development of international contacts with NGOs, but also to facilitate the development of course materials and to steer one or more courses through the university's curriculum-approval process.

In summary, SW 354 was developed at GVSU-SSW as one step in a natural progression in curriculum development, which is occurring in schools of social work across the world. There is now full recognition at GVSU-SSW—as at other schools around the country—that a xenophobic perspective on professional social work practice does nothing to prepare students or equip faculty to meaningfully participate in the globally focused problem solving that the emerging social, political, and economic realities of world affairs demands. The inclusion of SW 354 in the curriculum is seen as one means of addressing this need.

A HOST MODEL CASE STUDY

At GVSU, the host model is a collaborative arrangement between GVSU-SSW and a host university in another country that implements the jointly developed plans for students' international learning experiences. With this model, it is not necessary for SSW faculty to accompany students to the foreign institution, although this can be desirable. Also, with this model new faculty and staff coordinators in either location are not dependent upon a single person's knowledge or experience, and they can rely on past collaborative networks and the program administrative structures that are already in place.

The GVSU-SSW has had many years of successful partnership with the social work program at the University of Natal in Durban, KwaZulu-Natal, South Africa. This South African Service Learning Initiative, first proposed in 1997, developed much like the faculty-led program for El Salvador in that both were driven by faculty interest and experience.

In 1996, the GVSU-SSW was quick to understand that faculty members with experience in international settings were valuable resources for the university's administration because they could accomplish GVSU's newly established international objectives. Since that time, resources and support for international programs have been increasing with considerable encouragement from the SSW. Concomitant with the international objectives of GVSU, the administration developed new interest in and financial incentives for education through service learning for all disciplines. The SSW became the undeniable, if not universally recognized, "campus expert" on matters of service learning by virtue of the profession's hard-won curriculum model that requires a field practicum.

The Salvadoran home model and the South African host model both continue the tradition of educating students by combining service with learning. In addition, by giving students two distinct choices for achieving similar goals, these two models reinforce the social work principle of consumer choice in this "student-centered" program.

History of the Host Model Development

A 1997 proposal by the GVSU-SSW faculty was funded to explore international study options with universities in South Africa. In 1998, SSW faculty members visited South Africa to collaborate directly with the University of Natal. Their interest was in developing a university-supervised service-learning opportunity for GVSU students. The plan was to accommodate both BSW and MSW students who had chosen to investigate the comparative social policy issues that guide practice, or to examine comparative social work practices between the United States and South Africa.

Quite serendipitously, 1997 was the year that the well-respected University of Natal—chartered in 1904 and now serving about 17,000 students—developed plans to offer a 6-week International Winter School (IWS), during their winter break (June-August). The University of Natal's setting—a separate enclave within the city of Durban where students live in secure dormitories and have access to the university faculty, a substantial library, and Internet services, appealed to GVSU-SSW's faculty and the dean of GVSU's international affairs. Thus, the institutional objectives of the GVSU administration also came together to serve the SSW vision for a service learning in South Africa.

In 1997, the South African national Office of Education, as part of the Reconstruction Development Plan, required all institutions of higher education in South Africa to design community development initiatives. This lead GVSU educators to believe that a service-learning component might be considered by administrators and developers of the IWS program.

Credit for what now exists in South Africa for the GVSU-SSW graduate and undergraduate students goes to the IWS administrators, who are now within the newly organized Faculty of Community Development

Disciplines, which serves social work, psychology, anthropology, education, nursing, architecture, and planning. The coordinator of IWS was willing and able to divide the existing program into two 3-week modules to meet the time constraints of the GVSU students. The coordinator also expressed a willingness to modify the existing curriculum to incorporate service-learning experiences for both graduate and undergraduate students.

The flexibility and consent of the IWS coordinator gave GVSU faculty the license to share their vision for service learning with the chair of the social work department at the University of Natal. Together, the two programs laid plans for an experience in which BSW and MSW students would stay in South Africa for either 3 or 6 weeks, with 2 days each week spent on campus for formal learning about the history, politics, language, culture, and the field of social work in South Africa. This classroom element also includes arranged field trips off campus, use of the University of Natal's library, use of the Internet, opportunities for research, individual and group study, and formally arranged travel.

For the service-learning component, 3 days of each week are spent in social service agencies that have been chosen by the students, such as the Durban Child Welfare Association or The Agency For The Aged, both of which are NGOs. In these placements, BSW and MSW students commit to service, doing what needs to be done in understaffed and underresourced social service agencies. Course evaluation requires attendance at scheduled events, daily journal writing, and a substantive paper that is negotiated with each student before departure and evaluated by GVSU-SSW faculty with input from the University of Natal faculty. Following their return to the United States, students meet with faculty for debriefing, a formal evaluation of their experiences, and to provide feedback for future improvements. Returning students are also asked to participate in future orientation sessions to share their experiences with the next group of students going to South Africa.

The South African program requires the faculty coordinator to assume some unique and specific tasks. For the students to receive their study permits from the South African embassy, the process of formal application to the program must begin in the January before the summer of participation. First, students must apply to the University of Natal so that their letters of acceptance can be submitted to the regional South African consulate. In addition to these letters of acceptance, the consulate needs several other documents, including passports, completed embassy forms, proof of paid roundtrip travel arrangements, proof of medical insurance, and a letter from the dean of GVSU-SSW stating that all applicants are in good academic standing. The South African consulate general in Chicago has a specially appointed liaison who works with GVSU faculty to meet these requirements and suggests that applicants plan on 6 weeks for the processing of their paperwork. Since the processing of any one student's application will not begin until the entire packet is complete, students need to understand that their paperwork must be finished as soon as possible. This is especially true for those students who may wish to visit Europe or elsewhere before going to South Africa, as they will need their passports as well as the South African study permits.

The first five students traveled to South Africa in the summer of 1999. For this initial trip, the director of the GVSU-SSW graduate program accompanied the students and stayed for the 3-week module. In this way, another member of the GVSU-SSW became personally familiar with the University of Natal program faculty, the students' challenges, the university campus, the South African social service system, and the country in general. The director's visit also broadened the base of interest and experience for the South African initiative within the SSW.

Collaboration and Linkages

From the beginning, collaboration with foreign colleagues was central to the development of the host model and the South African initiative. Two visits to the campus of the University of Natal set the foundation for a substantial working network. On the GVSU-SSW faculty's second visit to the campus, in 1998, they learned that an IWS faculty liaison would be visiting the United States. An invitation was extended to visit the GVSU campus and to meet the social work faculty and dean, and the dean of international affairs. The SSW arranged for speaker forums across GVSU, so that the University of Natal and the IWS faculty liaison could be introduced to a broad spectrum of students and faculty.

Finally, and most recently, the GVSU-SSW faculty invited a social work educator from the University of Natal to join them for a paid sabbatical in the winter semester of 2001. This collaboration has made it possible for the director of the social work program at the University of Natal, Dr. Vishanthie Sewpaul, to speak directly with SSW students, faculty, and the International Committee, as well as the GVSU administration, as the two partner institutions strive for ongoing quality improvement for the South African project. The presence of Dr. Sewpaul also served to raise the visibility of South Africa throughout the SSW and has helped stimulate debates across the GVSU campus on global issues as divergent as AIDS, the oppressive nature of the U.S. economy in relation to South Africa, and global standards for social work education. This close association has also heightened GVSU-SSW's respect for the well-developed system of education for social work professionals at the undergraduate, graduate, and doctoral levels in South Africa.

In addition, GVSU-SSW facilitated speaker forums for our Dr. Sewpaul at the Council on Social Work Education's Annual Program Meeting, and at Midwest and Eastern U.S. universities. These events served to offer a reality-based view of more of the United States and to expand the professional network of Dr. Sewpaul.

Further, prior to the arrival of Dr. Sewpaul, the GVSU-SSW contacted the local HIV/AIDS service community, informed them of Dr. Sewpaul's expertise and interest in AIDS and of the length of the exchange, and invited these agencies to consider Dr. Sewpaul's presence at GVSU as a resource to be accessed. This community responded quickly with invitations for the visitor to address service professionals as well as agency clients. A Grand Rapids resource center for AIDS agreed to provide financial support for personnel in Durban, South Africa, to work with a support group of mothers of children with AIDS, which was developed by Dr. Sewpaul. This linkage has the potential of developing cross-national social work practicums for GVSU-SSW students, as well as creating an international agency partnership.

Another United States-South Africa link has developed through a West Michigan AIDS clinic, in which professional staff work with people from Africa who have AIDS or are HIV positive. Dr. Sewpaul was invited to serve as this local agency's consultant and support group leader to establish an autonomous support group among African individuals who live with HIV/AIDS in West Michigan. Most recently, this agency submitted a grant to fund a trip to South Africa for its GVSU-SSW practicum student, in the hope of developing an international link between HIV/AIDS service agencies.

GVSU-SSW looks forward to an ever-evolving relationship with the University of Natal that will fine tune this host model. It is expected that the collaboration will expand, improve, and solidify social work learning opportunities for both U.S. and South African social work students, faculties, and community professionals.

Student and Faculty Research

Unanticipated opportunities for research evolved from the first 2 years of this program when the faculty coordinator designed a study for five students based on the five "universal objectives of social work" identified by Minahan and Pincus (1977). As part of their service-learning assignment, these students were each awarded $500 by the GVSU Johnson Center for Philanthropy and Non-Profit Leadership to seek South African agency service examples as indicators of these objectives in order to confirm their universality (Minahan & Pincus, 1977; Tropman, 2000). As a result of this theory-building investigation, students experienced the universality of scholarly social work principles and gained additional insight into the utility of the advanced generalist curriculum model used at GVSU-SSW.

Although the host model does not require faculty participation, it is allowed. In addition, the host model offers opportunities for SSW faculty development and research. In 2000, the GVSU-SSW coordinator was granted faculty development funds to compare the South African and U.S. social-security policies for elders and to integrate these findings into the newly developed curriculum sequence on gerontology. Additional funds were awarded by the GVSU Johnson Center for Philanthropy and Non-Profit Leadership to explore opportunities for social work students to be placed in aging-focused NGOs to complement this gerontology sequence. With this financial support, the GVSU-SSW coordinator also registered as a postgraduate student seeking a placement in aging. This lead to a 3-week service-learning experience with the equivalent of a privately funded aging-focused agency.

While in South Africa, GVSU-SSW faculty was invited to address gerontology administrators on the tax structures that fund welfare in the United States and to conduct a workshop for South African aging-focused practitioners. In addition, the director of an NGO in Durban agreed to distribute and collect survey instruments that would make possible a South African working-mother study comparing previously collected 1988 apartheid data and postapartheid data from 2000. This study surveyed the attitudes of Black and White urban working mothers on the future of their children in South Africa. The responses of these women, 12 years later, should be especially interesting today in light of the changes brought about by the new South African constitution, which recognizes the citizenship and the political presence of the Black constituency.

Challenges

One difficulty associated with this project is that student participants must present evidence of their acceptance by the University of Natal before obtaining study permits from the South African embassy. This requires regular communication between the project's partners as well as efficient faculty and student time management so that the proper forms and documents can be processed well before the student's departure.

A more significant challenge is the preparation of students for what they will see and learn in the South African province of KwaZulu-Natal. The initial year, students were not prepared for the poverty and the discrimination they observed and the emotional response these conditions evoked. The pretrip orientation for the students now involves very frank discussions conducted by faculty and former student participants regarding the emotional aspects of international learning. Preparation also includes telling the students that they will not be prepared. Attendance is required at monthly orientation meetings, January through June. At these orientations students have the opportunity to hear from and question past participants, some who have volunteered to sign copyright releases for their daily journals. Interested students can now gain additional insight by reading these daily observations, impressions, and emotional responses.

Students are also introduced to the culture, history, politics, and geography of the country through discussions, guest presenters, readings, and videos. To give them some insight into the politics of apartheid, the film *Cry Freedom* is used to depict the activism of Steven Biko and other South Africans. To provide a visual preview of KwaZulu-Natal, students are shown a commercial travel video showing its cities and countryside. Perhaps the most valuable visual aid is a home video taken by a student participant. This video offers a graphic illustration of the realities of life in a beautiful and cosmopolitan city for those who live in the crowded squatter settlements, where the unemployment rate is just under 50%. Also pictured is the University of Natal's campus community and events in the city and the rural areas in which previous students were involved.

The principles of reciprocity and mutuality have yet to be fully addressed by GVSU as these international service-learning initiatives develop. GVSU-SSW now must consider accepting the challenge to find ways for South African students to experience service learning in the United States. This will mean a search for grants and funding to finance the experience. It will also require a "mentoring" SSW—with the responsibility for mentoring falling on the whole department rather than any single individual—and service plans that can be quickly put into place. The SSW will also need to socialize community agencies to the concept of international partnership and the concept of truncated practicums as service-learning opportunities. As the structure and process for international service learning matures, and more models develop, this mutuality would seem to be an inevitable outcome and obligation of all international partnerships initiated by U.S. universities.

Replication

Faculty experience, interest, and professional networks have been the most important resources for connecting NGOs and universities to GVSU-SSW. However, for faculties that have the interest, but limited institutional supports, experience, or networks, the needed resources can be as close as the office computer. Faculty at other universities who have participated in an international collaboration willingly share their knowledge. At GVSU, for example, information on the IWS was passed along to a former faculty colleague at Winona State University in Winona, Minnesota. This colleague's interest led to an invitation to Dr. Sewpaul to address an international forum at the Winona State campus. This interest has also led to a reciprocal invitation from the University of Natal to spend a sabbatical in South Africa. Following this sabbatical, the intention is to offer IWS opportunities to Winona State students.

Many foreign universities have websites filled with information useful to international exchange. Also, a phone call to the embassy of the country of interest can garner basic information. Once the vision for what is to be accomplished is in place, the disciplined work of long-distance development begins. This effort is truly a combination of 10% creative vision and 90% dedicated year-round collaborative discussions, reinforced by mutual enthusiasm and respect. If the host university is online, as in this case, the task is simplified and a working relationship can quickly develop. For countries without a moderately sophisticated infrastructure, developing the linkage will be more difficult.

Once communication about the initiative is established at the partner schools, then institutional regulatory and practice barriers on both campuses must be addressed. Safe and adequate student housing must be available, and the schedule for participation must be established. Also to be developed are the goals for service-learning opportunities, costs, criteria for acceptance, and designs for program application and evaluation.

Marketing the opportunity to students is also important. At GVSU the promotion of the international project is a shared experience among faculty on the International Committee. Former participants who willingly share their experiences with other students are probably the best source of advertising. Applications at GVSU go first to the international office, and must meet a December (BSW) or January (MSW) deadline. Applications then come to the SSW for final review and acceptance. The successful applicants are congratulated and then immediately immersed in the business of orientation.

SUMMARY

The GVSU home and host models for international service learning are a natural progression in social work education because the practicum has long been considered by many as the most important "course" a student takes in the professional curriculum. These new models of "truncated practicums" require the same qualities from faculty that all social work departments desire: experience, knowledge, enthusiasm, and organizational skills.

Student participants come away from these projects with a new respect for the diversity of perspectives that exist globally when the universal issues of oppression, in relation to race, gender, age, or socioeconomic realities, are addressed. They develop an awareness of their potential to stimulate collaboration between other countries and the United States in social welfare development, education, professional practice, and research. These future leaders of the social work profession now have added insights regarding U.S. culture and the accepted patterns, formal and informal, pro and con, that dictate public service development and delivery. In the process, they have gained experience in how public policy is applied through the association with both the government and nongovernment organizations that turn policies into practice. They have a new, more realistic awareness regarding the limited applicability of conventional U.S. education and professional practice when the culture or socioeconomic and political context is dramatically different from that of the United States.

Holistic Advantages

GVSU-SSW and its international partners, the NGOs and universities, have enjoyed mutual benefits from the infusion of enthusiasm through their association with idealistic social work students, through the collaborative planning, and through the reciprocal approach to plans for continuous improvement.

GVSU continues to widen its educational sphere, as it becomes increasingly involved in finding ways to attract students, faculty, scholars, and guest speakers who have international interests and experiences. The SSW has broadened its collegial affiliations and knowledge of international social work policy and practice, and is increasingly questioning the unilateral standards for human service education, for social work policy and practice, and for customary analysis and evaluation benchmarks. GVSU-SSW's international colleagues, on the other hand, have had the opportunity to assess and reassess the abilities of GVSU students, based on direct association rather than hearsay. Most important, GVSU's increasing participation in international activities, in response to the 1996 institutional plan to increase global initiatives across campus, has begun to combat the ethnocentrism that threatens this university community and most others in the United States.

This necessary shift to a more global perspective, energetically spearheaded by the SSW, has led to institutional changes at GVSU that include a more flexible and supportive approach to international initiatives by the dean of international affairs. These changes have also extended to the university's Johnson Center for Philanthropy and Non-Profit Leadership, as evidenced by the generous funding of SSW student and faculty service-learning proposals. Most recently, the SSW gained increased visibility when the university president's office financed the travel for two SSW educators to El Salvador after a devastating earthquake in order to express the concern and compassion of GVSU.

Ultimately, social work educators everywhere will be increasingly challenged to think globally and to advocate for institutional, economic, and political reforms cross-nationally. In the 21st century, it is imperative that social welfare services and practices for all people be designed to prevent vulnerability. GVSU-SSW has used service learning to confirm that global social welfare practice must enhance the human condition in a sustainable and relevant manner, and that professional collaboration cross-nationally must reflect a deep respect for human rights, human strengths, and cultural practices. These are the ongoing objectives for international service-learning in the School of Social Work at Grand Valley State University.

REFERENCES

Knowles, M. (1984). *The adult learner: A neglected species* (3rd ed.). Houston, TX: Gulf Press.

Minahan, A., & Pincus, A. (1977). Conceptual framework social work practice. *Social Work, 22,* 347-352

Tropman, J. E., (2000). *Successful community leadership.* Washington DC: NASW Press.

TEN

Developing Social Work Education in Lithuania: An International Consultation Project

Robert Constable, Regina Kulys, and W. David Harrison

From September, 1991 through the present, the authors have worked in various capacities to assist the development of the Center for Professional Education in Social Work in Kaunas, Lithuania. The Center, initially cosponsored by Caritas of Lithuania (a charitable-relief organization) and Vytautas Magnus University, was fully incorporated into Vytautas Magnus University in 1997. To support the project, the authors assembled a large and complex network that included Loyola University Chicago, the University of Illinois at Chicago, and the University of Alabama as major participants, together with diverse social work faculty from universities and agencies in the United States, the United Kingdom, Eastern and Western Europe, and Australia.

The Center's initial purpose was to "educate the educators," leaders and developers of social work in Lithuania. The initial formal proposal, completed in May 1992, stated the following goals:

a. to provide a basis for the development of the social work profession in Lithuania. . . to educate the educators and leaders of the Lithuanian profession. . .
b. to provide a basis for the development of Lithuanian social services through the provision of consultation. . . . The consultation process will eventually lead to a research focus. . . an important function of the Center. (Constable & Kulys, 1992).

In 1995, the first students graduated from the Center with master's degrees in social work, followed over the years by more than 100 others. As of 2002, five of these graduates have now completed their doctorates and at least six others are at various stages of this process. These master's and doctoral graduates are now in position to take on a leadership role in Lithuanian social work, but this progression will also take time. The thesis research required of each master's- and doctoral-

degree graduate has generally been fruitful for the development of Lithuanian social services, particularly in child welfare. In addition, continuing education and baccalaureate-level programs have developed later as offshoots of the original graduate program.

BACKGROUND OF THE PROJECT

With 3.7 million people, Lithuania is the largest Baltic republic. Its cultural and linguistic traditions are among the oldest in Europe and its religious traditions are profoundly interwoven with its culture. Occupied by Russia throughout the 19th century, Lithuania enjoyed 2 decades of freedom prior to 1940. The subsequent brutal colonization by the Soviet Union, the mass deportations of Lithuanians to Siberia, the eventual suppression of its religion and national culture, and the compounded tragedies and losses of the Second World War and its aftermath left deep, painful, and enduring scars on every aspect of the Lithuanian social fabric. In the first 4 years following independence, achieved in 1991, living conditions had in many ways worsened. This was particularly true for those who could not participate in the emergent free market: women, children, the elderly, people who were physically or mentally ill, and those caught in the correctional system.

In Lithuania in the 1990s, social work had never existed as a profession. Under Soviet rule, neither social nor personal problems could be dealt with as such and the most elemental realities were viewed in a political context. The family, for example, was the place where workers took care of a future generation of workers. There were some social benefits, such as daycare and assistance for certain groups (i.e., pensioners). Many of these benefits changed or disappeared in the transition to a free-market society with rampant inflation. Many social problems, such as children with disabilities, were largely hidden away in institutions. After Lithuania's independence, the shift from the previous political culture was uncertain and radical.

At the beginning of this transition, Dr. Robert Constable started working with Caritas of Lithuania as a consultant and gave a series of public lectures on social work. The lecture series was cosponsored by Vytautas Magnus University, which led Caritas and this school to plan to jointly develop the social work profession in Lithuania. The basic question in the development of social work education in Lithuania, which the visiting international faculty often discussed with their Lithuanian cosponsors, students, and graduates, was what type of social work practice would best meet the needs of Lithuanian society and culture. These concepts for practice became clearer as the program developed. It was assumed that no one Western model of social work would be fully adequate to the situation. Instead, answers would emerge from the Lithuanian social workers themselves in their individual work and in the cosponsored project.

There needed to be a balance of openness and specificity in the program. From the educational models developed to date in the West, neither social development, which excludes direct individual, group, and family work, nor a model of direct work, which excludes social development, seemed appropriate. In any case, each model presupposes the other. Within the Soviet political and educational system there was no lack of planning for others, but little understanding that people and social units could take appropriate charge of their own lives and could become agents for their own development. The fundamental principle, which emerged over and over again, was that the new social workers had to experience a practice relationship. This relationship had to be open and honest, respectful of human dignity and diversity, and oriented toward the goal of self-determination. Abstract ideas about these topics were inadequate, especially in work with new programs and social policies. The first and most difficult task for Lithuanian students who had been exposed in any way to Soviet society and Soviet education, was learning what was necessary for these values of openness, diversity, self-determination, and respect for persons to exist in their work. For this reason it was decided that the program should start with a direct-practice focus, accommodated to Lithuanian cultural values. Building on this initial emphasis on work with smaller units of persons, families, and agencies, the program would gradually broaden to include tasks in social development.

GOVERNANCE, SUSTAINABILITY, AND MUTUALITY

The Center for Professional Education in Social Work was supported by a complex, interactive network, involving Vytautas Magnus University, Caritas of Lithuania, the Lithuanian Bishops' Conference, the U.S. National Conference of Catholic Bishops, and the universities which individually supported and sponsored the work of the visiting international faculty. Until its full incorporation into Vytautas Magnus University in 1997, the Center had quasi-independent status, although it operated within the physical confines of the university and according to its rules. The Center was governed by a *taryba* (board of directors) drawn from the university, from Caritas of Lithuania, and from governmental and private sectors of Lithuania. During the first 6 years (1991-1997), Dr. Regina Kulys and Dr. Robert Constable served as codirectors and worked with the delegated Lithuanian administrators. The program's administration was inevitably diffuse with the codirectors dividing their time between the program and responsibilities in their home universities.

The Center's funding was provided in different ways by the university and by grants from the Lithuanian and U.S. bishops' conferences. An international network of 30 overseas faculty volunteers managed to get support from their home universities and other sources to take time off from their normal duties and work with this project. Among these faculty there were three Fulbright Senior Scholars and one master's-level Fulbright Scholar. A number of other international universities provided scholarships and assistantships to Lithuanian students, including Jagellonian University and the University of Lodz, Poland, and schools of social work and universities in Scandinavia, the United Kingdom, and Germany. The Center also drew support from the Soros Foundation and from the Magdehuis and the Prince Bernhard Foundations from the Netherlands as well as the United Nations Development Program.

Through consultation, the Center's administrators and faculty developed a complex, Lithuanian network of government ministries, professional schools, municipal welfare agencies, and academic institutions. A series of connections emerged with social workers in the Scandinavian countries and individuals from the profession as it was evolving in Estonia, Latvia, and Poland. Students, also part of the development process, created consultative relationships and workshops in public agencies and privately sponsored services emerging in Post-Soviet Lithuania. In the raw and uncertain climate of post-Soviet Lithuania, the Center's support network as a whole was diffuse, complex, unstable, and inherently conflicted.

The codirectors worked to develop and administer the Center, find resources, organize and match these resources with program needs, and help people to contribute their best to this ongoing process. The support network represented sectors of Lithuanian society that normally would not work readily or easily with each other. As foreigners, the codirectors were often in a position to mediate between these groups, assisting them to find common interests and to work together. This access allowed them to open opportunities for students and for the program. However, there was synergy among these sectors and the international network, only as long as the codirectors maintained certain mutually understood boundaries between the diverse groups and worked between these boundaries to develop outcomes which everyone would support. One example among many was the conflict between Vytautas Magnus University, which is based on secular assumptions and reflects to some extent the old system, and Caritas of Lithuania, a nongovernmental organization with religious foundations and a history as an underground, dissident organization. Facing these unstable conditions for development, the codirectors found themselves continually adapting and reorganizing the program in order to sustain its initial objectives. Despite inherent instabilities, they provided the continuity for the program to develop and eventually assume Lithuanian leadership.

The Center has been in operation for a decade (1992-2002), and has now been under Lithuanian leadership for almost 4 years. The program became sustainable only through a delicate balancing act between the different groups that supported it. Each sector would contribute what it could, remain in contact with the process, give direction, and receive information about the Center. Only gradually and with difficulty were the problems of mutual accommodation ironed out, but this has never been fully accomplished. In this sense there cannot be full mutuality between the supporting groups, and this is well understood and accepted by all, including the codirectors' own universities. Essentially the project had to wait until the first graduates entered the system at an appropriate level to see any results of this educational initiative. This waiting process continues, although the initial indicators are good. Graduates are entering the system and are gradually influencing it with professional standards accommodated to Lithuanian society and culture.

The visiting U.S. faculty's home universities supported the Center, when they could, through scholarships for students, sabbaticals, leaves of absence, informal arrangements, and other trade-offs. If the project had been a short-term consultation, it would have been easier for the universities to support. It was more difficult to sustain the project over the many years needed because there was a substantial, permanent drain on the energies of some of their most productive faculty. The necessary, although undesirable, result was that a long-term project participant simply took a reduced salary for the time spent working abroad, but continued meeting university expectations in other areas. Additional collaboration included six doctoral students the Center sent to two of these universities. This exposure contributed at least as much to the sponsoring universities as to the Lithuanian doctoral students.

Nevertheless, from the beginning the Center was not considered a project of any of these supporting U.S. universities. It was rather a Lithuanian program that used the best international resources available to accomplish its goals. During the initial 6 years of the project, rather than rely primarily on U.S. faculty, the codirectors actively drew from an international pool of senior social work educators with multicultural and multinational experience. None of the U.S. participants' home universities would have been willing or able to support the program in the way it was ultimately sustained by volunteer sweat and toil and by a network of diverse resources. These universities did receive a certain amount of credit for the involvement of their faculty and their sponsorship in the early years of the program, but the impact and value of this credit is limited. Financially stretched to meet the needs of their own students, it was remarkable that these schools supported the project as much as they did. It was only later, at the doctoral level, that a more established exchange of faculty and students was achieved. This collaboration program made a profound difference for those faculty and students.

PHASES OF PROGRAM DEVELOPMENT

Retrospectively, the program's development can be divided into four phases of activity. The first phase, from September, 1991 through September, 1992, was the development of support for this social work center. The second, from September, 1992 through May, 1993, was the start of the certificate program. The third, from 1993 through 1997, was the development of the master's-degree program. The fourth phase, from 1997 through the present, involved developing doctoral education and assisting the program and its graduates to move toward self-sufficiency with fewer overseas faculty. In all of these phases, a blend of international and Lithuanian faculty joined the program and developed their roles. There was also continual networking with other programs, institutions, and countries.

Phase 1: The Development of Support for a Social Work Program

In 1991, shortly before the collapse of the Soviet Union, Dr. Robert Constable of Loyola University Chicago was invited by Caritas of Lithuania to be a consultant; this was similar to the work he was doing with several Polish universities. In Kaunas, Lithuania, in September of that year, Dr. Constable delivered a well-attended series of lectures on social work that were cosponsered by Caritas and Vytautas Magnus University. The lectures used a frame of reference for social work that did not impose a narrow social work practice and education model, but was open to models which would emerge from these very different circumstances. The frame of reference related the constants in social work, professional values and scope, to the development of family and of social welfare, and as resources to help people reconstructing their individual environments and their systems of community assistance. Conversations with the first generation of students to graduate from the Center point out that these ideas crystallized the thinking of a number of people who decided to enter the program as soon as it was established. These prospective students were already established as engineers, physicians, teachers, architects, etc. (Harrison & Jaskyte, 1999). An initial proposal that outlined a social work program was elaborated with a sample outline of basic courses and field experiences. Vytautas Magnus University and Caritas agreed to support the program using local leadership.

The sponsorship of Caritas of Lithuania gave the program an excellent context of real human need and agency practice, as well as an optimal anchor in Lithuanian culture. Caritas represented the Catholic Church, which was only beginning to emerge from an underground mentality. By 1991, Caritas had used active international support to develop a number of loosely organized centers in Lithuania and to distribute medical supplies, food, and clothing. The president of Caritas, Sister Albina Pajarskaite, who had an advanced degree in the agricultural sciences, was particularly interested in the potential leadership of Lithuanian

social workers for rebuilding their society. Not everyone in Lithuania or in the Catholic Church shared her vision, but her presence was a powerful factor in the Center becoming a Lithuanian response to social concerns. However, the Lithuanian leadership for the proposed program, expected from discussions with Caritas and Vytautas Magnus University during Dr. Constable's visit, did not materialize. In response, Sr. Pajarskaite actively sought support from the National Conference of Catholic Bishops (NCCB) of the United States and personally asked Dr. Constable and Dr. Regina Kulys, from the University of Illinois at Chicago, to develop a social work program in Lithuania. Dr. Kulys' fluency in Lithuanian and familiarity with the culture was indispensable to this arrangement.

Vytautas Magnus University in Kaunas, which had been shut down shortly after the Soviet invasion in 1940 and reopened in 1988, had a mixture of overseas volunteer faculty, who would come and go, and local faculty, who had only known the previous Soviet educational system, and who had the effective power in the university. Reflecting the political realities of Soviet rule, some areas, such as the information sciences, were well developed; others, such as the social sciences, were not.

For Dr. Kulys and Dr. Constable, the desire to make the program Lithuanian as quickly as possible prompted a long-term development strategy. The substantial assistance of overseas faculty and resources would be needed to get the project underway, but this would only buy time for the more important project of developing Lithuanian leadership. However, the ready availability of Western volunteer faculty could prevent the emergence of Lithuanian leadership to appropriately fill the needs of the program. Therefore, when the administrators were not dealing with program development and management, much of their work would have to be the development of a Lithuanian, and later Baltic, network of support through consultation with schools, government ministries, and emergent programs.

After several months of discussion in the United States and later in Lithuania, Dr. Constable and Dr. Kulys wrote a proposal to the NCCB in May, 1992 to "assist in the development. . . of a Lithuanian Center for Social Work at Vytautas Magnus University" (Constable & Kulys, 1992). This proposal was accepted by the senate of Vytautas Magnus University with the expectation that the program would accept its first class in September, 1992. The program goals, stated in the proposal to the senate, specify the expectation that graduates would move into leadership positions and would become important players in the development of the human services. Therefore, as the program progressed, Lithuanian leadership would take over and the overseas contributions would be reduced. In May 1997, at the end of 5 academic years, the Center would incorporated into Vytautas Magnus University under Lithuanian leadership.

During this first phase, program governance was always a delicate issue because funds originated from the NCCB, were then transferred to the Lithuanian Bishops' Conference and Caritas, and finally expended directly by the Center at Vytautas Magnus University. This complicated funding process reinforced the Center's differences from the university's other programs and created resentment, which at times came out into the open. The project was simultaneously part of the university and separate from it. For the university's administration to accommodate Western-inspired professional education in a completely new discipline with Catholic sponsorship was not easy. Furthermore, Dr. Constable and Dr. Kulys, volunteers with full-time appointments in their home universities and continued expectations of academic productivity, were often unable to be onsite. Lithuanian faculty, appointed to assist in running the program, were not always able or willing to deal with emergent issues. The effective lack of an onsite advocate at the university created many difficulties in managing the program and in arranging and encouraging the eventual assumption of the program's leadership by Lithuanians. Until this transition took place there was a tendency to let the foreign consultants take responsibility for the project's governance.

The Center would be supported and governed by Vytautas Magnus University with the assistance of a taryba composed of representatives from the university, Caritas and the Catholic sector, and the public sector. The taryba reflected the many different viewpoints in the society of post-Soviet Lithuania. However, in its intent to include these diverse perspectives in the program's governance, the project created a difficult challenge for itself. Members of the taryba had very different approaches to decision making and conflict resolution. They operated in patterns mainly familiar to themselves, and finding substantive common ground between them would take a good deal of time to develop.

Phase 2: The Certificate Program

The initial program offered by the Center provided a certificate in social work for students who had already completed a professional degree in another discipline. In any case, no degree could be offered until it got formal university approval. When the master's degree was approved by the university, all of these students decided to take the master's program, even though its requirements, which included a research thesis, were more demanding than the certificate program. By spring, 1992, the first applicants were individually interviewed for admission to the certificate program. The commitment and energy of this first class has led them to continue their involvement in the program, in one way or another, to the present.

A central struggle for the certificate program was helping students to connect what they learned in the classroom with the realities they experienced in the field. Often it was difficult for the student and the professor to make this connection. For example, a student, having learned about worth and dignity of every person, found that some patients in a psychiatric hospital were tied to their beds for long periods of time. The students struggled to connect such practices, considered normal by the institution, to the values they were being taught. Expressing one's own thinking in the class and the field, being accountable for a helping process, helping a client (individual, group, or community) productively take charge of a process, respecting and valuing cultural differences, confidentiality, and dealing effectively with authority were all concepts which the Soviet system had excluded. Teaching them demanded a great deal of support, assistance, and translation from teachers and eventually from field instructors. The impact of this new awareness was that students realized that they had to find a role in the necessary reconstruction of the institutions they were serving and professors found that they needed to deal with the realities of this society in a constructive way.

The codirectors recognized from the beginning that field experience would need to have high priority. Vytautas Magnus University had great difficulty recognizing the field as a site for practical, more personally integrated learning and they were initially unwilling to grant credit for field experience or to engage faculty in these responsibilities. This issue became a point of constant negotiation between the foreign consultants and the university, and it has never been fully resolved (an accommodation was eventually reached). The strongest support for a fully developed field program comes from the profound impact these experiences had on the program's graduates. Rather than the classroom, the field was the place where students experienced conflicts between social work values, institutional practices, and their own fear and ambivalence.

A 2-year field experience was developed with careful field instruction and accountability. This experience was separated into a year of direct practice and a subsequent year moving toward social development practice. The broader focus of the 2nd year was also related to the research requirement of the master's degree, which was an individual project, approved by a research chair and a committee and published in the form of a master's thesis. Initially, overseas faculty were the field instructors, but later the program's graduates took on this responsibility. Field instructors supplied an intense tutorial relationship that helped the student to develop an internal sense of practice and an understanding of social work values, theory, and skills. Fortunately for the project, Dr. Lucia Valciukas, a very effective and compassionate educator from Australia who was fluent in Lithuanian, stayed in Lithuania for 4 full years, mentoring field instructors and supervising students.

Continuity, commitment, linguistic fluency, and true biculturalism were extremely important elements of the field program's success. Field sites emerged in the areas of family services, child welfare, social work in schools, mental and physical health, and in private, sectarian, and municipal social services. In each case, social work was a totally new profession and its values were quite different from many of the assumptions which guided the previous workers in these settings. While providing these direct services, students and faculty from the Center were, from the beginning, in a social development role, assisting in the creation of a new helping role in Lithuanian society. A good deal of faculty time was spent negotiating and managing the development of these placements, supervising the students, consulting with some of the field work program administrators, and later training program graduates to take on supervisory responsibilities.

Phase 3: Developing the Center's Master's-Degree Program

The Program. The initial, or foundation, year of the Center's master's-degree program consists of basic classes in Human Behavior and the Social Environment, Social Policy, and three discrete classes on practice methods with individuals, families, and groups. The 2nd year is devoted to social development practice and research to complete a master's thesis. This curriculum is meant to preserve a balance between generic and specific content. The major, semester-long courses are taught at a

fairly broad level so that students can make connections with a range of applicable concepts and can develop general skills. Numerous intensive 2-week workshops address different areas such as child welfare, case management, addictions, and mental health. In addition, students are encouraged and concretely supported to participate in work-study opportunities in other countries, including Poland, Denmark, Sweden, Norway, Finland, Germany, the United Kingdom, the Netherlands, and the United States. During these work study programs, students actually observe and work as social workers. These individually negotiated experiences are enormously important as they develop future leadership and, through the connections of the work-study student with other student participants, broaden the experience base of the Center's program.

When the master's degree program was approved in 1993, three elements were added to the former certificate program. First, research courses were now geared to the production of a master's thesis. A tutorial process was initiated to guide students through the completion of this thesis and its approval by a committee. Dr. David Harrison, from the University of Alabama, mentored students through this process and later taught Lithuanian faculty members to take his place. Second, courses in administration, policy, and social development were introduced in the 2nd year and integrated with the field experience. Finally, a separate social work library and computer center was being actively developed. There were contributions of books from U.S. universities and faculty; computers, shelves, and the librarians' salaries were supplied by two Dutch organizations, the Magdhuis and Prince Bernhard Foundations; and Vytautas Magnus University rehabilitated a large reading and book storage room. This library, reading room, and computer center eventually housed close to 90,000 contributed social work volumes in a diverse and relatively complete collection of books and journals.

With the Center's shift from a social work certificate to a master's degree, research became at least as important as the practice component. In fact, from the university's perspective research is the major component. In actuality, research does support social development practice and so the two components are not incompatible. The lack of descriptive research in basic human service areas in Lithuania provides students with many opportunities to focus on how people experience social problems and on initial experiments in new areas, such as school social work, foster care, and adoption. Many of these studies, when completed, were the first in their field in Lithuania. Later, they served as the basis for publications, international conference presentations, further research, practice, and program development.

The Faculty and Students. In the beginning, most of the program's faculty came from abroad; they are gradually being replaced by Lithuanian educators. Overseas faculty were drawn into the program through multinational networks, including such organizations as the International Association of Schools of Social Work and the Council on Social Work Education. The Center sought faculty who were experienced teachers, able to work in a foreign culture, innovative, diverse, and able to work with the program's Catholic sponsorship. Five foreign educators who were fluent in Lithuanian took substantial roles in the program. For the remaining faculty members, translators facilitated communication in and out of class when necessary.

From 1991 through 1997, a total of 30 overseas faculty, many of which were senior social work professors (including four Fulbright Scholars), volunteered to teach at the Center. Most were only able to make one trip, but others taught on a series of visits. Most of these volunteers had positions at other universities and had to arrange leaves of absence, sabbaticals, and vacations. The majority of the faculty were from the United States, but a substantial number came from other countries: Poland, Canada, the United Kingdom, Ireland, Australia, and Germany. The number and diversity of faculty allowed different students to get what they wanted and needed from the experience. These visiting educators found the Lithuanian experience a profoundly compelling one, which "challenged and drew out from us everything we were able to give and more" (P. Abels, personal communication, June 30, 1993). Each instructor found the students unforgettably avid and courageous learners who deeply validated social work in a totally different environment. These faculty emerged from this teaching experience with unforgettable memories of the students and their perspectives forever altered. The personal concern of Sr. Pajarskaite and others from Caritas for each of the volunteers helped the visitors to understand the Lithuanian economic, political, and socioeconomic context. Sr. Pajarskaite's astute observations, grounded in Lithuanian realities, oriented the work of the Center. In her profound realism, balanced by an insistence on the highest professional quality, she shaped the program goals and provided support and connections.

What the students "caught" from faculty was often more important than what was explicitly taught.

Students learned to get what they could learn from each teacher. They also began to understand that conflict can be productive: two professors, after arguing different positions on an issue in front of the class, would later go to a pleasant dinner together. Students also took an active part in faculty meetings and in curriculum development, and they had many informal teaching-learning contacts with visiting faculty. These students were initially unaccustomed to expressing their own ideas and to being treated with respect for their contributions. However, these same students would later take leadership roles in the development of a continuing education program, a comprehensive child welfare agency, and the Lithuanian social work profession. Many of these initiatives emerged from class discussion.

Harrison and Jaskyte (1999) analyzed the first two graduating classes' early contacts with Western faculty members. These students found many of the faculty's ideas interesting and new, but they often had difficulty connecting the concepts to their experiences and found them largely irrelevant to the world they knew. However, the modeling of relationships between the faculty members and the students, as well as between faculty members themselves, was very important. There was a parallel process among the students of trying to make sense of what professors, described as "the curly-haired one" or "the one who sits on the table," had to say. Sitting cross-legged on the table while lecturing was unknown to the Lithuanian university context. The gesture loosened the formal expectations of the teacher-student relationship. Some of the biggest obstacles to learning arose when the visiting professors persisted with their examples from afar, which often concerned services that were nonexistent in Lithuania. Other difficulties occurred when students felt that the instructors were growing frustrated by their slowness to learn or develop Western-style procedures and ideas. Only as the students gained some practical experience could they begin the more advanced filtering and application processes that are currently starting to take hold. Watt (1995) used focus-group work with students to confirm that connections have to be made between theory and practice and that observational, interactive, and experiential methods of learning are consequently very important. However, the visiting faculty often had only a short time to learn enough about the Lithuanian context to help students make these connections. Fortunately, a number of faculty made repeated trips throughout the program's development. These instructors were able to adapt their teaching to the Lithuanian situation with greater facility and also served as mentors for the less experienced faculty.

It is also very important to connect the program and its students with the experiences of other institutions. These linkages were made through conferences and exchanges with what has eventually become a network of developing programs in the Baltic states and Poland. It is also important to assist the students in experiencing different models of practice from Western Europe and Poland. Students continue especially to participate in work-study programs in Poland, which are extremely popular because they give the students a sense of different possibilities under similar conditions. Connections with social work programs in the other Baltic countries, Scandinavia, and Western Europe have been given high priority through a variety of conferences and exchanges. In January, 1994, the Center organized a very successful Baltic-Polish Conference on Field Instruction in Social Work, which was partially funded by the Soros Foundation (Constable & Kulys, 1995).

Phase 4: Developing Doctoral Education and Moving Toward Self-Sufficiency

The official transition of the Center to Lithuanian leadership and full incorporation into Vytautas Magnus University took place in May, 1997, but this shift was the fruit of several years' effort. The recent emergence of Lithuanian social work makes it difficult to find appropriate faculty and administrators. Additionally, the university's steadfast requirement (which came from the Education Ministry) that any professor teaching at the master's level must have an academic doctorate excludes many otherwise qualified Lithuanian faculty who might possess master's degrees or medical degrees. This condition also excludes the Center's graduates as well, although they do find some opportunities to teach as understudies to senior professors, or recently, at the BSW level. As a result of this situation, a relatively high number of the early graduates have achieved an academic doctorate, meeting the expectations of Western universities in shared-resource programs.

A top priority of the program was the maintenance of supportive and consultative contact with the program's graduates as they gravitate toward field instruction, research, doctoral study, program administration, or teaching. Graduates of the program also maintain a close network among themselves. They developed, funded, and continue to administer and teach a very successful continuing-education program for social work practitioners who work in municipal child welfare, aging, and other sectors. Some graduates are already administering programs in the public and the emergent private human service sectors of Lithuania. A major focus of the Center has been to help program leaders and teachers become credible scholars within the university system and who can contribute ideas and develop knowledge in a systematic way. A number of these doctoral students have affiliated their Lithuanian studies with doctoral programs in U.S. universities. The University of Alabama has pledged up to five funded places for Lithuanian social work students seeking their PhDs.

This project was sustainable because it was, from the beginning, conceived as a Lithuanian project and not primarily as a project of the consultants' home universities. It was propelled by the needs of Caritas of Lithuania, a nongovernmental organization, and by the continuing energies of its graduates. It was supported by an international network of faculty, foundations, and collaborating universities, which sacrificed as many scholarships and books and as much release time as they could afford. Although there was an active exchange of lectures during the first 5 years of the program, the emergent models of social work in Eastern Europe scarcely made a dent in the intellectual preoccupation of the visiting faculty's host universities. The beginnings of mutuality can be seen as the University of Alabama has effectively developed active support for collaborative doctoral education. Further, a class of master's-degree social work students did come from the University of Alabama to visit Lithuania for 2 weeks. These students learned a great deal during this very active exchange with Vytautas Magnus University students and others. In retrospect, given the sum total of their schools' resources, the authors are pleased with the support they received from their home institutions. Given another chance, they would not do it differently.

CONCLUSION

In this chapter, a number of assumed principles repeatedly emerged from the authors' experience and reflections. First, that the long-term and overriding goal of this project would be to assist Lithuanian social work educators in taking over the program and in developing Lithuanian social work. Secondly, that the education would be diverse and uniquely suited to Lithuania. The authors had some ideas of which practice models might work, but their key task was to identify possibilities and assist others in developing them. Therefore, the outcomes of this project could not be predetermined: no one, including the Lithuanian participants, knew what Lithuanian social work might be, or what was ultimately needed or wanted. Instead, the teachers were drawn from a variety of countries and philosophical backgrounds. The students were exposed to many successful practice models from different countries, but there was simultaneous demand from the Lithuanians themselves that these models be of high quality. All of the consultants needed to go into the field, testing and developing approaches appropriate to the specific environment. Finally, we learned that living out social work values in the daily exchange between instructors and students is the best way to teach these concepts. Students were excited by the values of worth and dignity of every person, of self-determination, of confidentiality, and many others, but at first they found these ideas strange and difficult in application. Particularly the first class of students, who had experienced firsthand the Lithuanian resistance movement, resonated with these values and said in different ways: "I want to live my life consistent with these principles."

REFERENCES

Constable, R. T., & Kulys, R. (1992). *Proposal for a Lithuanian center for social work*. Kaunas, Lithuania: Vytautas Magnus University, Archives of the University Senate.

Constable, R. T., & Kulys, R. (Eds.). (1995). *Social work field instruction in post-communist societies*. Kaunas, Lithuania: Caritas Press.

Harrison, W. D., & Jaskyte, K. (1999, March). *The cardinal components of instruction: Lithuanian students' first encounters with Western instructors*. Paper presented at the Council on Social Work Education's 45th Annual Program Meeting, San Francisco.

Watt, J. W. (1995) Student perspectives on social work education programs in the Baltic states and Poland: A focus group report. In R. Constable & R. Kulys (Eds.), *Social work field instruction in post-communist societies* (pp. 46-54). Kaunas, Lithuania: Caritas Press.

ELEVEN

Building a Social Development Approach to Social Work Education: The University of Toronto–Sri Lanka School of Social Work Project

Wes Shera

In 1982, the University of Toronto Faculty of Social Work and the Sri Lanka School of Social Work, in Colombo, Sri Lanka, established a 4-year inter-institutional cooperative program in the areas of curriculum planning, resource development, and the planning and teaching of courses. The project's overall objectives were to increase the capacity of the Sri Lanka School of Social Work to contribute to its country's development efforts and to improve Canadian social work educators' ability to provide appropriate technical assistance for these efforts. Several more specific aims were pursued in order to enhance the Sri Lanka School's production of competent graduates:

1. To cooperate in a planned program for the development of social work education
2. To upgrade the Sri Lanka School's curriculum within the context of social development efforts in that country
3. To strengthen the development of trained social work manpower in Sri Lanka at the diploma level and to begin plans for a master's-level degree
4. To jointly produce documentation, analysis, and evaluation concerning the project

The project was jointly funded by the Canadian International Development Agency (CIDA), the United Nations Children's Fund (UNICEF), the Ministry of Social Services in Sri Lanka, and the University of Toronto Faculty of Social Work (Abrahams & Shera, 1984).

BACKGROUND

At the time of this project, 1982-1986, Sri Lanka, formerly known as Ceylon, had a population of approximately 15 million. The country hangs like a teardrop off the southeast coast of India. It covers an area of about 65,610 square kilometers, approximately 430 kilometers long and 225 kilometers across at its widest point. The two major ethnic groups in the country were Sinhalese (72%) and Tamils (20%). Buddhism was the predominant religion (66%), followed by Hinduism (19%) and Christianity (9%; CIDA, 1981). From an international perspective, Sri Lanka was recognized for two major initiatives. First, Sri Lanka's policy of nonalignment has allowed it to formulate an independent foreign policy, promote its international interests, acquire foreign aid, and take leadership in the nonaligned movement. (Phadnis & Patnaik, 1981). Second, although it is in the bottom half of the World Bank's list of the poorest 40 countries, with an annual gross national product of just $200 per person, Sri Lanka has made remarkable improvements in literacy, life expectancy rates, and infant mortality and birth rates. Taken together, the government's social welfare policies, such as free rice rations, free education and health services, and subsidized food and transport, significantly reduced absolute poverty from 1953 to 1973 (Gunatilleke, 1981). During this period, Sri Lanka also had an impressive record of income redistribution to poorer sectors of society, especially in comparison to the performance of other Third World countries (Fields, 1980).

But as the country moved into the late 1960s and early 1970s, it began to encounter difficult structural problems with which it could not cope. Malnutrition, poor sanitation, and limited knowledge of hygienic practices prevented the further reduction of infant mortality rates. Significant percentages of school-age children either did not enter (15%) or did not remain in (30%) the school system (Gunatilleke, 1982). Many of those who completed their education were unable to obtain employment. Dependency on the centralized administration and on its delivery of services had reduced or failed to develop the capacity of local jurisdictions to address issues of social concern. In 1977, these factors and the poor performance of the economy precipitated a change in government and significant shifts in the country's development strategies. The new Jayewardene government initiated economic policies aimed at liberalization of the economy to promote growth, employment, and the production of exports. Specific steps included dismantling of price controls, provision of monetary incentives, reduction of consumer subsidies, devaluation of the rupee, and elimination of government import monopolies, which increased interest rates and encouraged foreign and domestic investment (CIDA, 1981). The government also undertook a new development initiative that concentrated on three lead programs: the acceleration of the Mahaweli irrigation/resettlement/hydro-electric scheme, an urban renewal housing program, and the establishment of a free trade zone north of Colombo (Hewavitharana, 1980).

Even though the economy exhibited some signs of improvement after 1977, numerous observers raised serious questions about both the economic and social aspects of the new development strategy. A few of these concerns included the ability of the country to achieve greater economic independence, the increasing gap between the rich and the poor, the disparities between urban and rural locales, and the exploitation of workers in the free trade zone. (Balasuriya, 1980; Dunham, 1982; Hugue, 1982).

SOCIAL WORK EDUCATION IN SRI LANKA

The Ceylon Institute of Social Work was organized in 1953 under voluntary auspices. Its major objective was to provide adequate facilities for the training of social workers in Ceylon. The first program of study was a year-long undergraduate certificate course in social work for a limited number of trainees. As the students increased in number, however, an expansion of facilities and staff became imperative. An interdepartmental government committee was appointed to study the various aspects of the Ceylon Institute's problems, and in October, 1964, it recommended the establishment of a professional school of social work under the Ministry of Social Services (Sri Lanka School of Social Work, 1978).

The first semi- or preprofessional course offered by this new school was a 2-year Diploma in Social Work. Training consisted of a year of full-time classroom study, then field work, participation in seminars, and completion of a final research report. In addition to the diploma program, other short-term courses and in-service training programs were continuously being given at the school.

In the years that followed, the school was unable to recruit adequately trained personnel to serve as faculty and staff, and to meet administrative requirements the 2-year course was reorganized into a 3-year part-time study program. The new goal was to improve the standard of Ceylonese social services through training programs made available to social workers in both government and voluntary social welfare agencies. In 1972, the constitution and the government were changed and Ceylon became the Republic of Sri Lanka; consequently, the Ceylon Institute became the Sri Lanka School of Social Work.

A perennial problem for the school has been the shortage of trained staff, and in 1975 it was forced to temporarily suspend its diploma program. The director and part-time lecturers concentrated on giving short-term courses for management-, intermediate-, and direct-service-level workers in the Department of Social Services and the Department of Probation and Child Care under the Ministry of Social Services.

In 1978, the 2-year social work diploma course was recommenced in another attempt to professionalize the training offered by the school and to provide opportunities for untrained personnel to become qualified social workers. In 1983, the school's faculty consisted of a director, a deputy director, three lecturers, two training officers, and one United Nations volunteer.

The government's accelerated development projects during the 1980s have had a range of implications for social policies and social workers in Sri Lanka. Projects such as the Mahaweli Development Plan, Integrated Rural Development, the Child and Youth Development programs, and New Human settlements demanded qualified social workers. Prior to its identification with these development initiatives, the profession of social work was unknown or generally accepted as only involved in the implementation of remedial welfare services.

The Sri Lanka School of Social Work was located within the Ministry of Social Services, which consisted of three major branches:

Social Services. This section of the ministry included public assistance; financial support for tuberculous and leprous patients; relief for victims of floods, droughts, and epidemics; rehabilitation and welfare of the socially disabled; family counselling; house of detention ordinance; and poor law ordinance.

Probation and Childcare Services. This branch of the ministry included welfare services for preschool children, juvenile correction services (including administration of remand homes and certified schools), prevention, childcare, adoption services, and probation services.

Sri Lanka School of Social Work. The school is the training arm of the ministry. The school's mandate is to provide professional social work education and paraprofessional training for the staff of the departments of social services, probation, and childcare services and other state-run agencies and voluntary organizations.

The services provided by the ministry have been mostly remedial and custodial, have generally involved the provision of material assistance, and have been temporary in nature and residual in scope. Just prior to this collaborative project, the school had been trying to organize a more relevant curriculum for training students to be more responsive to the growing development needs of Sri Lanka. There was evidence to suggest that, provided with the means and the wherewithal to carry on a developmental program, the ministry could implement some newer strategies while still providing vitally needed services, such as those offered to the poor and the disabled.

In its effort to help the ministry develop these new service units, the Sri Lanka School of Social Work felt it would benefit from collaboration with the University of Toronto Faculty of Social Work. The ministry also recognized the potential for a developmental program and supported the linkage project. It was hoped that the Sri Lanka School of Social Work, with Canadian assistance, would be able to help the ministry implement, on a larger scale, a developmental approach within its services.

THE LINKAGE PROJECT

The Canada-Sri Lanka Social Work Education Linkage Project originated through discussions between Dudley Dissanayake, director of the Sri Lanka School of Social Work; Dr. Michael Oliver, director of the International Development Office in Ottawa; and Dr. Caryl Abrahams of the Faculty of Social Work at the University of Toronto. The exploration of feasibility factors, participatory planning, and the definition of objectives and the process through which these objectives could be realized took place under a development grant provided by CIDA.

The project's objectives, as listed at the beginning of this chapter, were achieved through the following activities:

- Individual Canadian social work educators serving as consultants to their Sri Lankan counterparts in the areas of curriculum planning, social work education technology, resource development, the planning and teaching of courses in specific content areas, and strengthening field instruction components
- Continuous evaluation and documentation of this consultancy process
- Orientation programs
- Joint workshops
- Advanced educational opportunities for faculty members of the Sri Lanka School of Social Work

Some of these activities required long-term assistance, and they were completed by consultants who were willing and able to stay for more than 6 months. These activities included curriculum planning, designing the proposed MSW program, integration of the school's programs into a consistent, resource-efficient package, and project documentation.

Other objectives were met through short-term consultancies in areas such as group work, community development, research, social development, and social policy. Expert consultants were selected on the basis of a demonstrated capacity for flexibility, cross-cultural competence, and willingness to cooperate with Sri Lankan counterparts in both the consultation process and its documentation. These short-term participants provided advice in specified content areas for periods of approximately 3 months.

An area of particular significance to the success of this project was the development of appropriate local teaching resources. Videotapes, films, audiotapes, and written material were developed with the assistance of short-term consultants who had expertise in preparing locally relevant materials for instructional use. These consultants also provided integrative theoretical content and instruction for classroom use.

Consultants first participated in orientation sessions in both Canada and Sri Lanka to ensure consistency in expectations, procedures, and documentation, as well as to familiarize themselves with Sri Lanka. One unique feature of the project was the use of a single unit for the accommodation of all short-term consultants. There were a number of reasons for this decision, other than the appreciable savings compared to the typical living costs of bilateral short-term consultants.

The single accommodation promoted closer working relationships among the consultants and provided an informal setting that encouraged ongoing interaction with the Sri Lankan participants and reduced the social distance that would have been created by tourist-type accommodations. Additionally, this cohesive environment facilitated rapid cultural adjustment and ongoing orientation programs, as well as positioning the consultants to be more immediately productive.

The characteristics of the consultants involved in this type of cross-cultural project often determine its success or failure. The selection criteria used when considering candidates included the following: level of commitment to the project; ability to work as a team member (flexibility, cooperativeness); possession of a generalist orientation, but with an area of expertise; ability to model social development principles (especially in teaching); and availability at the appropriate time.

The Social Development Perspective

To ensure that both the consultants and their Sri Lankan counterparts operated from a roughly uniform mode, the social development model was agreed upon by the framers of the project, Dr. Abrahams and Mr. Dissanayake. They believed that this model would provide the most effective framework for the project's activities. Although there are many definitions of social development, Sanders (1982) described it comprehensively as a movement, a perspective, and a mode of practice.

> Social development as a movement embodies the philosophy of a positive, humane, people-oriented development in societies. It is centrally concerned with social justice and equitable distribution of resources. Other related concerns embodied in social development as a movement are commitment to the development and optimal use of human resources, involvement of people in their own development, integrated economic and social development and emphasis on the qualitative dimensions of development.

> Social development as a perspective embodies a fundamental philosophical stance in work

with people in a helping role that is positive, holistic, open to social change, and based on optimizing the inherent strengths and capacities of individuals, families and communities. It is a perspective that cuts across both direct and indirect practice. It represents a comprehensive, broad-based view and opens the door for the social work profession to go beyond the predominant, traditional remedial, reactive stance in response to human needs and concerns.

> Social development as a practice mode in social work is a reconceptualization in a more integrative, social change-oriented framework of practice skills in the macro area of practice (especially community organization, policy development, development planning, and administration) focusing on institutional renewal and development at varying levels. This development and change come about through capacity building in people and in the exercise of their collective strength (especially through the political process) to ensure greater responsiveness of institutions in resource allocation and policy decisions to people's needs, life styles and value system. (pp. x–xi)

Paiva (1982) challenges social workers to examine their functions vis-a-vis development in Third World countries and to move beyond traditional roles in order to bring about changes in social structures and institutions by developing the capacity of the people and their resources. Hollister (1982) warns us that there is no single correct curriculum for professional training programs in social development. Instead, each curriculum should include content relevant to the region being served, and each must be a realistic compromise between the amount of information that students should know and the practical limits on the available time for professional training.

The Sri Lanka School of Social Work and the Canadian Consultants

The Sri Lanka School of Social Work was in a unique position at outset of the collaborative project. A committed, thoughtful, and basically trained faculty already existed and social work was beginning to receive recognition for the part it could play in the development of the country. The Sri Lankan faculty had identified specific educational and technological areas with which they required assistance. The University of Toronto Faculty of Social Work had recognized expertise in the field of international social work and in social work in developing countries.

Three of the Canadian faculty members were familiar with Sri Lanka, including one educator who had worked in community development training in Sri Lanka and had a continuous interest in the country's social development. This expertise, combined with the recognition of changing processes for social work education in Canada and the influence of Toronto's multicultural communities, led a number of Canadian faculty members to address the transferability of teaching and practice technologies. Thus, it was assumed that by joining together, the consultants could upgrade specific areas of Sri Lankan social work education, plan curriculum development with particular attention to cross-cultural aspects, and continue to confront the issues of transferability.

A significant factor for this project was the increasing sophistication and awareness of best practices in international collaboration. When conducted on the basis of joint planning, with clearly identified goals, objectives, and rewards for both partners, any assistance project has an excellent chance for continuous development and successful completion. Sri Lankan faculty wanted to gain competence in curriculum planning and course design and delivery, while Canadian faculty wanted to learn about the transferability of social work education to developing countries and about how this learning might be of use in the multicultural environment of Toronto. This dual investment and reward system reinforced each participant's desire to make the project a success.

The Sri Lanka School of Social Work was the only institution in Sri Lanka that educated and trained the personnel who staff, supervise, and administer the government and nongovernment agencies engaged in youth development, women's development, regional development, urban and rural development, planned human settlements, correctional services, public welfare, public health, and services for the elderly and disabled. It is therefore important that this education and training be of excellent quality. The impact of the school can be understood by noting that over 700 applications are received annually for only 40 places in each class. The school's avowed emphasis on social development is congruent with the national development policy of Sri Lanka.

STRATEGIES FOR CONSULTATION AND EVALUATION

Although the social development model has been discussed primarily in terms of its relevance to the curriculum of the Sri Lanka School of Social Work, it is important to note the team attempted to model many of the principles of social development (Meinert, Kohn, & Strickler, 1984) during the consultation, including cooperation, participation, feedback, pragmatism, social planning, and reflective review. The consultative process that preceded the funding of the project incorporated both joint planning and mutual agreement on the parameters of the project. Although these elements were included in part due to the ethics of the consultant involved, it should be pointed out that in the international development arena there is a growing emphasis on making the full agreement of the host country a prerequisite for funding.

A six-stage framework, developed by Jacobsen (1974), was modified and used to guide both the consultation and the evaluation strategies used in this project. The six stages were as follows:

1. Entry into the organization
2. Relationship building
3. Organizational assessment
4. Contract development
5. Instituting, monitoring, and modifying a set of interventions
6. Evaluation and termination

The entry phase involves those interactions and processes by which the consultant and organization "check each other out" and explore their mutual willingness to continue. Relationship building is initiated during the entry phase, but it requires greater energy and development as the consultation continues. Organizational assessment describes those activities that help a consultant understand the structure, processes, and environmental relationships of the host organization. This assessment typically has implications for further relationship building and for the nature and timing of specific interventions. The contract is a written or verbal agreement between the consultant and the host organization that specifies the parameters of the consultation. The interventions performed by the consultant and her or his host counterparts are those activities that are intended to bring about changes that the organization feels are required. The evaluation and termination phase includes both an assessment of the effectiveness of the consultation project and a gradual process of separation that leaves the host organization with the capacity to address the remaining issues in an independent and positive manner.

PROJECT OBJECTIVES AND ACTIVITIES

A wide range of activities were undertaken to achieve the specific objectives of the project:

1. Upgrading of the Sri Lanka School of Social Work's curriculum within the context of social development efforts through the development of educational technology and course syllabi within an integrated plan. Activities to achieve this objective included:

   - Social development workshops
   - Collaborative revision of course syllabi

   In the workshops, the Canadian consultants and Sri Lankan counterparts reviewed the curriculum to achieve an overall social development focus. Through purposive planning and continuous modeling, the workshops progressed from expert-led consultations to significant forums of coleadership, participatory agenda development, and inclusive discussion. Workshops were conducted to develop the teaching staff's ability to design and improve curricula, to use a variety of pedagogical strategies, and to revise their individual courses. As a result of this process, the entire curriculum was examined and all courses were revised to be congruent with the social development perspective.

2. Upgrading the Sri Lanka School of Social Work curriculum through the initiation and development of field instruction technology and centers. Activities to achieve this objective included:

   - The development of field instruction competency for Sri Lankan faculty members
   - The provision of training courses for Sri Lankan agency supervisors
   - The development of Sri Lankan faculty members' ability to train field instructors
   - The establishment of field-teaching centers
   - The creation of guidelines for field instructors

3. Upgrading the Sri Lanka School of Social Work curriculum by preparing bibliographies and other teaching materials from both local and foreign sources. Activities to achieve this objective included:

   - The production of course bibliographies
   - Workshops on teaching technologies
   - Study tours to Canada for Sri Lankan faculty

4. Upgrading the Sri Lanka School of Social Work curriculum within the context of social development efforts through the identification, organization, incorporation, and transformation of local data into indigenous teaching materials. The activities undertaken to achieve this objective included:

   - The collaborative preparation of a field instruction reader
   - Systematic collection of teaching resources
   - The development of a manual for field instructors training courses
   - Field visits and onsite consultation with agency supervisors
   - Observation and feedback on the classroom teaching techniques of Sri Lankan faculty
   - Initiation of a lab-training program for students

5. Upgrading the Sri Lanka School of Social Work curriculum within the context of social development efforts by expanding teaching and learning resources. Related activities included:

   - Onsite consultation, including field and classroom observation, research-oriented field visits, workshops, and individual consultation
   - Review of social development projects for inclusion in the overall curriculum
   - Preparation of a dictionary of professional terms in Sinhala (the primary language of Sri Lanka)
   - Review of physical facilities, audio-visual equipment, and library vis-a-vis their capacity and appropriateness for supporting the social work program

6. Cooperation in a planned program designed to continue the development of social work education in Sri Lanka by increasing faculty expertise in curriculum planning, field instruc-

tion, social work teaching technology, and practice theory. Activities undertaken to achieve this objective included:

- A collaborative process of individual consultation for increasing the expertise of Sri Lankan faculty members in curriculum planning, field instruction, and teaching
- International study tours for Sri Lankan educators
- Specialized study programs for selected faculty members
- Preparation of a planning document for the Sri Lanka School of Social Work

7. Cooperation in a planned program designed to develop social work education in Sri Lanka by providing opportunities for educators in Sri Lanka and Canada to acquire and demonstrate new teaching and practice methodologies and to develop practice models and social work theory relevant to the Sri Lankan context. Activities included:

- Collaborative work to build the new Sri Lanka School of Social Work curriculum
- Weekly meetings for Canadian consultants to reflect on the nature of their cross-cultural work
- Linkage-project coordinator meetings
- Use of a workshop or seminar format in the consultation process
- Shifting responsibility for project-orientation activities from Canadian to Sri Lankan educators
- The use of 6-month progress reports
- An extensive internal process for evaluation
- Collaboration on the development of a diploma program and a proposal for a degree program

ISSUES AFFECTING IMPLEMENTATION

The implementation of this project was significantly affected by several factors beyond the control of the Canadian consultants and their Sri Lankan counterparts. In Abrahams' (1986) final project report, these events and issues are identified as follows.

Civil Disturbances

Civil disturbances caused by warring factions of Tamil and Sinhalese extremists began on July 25, 1983. Hundreds of people were killed, thousands of others ended up in refugee camps, and the project came to a standstill. The Canadian consultants were called upon to work in the refugee camps. This experience was used by these faculty members to generate case examples for use in the classroom. Other natural disasters, such as periods of drought and flooding, also took faculty time away from project activities. It is important to note that much of what occurs during international projects is beyond the control of those involved and can have a major impact on the success of the project.

Technical Resources

A lack of resources, particularly UNICEF's inability to provide a vehicle for the project, hampered the work. Even when vehicles were available, the process of booking drivers and negotiating through the necessary bureaucratic procedures was time-consuming and cumbersome. This was a particularly critical problem during field work in rural areas outside Colombo.

Support Staff and Resources

It was very difficult to recruit the support staff that were to be provided under the collaborative agreement, primarily because of the requirement that they speak English. Eventually, an English-speaking secretary was hired from the private sector. Other resources supplied by the Ministry of Social Services, such as photocopying, office supplies, and translators, were available, but there were often shortages and breaks in these services.

Administrative Personnel Changes

Turnover in key Sri Lankan positions, such as the director of the school, the registrar, and the head of the ministry, had an impact on the project. Delays in replacing these individuals and the process of orientation for new personnel led to delays in the overall work of the project. In international collaborations of this nature, the support and leadership of key administrators is critical. The patriarchal, bureaucratic characteristics of the systems encountered during this project frequently prevented the Sri Lankan faculty from moving forward as a collective.

LESSONS LEARNED

The activities of the Canadian consultants, the Sri Lankan counterparts, and the different institutional administrators and the results of these activities indicate that the goal of cooperation for the improvement of social work education in Sri Lanka was met. The social development model of consultation enhanced the cooperative nature of this project. The model, as applied to curriculum development, the process of the consultation, and the content of the new Sri Lankan curriculum, provided all of the participants the opportunity for continuously examining both the content and the process of the project (Abrahams et al., 1985). The Sri Lankan faculty continually increased their ability to learn, model, and deliver social development content despite inadequate resources. High quality social work education cannot take place without the necessary resources. Concern was expressed regarding the continuing deficiency of the educational resources, such as library holdings, and physical facilities needed to support the program.

A significant factor for the development of social work education during this project was the ease with which changes were made and institutionalized within the framework of the ministry. The willingness of the head of the ministry to participate fully in the restructuring of the program provided encouragement for the consultants and the counterparts alike. Illustrative of this commitment was the draft planning document (for the proposed degree program), which was requested by and accepted, in principle, by the ministry.

The Sri Lanka School of Social Work increased its expertise in curriculum planning and in field instruction within the context of ongoing social development efforts. The focus on social development for the curriculum was initiated with workshops and individual consultation. This work, which upgraded the curriculum for the diploma program, was completed using a collaborative process of curriculum review and improvement. The social development orientation was clearly articulated in every course and students and graduates were committed to this approach for practice. The impact of this new initiative became evident in the increasing number of field-learning opportunities being offered to students from government development ministries, nongovernmental agencies, and individual communities.

There was a clear transition for all of the Sri Lankan faculty from social work practitioners and trainers to social work educators. Their increased competence includes the ability to carry forward the development of Sri Lankan field instruction. The creation of the Field Training Centres was less complete; this process takes many years, but the first steps in definition, design, and establishment of the pilot centers were undertaken. The Sri Lankan teaching faculty also demonstrated their ability to implement what they had learned for the construction of a degree program.

Sri Lankan graduates and current students were able to articulate the knowledge and skills they had learned, and they believed that these additions would be helpful for their employment aspirations. This is particularly true for the majority of students, who are employed in development fields, but all participants were found to be enthusiastic about social development and the contributions they could make in the community as change agents.

The processes of evaluation demonstrated the capacity of both the Canadian consultants and their Sri Lankan counterparts to jointly analyze the work they had undertaken. Using joint evaluation as a means of feedback and as a planning tool increased the participants' commitment to progress toward their goals, modeled principles of social development, and provided an important accountability function.

The documentation of the activities and the impact of the linkage project has provided a resource for others who wish to engage in similar activities. This documentation includes a series of six project reports published by the Faculty of Social Work at the University of Toronto, under the leadership of Caryl Abrahams (e.g., Abrahams et al., 1985; Abrahams, 1986). Several articles and book chapters have been produced (Abrahams & Shera, 1984) and numerous papers have been presented at international conferences, such as the International Association of Schools of Social Work meetings which were held in Montreal, Canada, in the summer of 1984 (Abrahams et al., 1985). Shera (1984) also presented a paper on evaluating the transfer and development of social work education technology in a developing country at the American Evaluation Association Conference.

The impact of this project on the Faculty of Social Work at the University of Toronto and the individuals involved was profound. Significant expertise was created in working collaboratively with international partners on development projects. This expertise included not only a refined body of knowledge and enhanced skills, but also important personal awareness about the use of self in cross-cultural encounters. The Faculty of Social Work subsequently received numerous requests for assistance, augmented its support of international students, and increased its involvement in a range of global activities. The educators who had participated in this project continued, over time, to be involved in a range of international activities. The author, who was one of the participants, has used this model of consultation in subsequent projects in Shanghai, China, (Shera, 1988, 1992); Mexico City, Mexico (Traub-Werner, Shera, Rodriguez Villa, & Tello Peon, 2000); and more recently in Beijing, China (Tsang, Yan, & Shera, 2000).

In August, 2000, the author had the good fortune of meeting the current director of the Sri Lanka School of Social Work, Piyasena Kotelawala, at the International Association of Schools of Social Work conference in Montreal, Canada. Mr. Kotelawala was one of the faculty members involved in this collaborative project many years ago. As a follow-up to this discussion, he commented by email on the long-term impact of the project for Sri Lanka, stating that it had

- Produced a development-oriented social work diploma curriculum which is still relevant today
- Introduced a community-based field curriculum
- Introduced the social development practice model
- Helped faculty members improve their teaching skills and be more aware of international practice
- Developed cross-cultural teamwork which was very significant to the achievement of the project's objectives

He also indicated that the Sri Lankan MSW program would begin in 2002 and that the linkage project had contributed to this development by building the foundations of the current social work program. It is this type of feedback that encourages social work educators to continue to make both professional and personal commitments to these important international linkage projects.

REFERENCES

Abrahams, C. (1986). *Final report.* (Publication No. 6, The Canada-Sri Lanka Social Work Education Linkage Project). Toronto, Canada: University of Toronto, Faculty of Social Work.

Abrahams, C., Bernas, P., Bogo, M., Chandrasekere, S., Herington, W., Kotelawala, K., & Shera, W. (1985).

IASSW, IUCISD presentations. Montreal, Canada, 1984 (Publication No. 5, The Canada-Sri Lanka Social Work Education Linkage Project). Toronto, Canada: University of Toronto, Faculty of Social Work.

Abrahams, C., & Shera, W. (1984). The Canada/Sri Lanka Social Work Education Linkage Project. In D. Kimberley (Ed.), *Beyond national boundaries: Canadian contributions to international social work and social welfare* (pp. 4-22). Ottawa, Canada: Canadian Association of Schools of Social Work.

Balasuriya, T. (1980). Our free trade zone: Is it development? *Logos, 19*(2), 1-37.

Canadian International Development Agency. (1981). *Sri Lanka—Post Report.* Hull, Canada: Author.

Dunham, D. (1982). Politics and land settlement schemes: The case of Sri Lanka. *Development and Change, 13*(1), 43-61.

Fields, G. (1980). *Poverty, inequality and development.* Cambridge, United Kingdom: Cambridge University Press.

Gunatilleke, G. (1981, November). Wealth and welfare. *New Internationalist,* 7-9.

Gunatilleke, G. (1982, July). *Changing needs of children.* Colombo, Sri Lanka: UNICEF Print Pack Ltd.

Hewavitharana, B. (1980). New patterns and strategies of development for Sri Lanka. *Economic Bulletin for Asia and the Pacific, 21*(1), 20-44.

Hollister, D. (1982). The knowledge and skills base of social development. In D. Sanders (Ed.), *The developmental perspective in social work* (pp. 31-42). Honolulu, HI: University of Hawaii, School of Social Work.

Hugue, A. S. (1982). The Mahaweli Development Project: An economic disaster? *Asian Profile, 10*(1), 97-105.

Jacobsen, J. (1974). *Program evaluation and psychological consultation.* Unpublished monograph, Community Mental Health Program, University of Michigan.

Meinert, R., Kohn, E., & Strickler, G. (1984). International survey of social development concepts. *Social Development Issues, 8*(1/2), 70-88.

Midgley, J. (1995). *Social development: The developmental perspective in social welfare.* London: Sage Publications Ltd.

Paiva, F. J. (1982). The dynamics of social development and social work. In D. Sanders (Ed.), *The developmental perspective in social work* (pp. 1–11). Honolulu, HI: University of Hawaii, School of Social Work.

Phadnis, U., & Patnaik, S. (1981). Non-alignment as a foreign policy strategy: A case study of Sri Lanka. *International Studies, 20*(1/2), 223–238.

Sanders, D. (1982). *The developmental perspective in social work.* Honolulu, HI: University of Hawaii, School of Social Work.

Shera, W. (1984, October). *Evaluating the transfer and development of social work education technology in a developing country.* Paper presented at the Joint Conference of the Evaluation Network and Evaluation Research Society, San Francisco.

Shera, W. (1988). The role of educational institutions in development: The Chinese case. *Social Development Issues, 12*(1), 33–41.

Shera, W. (1992) Educational evaluation in China: An analysis of current practices. *Evaluation and Program Planning, 15*(1), 45–53.

Sri Lanka School of Social Work. (1978). *Program prospectus 1978.* Colombo, Sri Lanka: Author.

Traub-Werner, B., Shera, W., Rodriguez Villa, B. M., & Tello Peon, N. (2000). International partnerships: A Mexico–Canada social work education project. *Canadian Social Work, 2*(1), 184–197.

Tsang, T., Yan, M., & Shera, W. (2000). Negotiating multiple agendas in international social work: The case of the China–Canada collaborative project. *Canadian Social Work, 2*(1), 147–161.

TWELVE

South–North Development Partnership: Lessons from a Nicaragua–Canada Experience

Maureen Wilson

This chapter describes an experience of South–North development cooperation between the Escuela de Trabajo Social (school of social work; ETS) at the Universidad Centroamericana (UCA) in Managua, Nicaragua and the Faculty of Social Work, University of Calgary in Canada. It will describe how this partnership began, the needs it was designed to meet, its goals and objectives, its activities and accomplishments, the evaluation of the project, and lessons learned from the experience.

THE CONTEXT

The setting for the emergence of social work in Nicaragua, as in much of Latin America, was provided by the Kennedy administration's Alliance for Progress. The 1959 victory of the Cuban revolutionaries had threatened U.S. interests throughout Latin America, which led the United States to promote a model of development in the region intended to reduce social discontent and prevent further such revolutions. Thus at a meeting in Punta del Este, Uruguay in 1961, the Alliance for Progress was created to advance the implementation of an approach to development that would avoid radical changes in existing socioeconomic structures. At this meeting, the U.S. delegation proposed the granting of $20 billion in credits to Latin American countries, to be used for the development of agriculture, industry, education, and health care. The U.S. proposal involved a plan to stimulate development in this region through the injection of massive foreign investment, which was expected to be associated with an increase in employment opportunities, more equitable distribution of national income, stabilization of prices for basic

products, reduction of infant mortality, improvement of public health services and housing, elimination of illiteracy, and expansion of vocational, secondary, and higher education (Wilson, 1996).

A social service bureaucracy was created in Nicaragua in the early 1960s to take advantage of the U.S. foreign aid programs introduced as part of the Alliance for Progress initiatives. There was a need for social workers to carry out some of these programs, and during this period schools of social work began to open throughout Latin America. In Nicaragua, social work education began in 1961 with the establishment of a program by the Nicaraguan Institute of Social Security to fill the need for interviewers to handle applicants for pensions and other social benefits (Téfel, Lopez, & Castillo, 1985). In 1964, the first 13 social workers completed this training; in the following year, the program moved to the National Autonomous University of Nicaragua (UNAN). The curriculum of the UNAN School of Social Work was greatly influenced in these early days by what the Nicaraguans described as the functionalist perspective of North American thought. The social worker was seen as politically neutral and there was an emphasis in social work on the "social assistance" function (ETS, 1985).

It soon became apparent, however, that the Alliance for Progress programs were not delivering the expected results. Few benefits trickled down to the mass of the people, and in Nicaragua these new programs served largely to provide employment and opportunities for personal enrichment of the elite and its middle class allies (Walker, 1985; Téfel, Lopez, & Castillo, 1985). Throughout Latin America, the gap between rich and poor widened, and a heavy proportion of the U.S. disbursements went "to military regimes that had overthrown constitutional governments" (Hansen, 1967, p. 1).

The support is gratefully acknowledged of the Canadian International Development Agency for financing for the project upon which these reflections are based.

While forces were gathering in Nicaragua to overthrow the corrupt Somoza dictatorship, throughout Latin America social workers were engaged in a reexamination of their roles and their perspectives on practice. This "reconceptualization movement" involved a new emphasis on the role of social work in the promotion of social change, employing Freire's methodology of popular education (Freire, 2000). Thus social workers would work more directly with the poor, accompanying groups as they analyzed their positions in the historical moments in which they live, and in determining courses of action for themselves. In this practice model, social workers would not see themselves as politically neutral, but rather as actively taking the side of the poor. In their search for models more appropriate to their reality, Nicaraguan social workers and educators were drawn to this perspective, and their curriculum shifted away from the *tecnicismo* that had characterized the school's curriculum throughout its first 13 years and toward an emphasis on "theoretical development" (ETS, 1984; roughly translated, *tecnicismo* means an overemphasis on technique, at the expense of clear insight into the nature and significance of the dynamic context in which the work is occurring). However, in the effort to overcome this blind *tecnicismo* and produce social workers capable of the social analysis necessary for the promotion of social transformation, the school's program developed some imbalance. During this transitional period, the high level of theoretical content was not well articulated with concrete practice methods.

Following the July, 1979 victory of the *sandinista-*led forces, social work entered a period of crisis in Nicaragua. The prevalent view of social work within the revolutionary alliance at that moment was that its essential function had been to mediate between the social classes, which contributed to the perpetuation of the old regime. In this view, the revolution and the subsequent emergence of a just society would render the profession unnecessary. Thus, in 1980 Nicaragua's only school of social work was closed to new admissions. The country's social work community quickly mobilized itself in response, holding a national meeting to deliberate collectively on what should be the content of social work education to prepare professionals to address the new reality. Following the meeting, the social work community was successful in persuading authorities of the need for social workers to implement the nation's new social policies.

After a move from the UNAN to the traditionally more conservative Universidad Centroamericana, and a

revision of its program, in 1984 the social work school was reopened. The new mission statement of the School declared that its graduates should be prepared to facilitate the democratic process of popular participation in the structural changes required to achieve a more just and egalitarian society. Basing a new definition of social work on service to the process of social transformation, the mission statement observed that intervention at the microsocial level must serve the interests of the popular sectors, involving "the sensitization and organization of these popular sectors [which] allows them to make themselves subjects of their own transformation" (ETS, 1984, p. 2; all translations are by the author). The overriding mission of social workers, then, is to enhance "the organized participation of the people in the development of the society. . . as the practice of popular democracy" (ETS, 1984). The methodological keys to this mission are to be found in the methods of popular education, or "education for critical consciousness" (Wilson, 1993a, p. 309).

ORIGINS OF THE COLLABORATIVE SOCIAL DEVELOPMENT PROJECT

In 1986, the author made a personal visit to Nicaragua, during which I was able to meet a number of the faculty members of the Escuela de Trabajo Social (ETS) at the Universidad Centroamericana (UCA). I had joined Prof. Mona Acker of the University of Regina, in Canada, on a visit hosted by Lic. Xanthis Suárez García, then president of the Asociación Nicaragüense de Trabajadores Sociales (the Nicaraguan Association of Social Workers). A University of Regina delegation had made a trip to Nicaragua the previous year as a return visit following their 1984 hosting of Ms. Suárez's trip to Canada (at the time of the International Association of Schools of Social Work–International Federation of Social Workers meetings in Montréal). In subsequent correspondence, these colleagues in Managua identified some development needs and priorities of the Nicaraguan School: improvement of the qualifications and the capacities of the teaching faculty and the development of a Social Action Documentation Center. At the outset of this project, the ETS had no faculty members with postgraduate degrees. Further, a number of members of the teaching faculty, having been recruited immediately upon graduation, lacked practice experience. A small building had been donated by a Dutch group for a documentation center, but it contained little in the way of materials beyond some outdated English-language texts.

Together we began to explore ways in which Canadian resources might be mobilized to assist the Nicaraguan school in its efforts to educate social workers in ways appropriate to the Nicaraguan reality. With the aid of a small developmental grant from the Canadian International Development Agency (CIDA), University of Calgary Librarian, Sharon Neary, and I made a planning visit to Nicaragua in 1987. At that time, a proposal was jointly developed by Nicaraguan and Canadian participants for funding for a project to support the realization of these goals. In 1988, funding was approved by CIDA for a 5-year project. Late that year, Nicaraguan and Canadian counterparts began a joint process to determine, priorize, and implement means of meeting the project's goals.

PROJECT GOALS AND OBJECTIVES

Broadly speaking, this collaborative project was designed to enhance Nicaragua's ability to effectively plan, implement, and evaluate social policies and community-based programs through the application of its preferred model of popular participation. The specific goal was to assist in the development of the human resources necessary to support these functions by strengthening the resources and capabilities of the country's only school of social work. Thus, the focus of the project's activities would be on upgrading the teaching faculty's capacities and improving the programs and the infrastructure needed to support research and teaching at the ETS.

This project emphasized the objectives of improving the levels of knowledge and skill of the teaching faculty and enhancing UCA's capability to produce social practitioners/researchers competent in popular education/participatory research approaches to practice. This enhancement included the aim of developing the school's Social Action Documentation Center: building its collection of learning resources; improving its technical services for more effective organization, documentation, and access to these resources; and providing skill development to enable documentation-center staff and ETS teaching faculty, respectively, to provide technical services and to access these resources. In keeping with the school's philosophy, the Social Action Documentation Center was to be designed to be welcoming and accessible as a resource to grassroots community groups and nongovernmental organizations (NGOs), as well as students and faculty of the university.

PROJECT STRUCTURE

The planning and development of the project were carried out through a participatory process reflecting a shared philosophy of *acompañamiento*, (or accompanying the process) among the partners (Prado Hernández & Wilson, 1988, 1989, 1990, 1996). This philosophy has been described as an approach to the development relationship which embodies "a process of sharing and mutual support. . . a form of development cooperation that goes beyond the financial relationship and is based on mutual knowledge, a common commitment, and solidarity" (Clinton, 1991, p. 63).

Strategies for achieving the project's goals and objectives were developed, and amended as needed, jointly by the partners. The project's administrative structure made the director of the ETS, Lic. Iris Prado Hernández and later Lic. Giomar Talavera, the Project Director. I served as the Canadian Coordinator and reported to this Project Director (through me, the Canadian information systems and short-term subject specialists also reported to the Project Director). Two advisory committees were established, one based in Canada and one in Nicaragua. The application of the *acompañamiento* approach was to be facilitated by the wide participation of all members of the ETS in each of the project phases and by the decision to base the Canadian Coordinator and the information systems specialist (Sharon Neary for 2 years, followed by Maryon McClary of the University of Alberta Libraries) onsite in Nicaragua during the first part of the project (1988-1990), gradually reducing this time in the field over the final 2 years (1991-1993). During the latter half of this time, the project was also to benefit from the extended onsite presence of two University of Calgary graduate students who were to participate and carry out thesis research in association with the project.

PROJECT ACTIVITIES AND ACHIEVEMENTS

Contextual Issues

As a result of an ongoing process of reflection and evaluation carried out by Nicaraguan and Canadian members of the team, it was possible to make frequent modifications to project plans and activities in order to address emergent conditions in the university and in the country. Therefore, the achievements of the project included not only developments in initially targeted areas, but also in relation to other needs identified later (see Wilson 1988-1993).

Political and economic conditions in Nicaragua impacted the processes and outcomes of this project in a variety of ways. During the first 2 years of the life of the project, these concerns were largely of an economic nature. Exceptionally low salary levels for university professors, for instance, had led to such instability in the makeup of the Nicaraguan team that it was decided to defer plans for scholarships for graduate study abroad until the project team could be reasonably assured of having recipients sufficiently committed to the program to be likely to return to their positions on completion of their studies. Accordingly, funds designated for graduate scholarships were initially redeployed to workshops and short courses for faculty, students, and community members. Low-intensity warfare, beginning in 1981, between the *sandinista* government and the U.S.-backed *contras* also had an impact on the work of the project. Beyond the obvious impact on the economy of committing half of the national budget to defense, the fact of war inhibited the project's ability to work in regions of the country affected by military activity.

In 1990, midway through the project, a national election resulted in the installation of a government less supportive of the development approach upon which this project was founded, which initially threw the Nicaraguan team into crisis. This situation produced a reevaluation of the goals and objectives of the project in the face of the new sociopolitical reality and a reaffirmation of commitment to the original goals of the project. The effects of the new government policies were mitigated somewhat by the comparative stability of the university environment, which is a result of the relative autonomy of universities in Nicaragua. The project was nonetheless frequently affected in one form or another by the uncertainty and political and economic disorder of the period. For instance, massive strikes against policies of the new government, involving the universities as well as other social sectors, meant prolonged periods of closure of the program and a slowing of progress toward project objectives.

Academic Upgrading

Academic upgrading was carried out through the provision of scholarships for graduate study for ETS faculty, as well as through short courses, workshops, and apprenticeship placements. Early concerns about the stability of the Nicaraguan team's composition led to a temporary redeployment of some of the funds originally designated for postgraduate-study scholarships. In view of the relative lack of concrete experience of some

faculty members with the School's preferred methodologies of popular education and participatory research, a scheme was devised in which inexperienced faculty members fulfilled 2-month supervised placements in established projects that employed these methods. Four placements of this nature were successfully completed, with projects in Peru and Mexico. In addition, a variety of workshops and short courses were made available to faculty members, some mounted inside Nicaragua by this project and open to the wider community as well as other programs in Brazil, Peru, Mexico, Argentina, Canada, the United States, and Austria. Sixteen workshop experiences were provided to faculty members in this way.

ETS faculty members made the mutual commitment to temporarily assume the duties of those who were absent to participate in these project experiences. Following their participation in these programs, faculty members reproduced their experiences in order to multiply the benefits for other faculty members, students, and community members. As previously noted, in 1988 none of the ETS faculty members had any academic degree beyond the undergraduate level (the *licenciatura*). Over the life of this project, three faculty members were funded to pursue master's degrees (one in Costa Rica and two in Mexico). Two other faculty members later enrolled in a graduate program in Honduras with assistance from the Peru-based Centro Latinoamericano de Trabajo Social (Latin American Center for Social Work [CELATS]).

Curriculum Development

Curriculum development was addressed through invited consultations and critiques on the social work program, intensive workshops designed to review and to reconcile teaching content and methodology with the school's objectives and mission statement, and workshops designed to address areas in which the Nicaraguan team identified the need for an improved knowledge base.

Following a participatory process in which criteria and priorities were established regarding characteristics and areas of expertise required of short-term consultants and specialists, this aspect of the project was carried out with the assistance of specialists from English and French Canada, Mexico, Peru, and Chile. Based on the minimum criteria of fluency in Spanish and an understanding of the popular education and participatory action research emphasis of the school, these foreign consultants were selected for their expertise in the areas of gender relations, participatory research, community development, popular education methodology, distance education, social work curriculum design, and community practice methods.

Results of these inputs were a comprehensive review of the curriculum and the development of a program more clearly directed to the preparation of professionals to work with the popular sectors in social development. Specific attention was given to the integration of theory and practice in the curriculum, the bringing of training in research methods into closer congruence with practice needs of the social worker, issues of gender in the curriculum, concretizing of educational goals to facilitate defining and teaching of specific skills, and the application of popular education and participatory action research methods to each of these issues.

The Social Action Documentation Center

Some 6,000 Spanish-language resources (books, audiovisual items, periodicals, and documents) were acquired for the Social Action Documentation Center, which became widely recognized as exceptional in its depth, currency, and comprehensiveness in the areas of Latin American social work and social policy and in its broad scope in related areas of study. The Center came to be heavily used by students and faculty and was regularly visited by members of the community, graduates of the program, NGOs, and other researchers. It was also the only open stacks collection on the UCA campus, and it had been fully processed for effective access by subject using a combination of CELATS and United Nations Educational, Scientific, and Cultural Organization classification systems. However, following the conclusion of the CIDA-funded portion of the project activities the Center, intended to be open to community and popular organizations as well as students and faculty, was moved by the university's administration to the university general library (Laforce 1998).

Social Information and Research Support System

In the course of this project, a need was identified for research resources to support efforts to address social problems, from the local community level to the national social policy planning level. Because of the lack of resources for planning and monitoring in the area of social development, the notion was conceived that a cooperative social information and research support system be developed. With the assistance of a grant from the Canadian International Development

Research Center (IDRC), project participants undertook a feasibility study for the development of such a system. The participatory process of this study was joined and studied for purposes of thesis research by a University of Calgary graduate student in Communication Studies. This spin-off project developed a life of its own, and attracted the interest of funders promoting regional-level planning. The project partners thus developed an ambitious proposal for a regional (Central American) program: the development of a Central American Center for Social Development (the Coordinadora Regional para el Desarrollo Social). Following wide consultation in both Canada and Central America, this program became the basis for a variety of project initiatives involving several Canadian universities and NGOs.

Canadian Student Benefits

In addition to indirect learning from the experience of the Canadian professors who participated in this work, Canadian students benefited from this project in a variety of ways. Two students from McMaster University in Hamilton, Canada, carried out senior-year practicums in Nicaragua with the supervisory assistance of this project. In 1988 and 1990, students in the University of Calgary's Latin American Studies summer field schools met with project participants and visited project activities. Although insurance difficulties aborted a field placement for four University of Calgary under-graduate students, a social work practicum assignment to this project was successfully completed by a University of Calgary graduate student.

The presence of this graduate student onsite in Nicaragua for a 4-month period helped facilitate a participatory project evaluation process that involved both Nicaraguan and Canadian participants, while also allowing the student to conduct thesis research. Similarly, the previously mentioned Communication Studies graduate student was able, through a participatory process in the development of a proposal for the Central American Center for Social Development, to examine the notion of dialogue in the relationship between participatory action research and development communications.

Public Education

Participants created or availed themselves of a variety of opportunities to increase public awareness of the issues addressed in this project. In Canada, these opportunities have included public speaking engagements, interviews for print and electronic media, and papers presented at academic and professional meetings. Over the course of the project, Nicaraguan and Canadian participants made presentations on this project at conferences in Austria, Mexico, Peru, Australia, the United States, Canada, Argentina, and Costa Rica. Among these presentations was a half-day workshop hosted by Canadian and Central American participants during a Canadian Learned Societies Conference in Ottawa in June 1991. This session included sharing and critical reflection on this experience of collaboration by Southern and Northern participants, and a discussion of the journey from this project to the development of a proposed Canada-Central America Partnership for Social Development between a newly formed Canadian Consortium for International Social Development and the Central American Center for Social Development. The session was videotaped and funds were obtained to assist in editing and producing the video (Wilson, 1994).

PROJECT EVALUATION

Evaluation and reflection on this project's process and outcomes were carried out on an ongoing basis, with periodic workshops that involved Nicaraguan and Canadian participants assessing project developments and planning modifications as required. The project was evaluated in a number of ways: by the participants' structured and ongoing reflection, by graduate student participants conducting thesis or practicum work, and twice by external evaluators contracted by the funder. One of the implications of the project's participatory design was that goals, objectives, and strategies would be in an ongoing process of review and reexamination by the partners. Therefore, while the broad goals and objectives of the project remained unchanged, with cooperation of the funder the design of individual components was modified through this process, in response to changing circumstances.

In general terms, the outcomes, while somewhat different from the initial expectations, were judged by both partners as more than satisfactory in relation to the original objectives of the project in each of the areas of academic upgrading, curriculum improvement, and development of the Social Action Documentation Center. The final CIDA-commissioned project evaluation concluded that the project had significant achievements:

The Social Development project attained notable results by strengthening the knowledge, skills and capabilities of the only Nicaraguan School of Social Work, and graduates (30 per year) still find employment in their area of expertise. . . . At the community level, the project supported the training and strengthening of various organizations involved in community development.

. . . many of the graduates now occupy strategic posts in the Government or in international or local NGOs. Their presence in decision-making positions allows them to use their knowledge in planning, implementing and evaluating social programs (Laforce, 1998, pp. ii-iii).

Project Strengths

The project management structures were coherent with a partnership approach, and management structures encouraged the development of shared ownership and decision-making, trust and mutual gain. . . .

The participatory approach and "horizontal management" that characterized this partnership project is considered one of the most positive parts of the learning process by local [Nicaraguan] partners. The Nicaraguan representatives learned a lot from what they call the "horizontal management" approach favoured during project implementation. It was the very first time they participated in a cooperation project that involved them in all stages of the project. The Nicaraguan Project Director even participated in various international seminars to present the management approach as a model to be developed for all institutional cooperation projects. (Laforce 1998, p. 23)

An important strength of this project is in the process through which it was developed. It was based upon an initiative and a set of development priorities of the Nicaraguan school, with the Canadian counterpart then determining how they might respond to these needs while leaving control of the development process in the hands of the Nicaraguan partner. This arrangement was made possible by the shared commitment of both the Canadian and Nicaraguan participants to *acompañamiento* as a process through which to carry this out.

This process of *acompañamiento* was greatly facilitated by the extended Canadian presence onsite during the project (Laforce, 1998). This allowed not only for joint participation in the ongoing process of evolution of goals and strategies for the project, but also for the sharing of the difficulties, limitations, and joys of daily life in a society in transformation. In part, this involved an understanding that a two-way learning process would be involved, an expectation which was clearly realized. This *acompañamiento* was identified in the final evaluation by the Nicaraguan participants as a significant strength of the project.

The nature of the external environment, in relation to both the university and the national context, was a factor of strength at the commencement of the project. The priorities of the government in power at that time, as well as those of the UCA, were both congruent with and supportive of the project's goals and approach. Although this environment later became less favorable, the initial supportive context had contributed to the development of sufficient commitment and momentum that these did not falter in the face of the changes.

Unanticipated Benefits

The flexibility incorporated into the project design and the funder's willingness to respond to justifiable requests for modifications combined to permit unanticipated beneficial results in several ways. Sometimes these benefits were purely serendipitous. When inflation and currency reforms in 1988 created a situation in which photocopies were to cost $3.00 U.S. per page, a photocopier was purchased for the project. Toward the end of the initial year of the project, faculty members were asked which of the project inputs had had the greatest impact on their work; thus far, the unanimous response was that it had been the purchase of the photocopier.

From the perspective of the Nicaraguan participants, a noteworthy benefit of the project was in the improvement of social work's profile as a professional program within the UCA. This was seen as being in part due to the increased legitimacy lent to the ETS by the presence of an international project and in part due to an increased assertiveness and sense of empowerment of the Nicaraguan faculty members as a function of the

external reinforcement of the group's philosophy and collective style of operating.

The redeployment of resources originally designated for scholarships during the first part of the project to workshops, short courses, and supervised apprenticeships abroad produced a number of unanticipated benefits. First, this considerably enlarged the number of persons able to directly benefit from training opportunities. Second, the contacts and interactions with persons and programs of other countries—apart from the formal programs—was extremely enriching for the participants; ideas picked up during these experiences have found their way into the work of the Nicaraguan partners in a wide variety of ways. Donations of educational materials have also resulted from these contacts, as have valuable long-term relationship networks.

Visits to Canada by Nicaraguan participants produced connections with organizations and individuals here which have led to further collaboration. During the final phase of the project, for example, the visit to Calgary by the current and former directors of the Nicaraguan program resulted in a formal agreement to develop a linkage between the independent Arusha Learner Center and the UCA Social Action Documentation Center. Linkages between Canadian and Nicaraguan social work associations, and similarly between student social work groups, were also pursued.

The participation of Canadian students, not part of the original project design, was evaluated positively by both the Nicaraguan participants and the Canadian students. The contribution of these Canadian students was particularly noteworthy in relation to project development, project evaluation, and the facilitation of linkages between Nicaraguan and Canadian groups. Out of needs identified in the course of this project, an initiative emerged for a Canada-Central America Partnership for Social Development, with founding members largely consisting of persons involved in this project.

The acquisition of additional resources for this project and for the ETS was facilitated by Canadian team members and included a $3,000 grant from the Edmonton-based Clifford E. Lee Foundation for the purchase of educational materials; International Council on Social Welfare, Canada, support (with CIDA assistance) for three Nicaraguan participants to visit Canada to study the potential for development of a social information network; a grant of $2,500 from the Association for Canadian Studies to explore the possibility of interuniversity collaboration between the

Université du Québec à Montréal and the University of Calgary for the continuation and expansion of this work; the donation of a vehicle by the Ontario-based organization Trucks for Nicaragua; support through the Calgary-based Arusha Learner Center for infrastructure sustainability for the UCA Social Action Documentation Center; and liaison with a group from the University of Washington through which various additional donations were received.

Gender Issues

A file review of Canadian Partnership Branch on Basic Human Needs Programming considered that the Social Development Project was one of the few capacity building projects that "ensured the full participation of women as beneficiaries and made a clear commitment to gender equity and redressing historical inequalities by ensuring that women predominated in training and in the provision of scholarships." (Laforce, 1998, p. 19)

This project was one in which both participants and beneficiaries were overwhelmingly female. Ninety percent of the teaching staff of the Nicaraguan program were female, and the Canadian team was predominantly female as well. Those who benefited from the scholarships, workshops, and technical training were all female (Centeno, Espinoza, Whitmore, & Wilson, 1991). The improvement of the ETS educators' knowledge of alternative paradigms for understanding issues of gender and development and the incorporation of these concepts into the curriculum are also considered significant contributions of this project (Wilson & Whitmore 1994, 1995).

Sustainability

At the end of the funded project, all of the scholarship recipients had returned to Nicaragua and their positions at the UCA. The benefits of short courses, workshops, apprenticeship placements, and consultations with short-term specialists provided through this project continue to be felt in the curriculum and consequently in the practice of the graduating students:

One of the most positive aspects of this project is its collaborative and participative approach, which was based on identification of needs by the local partner and followed by shared management of the project at all stages. This is

one of the reasons why the Nicaraguan partners are still very committed to the project and manage to keep the benefits of the project alive, within financial and institutional limits. The extended Canadian presence in the field, strong commitment, sensitivity to the local context and the high respect for local partners on the part of the Canadian resource persons are important elements in the success of this project. (Laforce, 1998, pp. 29-30)

While formal project activities terminated at the end of 1993, contact has been maintained between the principal participants, who continue to consult with each other and to present their collaborative work at conferences and workshops. There have also been subsequent Canadian student field placements in Nicaragua.

Students, faculty, and community members had become accustomed to accessing the resources of the UCA Social Action Documentation Center to enhance the quality of their teaching, research, and community work. Concerns regarding the ability to keep the collection up-to-date were addressed in several ways. Contacts made by the center's staff ensure that donations to the collection would continue and that the staff would be aware of other collections from which materials might be borrowed or to which users might be referred. Fundraising ideas (selling duplicated materials, small charges for video presentations, proposals to foreign funding sources) had been developed as ways of maintaining subscriptions and purchasing new materials. The UCA had indicated that it recognized the center's need for additional space and staff. Attention had been given to the development and sustainability of the outreach and social action functions of the Center through the assignment of staff to these functions, and through the development of a twinning relationship with the Arusha Learner Center in Calgary. However, following the completion of the initial CIDA-funded project and the departure of the Canadian participants, the UCA administration moved to centralize all university library resources. Thus,

the Documentation Center does not operate as initially planned and implemented, the books and other written and audio-visual documentation were transferred to the central library, and the Documentation Center does not play the expected role of a Learner Center accessible to and used by the community and grassroots organizations. (Laforce, 1998, p. iv)

Project Limitations

Limitations on what could be achieved by this project were presented by ETS's external environment, including both the university context and wider social and economic forces. Progress toward the implementation of several project components was delayed by political and economic disorder in the country at several points during the project, by the difficulties of daily life in Nicaragua, and by the struggles of the Social Work program to maintain its position in the university in the face of internal restructuring.

A flaw in the design of this project was in the lack of resources allocated for research and particularly for evaluation of the project itself. That research was not included as an activity of the project at its inception, with resources assigned to this function, reflected the funder's reluctance at the time to finance research activities. Later attempts to remedy this situation unfortunately coincided with budget cuts at both CIDA and IDRC. However, with respect to evaluation of the project itself, we were able to avail ourselves of the opportunity to make the project the subject of graduate student thesis research.

With regard to development of the Social Action Documentation Center, a significant limitation was the state of library education in Nicaragua, which had not adequately prepared the center's staff to manage, acquire, organize, and process materials in an automated environment and with a sizeable budget for educational materials. Therefore, more time than had been anticipated was spent training and consulting on basic library procedures. Low salaries, status, and morale in the Nicaraguan library community limited the onsite collegial support and slowed the process of exploring new methods and service options. Development of the center was further limited by a lack of adequate space for materials and users and by low levels of staffing.

The effective use of short-term Canadian participants was limited by the lag time between their selection and recruitment and their actual appearance onsite in Nicaragua, which was largely imposed by the exigencies of planning for the Canadian academic year. In some cases this delay meant that those involved in establishing priorities and selecting appropriate consultants were no longer part of the project team by the time their initial visits were realized. A further limitation on occasion was presented by the coinciding of local political disorder with these scheduled visits.

Faculty members' obtaining of graduate degrees with the assistance of this project, in the face of low university salaries, also created a situation of risk that these now more highly qualified *docentes* might ultimately leave their university positions to accept others offering better financial rewards.

Overall, as it was noted in a CIDA-commissioned performance review of this project: ". . . the opportunities to apply the popular participation model put forth in the improved curriculum are limited by the social orientation of the two governments elected since 1990" (Laforce, 1998, p. ii).

LESSONS LEARNED

Many lessons were learned by the participants in the course of this project, particularly with respect to project management and process, and also related to aspects of North–South relationships.

Project Management and Process

- Horizontal/participatory management

"One of the major lessons learned by the participants was that the horizontal management approach for joint management of partnership projects could work and that the approach was replicable" (Laforce, 1998, p.24). "The participatory approach and 'horizontal management' that characterized this partnership project is considered by local partners as one of the most positive elements of the learning process" (Laforce, 1998, p. iii).

The structure of this project, with control of the design and process of the inputs lying with the Southern partner and *acompañamiento* and shared by the Canadian partner, was positively evaluated by both partners. Our experience would suggest that such a participatory process, while more time-consuming in the short run, tends to produce commitment, investment, and "ownership" in the project which pays off over the longer term. We believe, however, that it would be less likely to be effective if not accompanied by a shared understanding and commitment by both partners to this way of operating (Whitmore & Wilson, 1995, 1997). Both the Nicaraguan and Canadian participants in this project were of the view that the accompaniment model functions best with the extended on-the-ground presence of the foreign partner.

- Process goals

It is recommended for the planning and evaluation of such projects that process/empowerment outcomes be identified along with more "concrete" project objectives (Wilson, 1994). "With respect to the overall performance of the project. . . . The participating partners consider that one of the most notable results of this project was related to the collaborative relationship between the partners, team-building supported by a high level of participation, increased self-confidence and feelings of empowerment and independence on the part of the Nicaraguan partner" (Laforce, 1998, pp. 29-30).

- Selection of project personnel

Our experience reinforces some of the findings of Kealey (1990) regarding the importance of appropriate personal characteristics in overseas development workers: empathy, interest in the local culture, flexibility, tolerance, initiative, open-mindedness, and sociability. Given the generally higher rating of women on these indicators, a strengthened presence of women should be expected, including at the level of project/program management.

- Flexibility

Our experience of the frequent need to modify the program design in response to emergent conditions points to the importance of flexibility on the part of both partners, as well as the funding agency. The perception of both Nicaraguan and Canadian participants was that CIDA was extremely open to justifiable requests for modifications. It is important to recognize that one is not necessarily "stuck with" aspects of program design which turn out to be ill-conceived or which become, over time, less appropriate.

South–North Relationships

- South–North technology transfer

It is important to understand that there is a two-way learning process involved in this kind of an experience. A consequence of the economic globalization process has been the globalization of poverty, and

> the creation of a "global South" which transcends traditional North–South borders. . . . The creation of a distinguishable global north and south as distinct from the traditional north and south should give impetus to alliance building amongst like-minded groups. (Malhotra, 1997, p. 1)

Given the current conjuncture, in which there is an increasing convergence of circumstances between underclasses in the North and in the South, in many ways those of us in the North have much more to learn than to teach in relation to social work practice in Southern countries.

- South–South exchanges

The fruitfulness of the opportunities for contact between Nicaraguan participants and other Latin American colleagues was an extremely striking aspect of our experience. The richness of the learning experiences obtaining for project participants though opportunities to travel abroad through this project suggests a need to reframe the Northern role in such exchanges. These kinds of opportunities should be maximized in the planning of projects of this kind, through the use of "Southern" resource persons whenever possible, and through the facilitation of overseas participants' attendance at conferences, workshops, and formal education institutions in the "South." Rather than thinking about isolated linkages between Northern and Southern partners, it might be more appropriate for the relatively resource-rich Northerners to play a facilitating and supportive role in not just North–South, but also South–North collaboration.

- Northern benefits

Northern benefits and participation, and the effectiveness of this kind of a South–North partnership, can be enhanced by systematically providing participation opportunities for Northern students in the planning stages (bearing in mind the selection criteria mentioned above) and by developing consortium arrangements involving other universities and NGOs to enhance the resources, expertise, and capabilities of the Northern end of the partnership.

- Issues of dependency

During the inbound flight on my first trip to Nicaragua, I encountered an acquaintance from Mexico who told me a story about his recent visit to Nicaragua. At that time, begging was virtually nonexistent in Nicaragua, and he witnessed his Nicaraguan companion sternly lecture a child beggar on the inappropriateness and lack of necessity for this activity in a society in which people found collective solutions to their issues of need. The child was then directed to a center where his needs could be addressed. Later my acquaintance was conducted on a tour of a local Nicaraguan social project, following which he was presented with a list of things needed by the project. He pointed out to me the inconsistency of his companion's castigation of the child's begging with this more sophisticated version of essentially the same activity.

When I assumed my role with this project, I was determined that my Nicaraguan colleagues would not be subjected to this indignity. Therefore, when needs were identified for additional resources to carry out some activity, I would quietly go about the "dirty work" of identifying potential funding sources and writing the required grant proposals, only letting our Nicaraguan partners know about this when there had been success in acquiring these resources. This practice was based on the reasoning that once the war had ended and it was once again possible to redirect state resources to social programs, this kind of "begging" would no longer be necessary.

Both partners later identified this as having been a mistake. In fact, as the history of Nicaragua evolved, the skills of writing grant proposals were to become more important than we could have ever anticipated for the development and sustainability of social projects. Although the war ended with the change in government, this change also meant drastic cuts to social programs, reinforced by externally imposed neoliberal policies that shifted expenditures from the social sector to the "productive" sector. Thus, some important capacity-building was now needed in the skills for writing successful project proposals. The Nicaraguan school later moved to address this issue, even introducing it as part of curriculum content.

The issue of language clearly involves questions of power and control. Translations almost inevitably miss the nuances of culture. More than mere words that can be translated, language reflects culture, history, a way of thinking, a worldview, how one expresses feelings and ideas, and how people relate to one another. Had our colleagues been required to interact with us in our language, it would have meant working with ideas formulated and expressed within the conceptual framework of a foreign language. This can be, at best, a subtle means of controlling the process and, at worst, another form of cultural imperialism. In this context, we were fortunate to be able to work in Spanish and also to recruit resource personnel capable of functioning in that language. We further suspect that our having to communicate exclusively in our imperfect Spanish had some leveling effect, particularly in redressing the imbalance created by our greater access to material resources. It is recognized that first-language collaboration may not always be possible, but careful attention should be given to the distortions created by the inability to work in this way.

SUMMARY AND CONCLUSIONS

This 5-year collaborative project was designed to enhance Nicaragua's ability to effectively plan, implement, and evaluate social policies and community-based programs through the application of its preferred model of popular participation. It attempted to assist in the development of the human resources needed to support these functions through strengthening the resources and capabilities of the country's only school of social work. The focus of the project was on upgrading the capabilities of the teaching faculty and improving the programs and infrastructure needed to support research and teaching at the Escuela de Trabajo Social at the Universidad Centroamericana in Managua.

The *sandinista* experiment in participatory democracy (1979-1990), which provided the context for the development of this project, was undoubtedly flawed and, largely for reasons of international pressure, was perhaps doomed to be aborted. Nevertheless, it did provide, for a brief moment in history, a supportive environment for the exploration of democratic, participatory approaches to development (Wilson & Whitmore, 2000).

The planning and development of this project was carried out through a participatory process reflecting a shared philosophy of "accompaniment" among the partners. The application of this approach was supported by a design allowing the Canadian project coordinator and information systems specialist to maintain an onsite presence during the first half of the project's life, with a progressive reduction of this presence as the project developed. We found the "accompaniment" approach to our relationship with our Nicaraguan partners to be a satisfying one, precisely because of its inherent clarity about who owns and controls the process: our partners do. It is *we* (the outsiders) who accompany *their* process: "This 'accompaniment' was identified by the Nicaraguan participants as a significant strength of the project" (Wilson, 1993b, p. 10).

Implicit in *acompañamiento* are the concepts of empowerment and participation. At the 1989 Conference of the International Association for Participatory Research in Managua, Nicaragua, neither prominent Colombian writer and activist Orlando Fals Borda nor his interpreter was able to produce a Spanish translation for the English term *empowerment*. The translation eventually agreed upon by those present was *poder popular* (people's power). The explanation of this difficulty is likely in that in the language and culture of English-speaking North America, empowerment tends to be assumed to be something vested in the individual; in Latin America, this is more likely to be seen as vested in a collectivity (a family, community, or people). With respect to *participation*, Fals Borda notes

> to participate means to break up voluntarily and through experience the asymmetrical relationship of submission and dependence (implicit in the subject/object binomial). This is the essence of participation. (Fals Borda & Rahman, 1991, p. 5)

These themes capture important elements of what is meant by *acompañamiento*.

Is it possible, then, for First World professionals and educators to usefully contribute to the development and support of indigenous models of social work in the Third World, or will their involvement inevitably constitute "professional imperialism"? Reflections on the experience described here produce a qualified "yes" as a response to this question, based on the application of the following set of principles for the participation of outside collaborators (see also Wilson & Whitmore, 1995):

- Collaboration must be nonintrusive. We must understand and respect that it is our partners' process and that decisions and the decision-making process will be different from what ours might be. The host must retain ownership both of what occurs and of the process.
- Mutual trust and genuine respect are basic necessities for successful collaboration. These involve a fundamentally accepting attitude toward people and their ability to understand and address their own realities, however different this may be from one's own. Mutual trust and respect also require patience, and will not be achieved instantaneously. It is understandably common for outsiders to be initially mistrusted; trust and respect may take months or years to be earned.
- There needs to be a common analysis of what "the problem" is. This will involve a generally shared belief system or ideology, and a shared understanding of the role of global structural issues in international relationships and of their effects on local organizations, communities, and individuals.
- Northerners must understand that we also have a stake in what happens in other parts of the globe.

This is the meaning of solidarity: an understanding of our common destinies, our common purposes, and our common humanity. It is people coming together and sharing; people taking care of each other; people sharing a journey.

- "Accompaniment" implies mutuality and equality in the relationship. It does not mean giving up our own identity, for we have rights, too. We need to declare our own agendas and interests and to be clear about what we want to get out of the collaboration. All parties need to give and to receive; otherwise the relationship lacks the required mutuality.
- There must be an explicit focus on process in international development collaboration. This requires the involvement of both intellect and emotion. It means understanding who we are as people and developing more than a detached working relationship. It means understanding another's culture, the social construction of time, of how people relate and the roles of informal interaction, and of rituals for preparing and eating food. Accompanying the process means just that: we cannot accompany a product.
- Where possible, the process should occur in the host country's own language or languages. Language is not simply a technical matter; it is a form of cultural expression that embodies a way of thinking and of understanding the world. It is also a matter of power.

In these ways, the application of the principles for *acompañamiento* as a process may help make our Southern partners genuine agents of their own change processes, rather than passive recipients of development assistance.

REFERENCES

Centeno, R., Espinoza, A. I., Whitmore, E., & Wilson, M. (1991). *Women at the gender barricade: Obstacles and rewards in North-South collaboration.* Presented at the 5th International Forum of the Association for Women in Development, Washington, DC.

Clinton, R. L. (1991). Grassroots development where no grass grows: Small-scale development efforts on the Peruvian coast. *Studies in Comparative International Development, 26*(2), 59-75.

Escuela de Trabajo Social. (1984). *Modelo del profesional de trabajo social.* Managua, Nicaragua:

Facultad de Humanidades, Universidad Centroamericana.

Escuela de Trabajo Social. (1985). Práctica historica del trabajo social en Nicaragua. *Revista de Trabajo Social*, 1, pp. 3-6.

Fals Borda, O., & Rahman, M. A. (1991). *Action and knowledge: Breaking the monopoly with participatory action-research*. Croton-on-Hudson, NY: Apex Press.

Freire, P. (2000). *Pedagogy of the oppressed*. New York: Continuum.

Hansen, S. (1967). *Five years of the Alliance for Progress*. Washington, DC: Inter-American Affairs Press.

Kealey, D. J. (1990). *Cross-cultural effectiveness: A study of Canadian technical advisors overseas*. Ottawa, Canada: Canadian International Development Agency.

Laforce, J. (1998). *Basic human needs performance review: Nicaragua Social Development Project evaluation report*. Ottawa, Canada: Canadian International Development Agency.

Malhotra, K. (1997). *An essay for Oxfam International*. Unpublished manuscript.

Prado Hernández, I., & Wilson, M. (1988, July). *Revolutionary social work: Professional education in Nicaragua*. 24th International Congress of Schools of Social Work, Vienna, Austria.

Prado Hernández, I., & Wilson, M. (1989, June). *Combatiendo el imperialismo profesional: un proyecto nicaragüense-canadiense de colaboración*. Presented at the 1989 Regional Conference of the Inter-University Consortium for International Social Development, Pátzcuarco, Mexico.

Prado Hernández, I., & Wilson, M. (1990, August). *International social development: lessons from Nicaragua*. Presented at the 25th International Congress of Schools of Social Work, Lima, Peru.

Prado Hernández, I., & Wilson, M. G. (1996, February). *International partnerships in project management: Lessons from Nicaragua*. Presented at the International Participatory Development Symposium, University of Calgary, Canada.

Téfel, R. A., Lopez, H. M., & Castillo, J. F. (1985). Social welfare. In T. Walker (Ed.), *Nicaragua: The first five years*. New York: Praeger.

Walker, T. (Ed.). (1985). *Nicaragua: The first five years*. New York: Praeger.

Whitmore, E., & Wilson, M. (1997). Accompanying the process: Social work and international development practice. *International Social Work*, 40(1), 57-74.

Wilson, M. G. (1988-1993). *Universidad Centroamericana-University of Calgary Collaborative Social Development Project: Interim narrative reports* (No. 1-10). Reports to the Canadian International Development Agency, Ottawa, Canada.

Wilson, M. G. (1993a). What difference could a revolution make? Group work in the new Nicaragua. In J. A. Garland (Ed.), *Group work reaching out: People, places, and power*. New York: Haworth Press, 301-314.

Wilson, M. G. (1993b). *Universidad Centroamericana-University of Calgary Collaborative Social Development Project: Final narrative report*. Report to the Canadian International Development Agency, Ottawa, Canada.

Wilson, M. G. (Executive producer). (1994). *Combating professional imperialism: Issues in international development partnership* [Video]. Calgary, Canada: University of Calgary.

Wilson, M. G. (1996). Strategies in international social development: Canada and the rise and fall of the Sandinistas. In B. Kirwin (Ed.), *Ideology, development and social welfare: Canadian perspectives* (3rd ed., pp. 165-187). Toronto, Canada: Canadian Scholars' Press.

Wilson, M. G., & Whitmore, E. (1994). Gender and international development praxis. *Social Development Issues*, 16(1), 55-66.

Wilson, M. G., & Whitmore, E. (1995). Accompanying the process: Principles for international development practice. *Canadian Journal of Development Studies*, 15(2), 61-77.

Wilson, M. G., & Whitmore, E. (2000). *Seeds of fire: Social development in an era of globalism*. Croton-on-Hudson, NY: Apex Press.

THIRTEEN

Russian–American Summer University: An Evolving Coalition

Wayne Evens, Marjorie J. Malkin, Mizanur R. Miah, Ivan Nikolov, Kathleen Welshimer, Sue Tebb, Patsy D. Tracy, and Martin B. Tracy

This chapter is a case illustration of an ongoing 9-year collaboration (1994-present) in Russia and the United States between two coalitions that are composed of academic faculty and staff, social service practitioners, government and nongovernmental agencies, and municipal government entities (a list of principal Russian and U.S. participants can be found at the end of this chapter). The main projects are the Russian-American Summer University and a women's leadership program. The initial collaboration was between Southern Illinois University at Carbondale and two cities in Russia: Togliatti and Samara. These cities are about 40 miles apart on the Volga River in the Samara Oblast, a province 600 miles southeast of Moscow. Togliatti has over 800,000 inhabitants and Samara's population is 1.3 million. Togliatti was built in 1954, after the construction of a hydroelectric dam on the Volga caused the village of Stavropol to be flooded. In the 1960s and 1970s, two additional manufacturing and residential areas that were separated by large forested areas were built. The largest industrial facility is the Volzhsky Automobile Plant, which manufactures the notorious Lada. The city of Samara was closed to foreign visitors for many years because it was the location of the training center for Russian Cosmonauts and Aeroflot pilots and a center for military production. The city was previously the site of an underground bunker prepared for Joseph Stalin during World War II, and it was the first place that a young Vladimir Lenin practiced law.

INSTIGATING FACTORS

The School of Social Work at Southern Illinois University at Carbondale (SIUC) was initially interested in establishing a relationship with academic institutions and social service agencies in Russia for the purposes of faculty and student exchange, possible practicum sites, and potential joint research projects. The first contacts were initiated by the school in 1993, with the Association of Russian Social Workers (ARSW). This effort was designed to establish linkages and to help Russian colleagues generate support for social work education in their country. The Russians were hoping to use these contacts with U.S. academic entities as leverage for institutional development and funding from the Russian government.

In 1994, the associate director of the SIUC School of Social Work was sent to participate in an international conference organized by the ARSW in Samara, Russia. At the ARSW conference, the associate director was approached by the founder and president of the Togliatti Social and Economic College (TSEC), who expressed an interest in finding a U.S. university to which she could send faculty and students for social work and English-language training. The subsequent visit of TSEC faculty to SIUC in the fall of 1995 provided the momentum necessary to firmly establish this collaboration.

GOALS OF THE COLLABORATION

The collaboration assumes that human problems have many similarities, even though culture may affect how these problems are expressed; therefore all program participants can and do learn from each other. Thus, the model for all exchanges has been a "meeting of peers" rather than a "teaching" model. The central goal of this project has always been to provide mutual benefits to all participants through interactions created by jointly planned and executed initiatives. The functional role of the U.S. partners has been primarily to consult with the Russian partners to determine their own needs, to plan their curriculum, and to coteach lectures, seminars, and workshops.

This partnership is based on the presumption that the best assistance the U.S. coalition can provide is a description of current prevention and treatment processes for social problems in the United States. Within this context, the underlying philosophy encompasses the following principles:

1. Training must reflect the fact that U.S. faculty and practitioners cannot fully understand Russian culture and cannot expect U.S. social service prevention and treatment approaches to work without significant modification.
2. Training for basic techniques of prevention and treatment should be culturally adapted by the Russian partners for local use.
3. Training should emphasize pragmatic techniques instead of theory.
4. Training methods should focus on experiential learning instead of lectures.
5. Training should be interdisciplinary and should involve a broad spectrum of academic institutions, social service agencies, and government programs.
6. Training should be based on the recognition that the Russian partners are equals.

Therefore, the Russian participants decide for themselves how to adapt, if at all, the training presented by the U.S. partners based on their own educational, cultural, social, and economic conditions and experiences.

COMMON INTERESTS AND EXCHANGES

Following the Russian faculty's visit in the fall of 1995, the TSEC president came to SIUC in the spring of 1996 to discuss shared interests in several areas relative to education and social services, in particular school-based social services. A working plan was developed for the following 2 years. This plan included the exchange of two faculty members each year, tailored instruction at the Center for English as a Second Language at SIUC, and assistance for the Russian partners in the development of social work curricula and training materials. A Memorandum of Understanding between SIUC and TSEC was signed by the institutions' presidents to formalize the partnership and to pave the way for future collaboration.

During the summer of 1996, TSEC students and faculty visited SIUC for a month of advanced language training, cultural exposure, and an introduction to U.S. human services. In the meantime, a joint grant from the Eurasia Foundation and U.S. Agency for International Development (USAID) Russia was developed in collaboration with the SIUC Masters of Public Administration program. The grant made it possible to provide six Russian professionals with an intensive month-long program in the United States during the 1997 spring semester that focused on curriculum development issues in public administration and social services.

Also, in the summer of 1996, representatives from SIUC visited Togliatti and Samara. This trip provided the SIUC representatives an opportunity to experience TSEC and to meet with government and agency administrators. The SIUC delegation also established contact with the rector of the Institute for Teacher Re-Training and Staff Development in Education (SIPKRO, from the Russian) in Samara, which provides continuing education programs in the Samara Oblast. The trip also allowed for a cursory assessment of the Russian situation, in terms of the level of social work education, the extent of social services, and the degree of formal and informal collaboration among service providers, social service agencies, educators, government officials, and TSEC. In addition, the visit was aimed at helping to solidify the administrative protocol between the various institutions and organizational entities and to clarify the goals of the partnership.

In 1997 the president of TSEC obtained additional funds from the joint Eurasia Foundation and USAID grant and provided resources for 10 additional Russian educators to visit SIUC to develop curriculum materials and train in public administration (legal and financial aspects), social work (unemployment and social problems), and data management. This training program was titled, Contemporary Problems of Professional Training of Specialists in Social Pedagogy and Social Work: Expertise, Solutions, Prospectives. Community practitioners and SIUC faculty from the School of Social Work, the Rehabilitation Institute, the Department of Political Science, and the Masters of Public Administration program conducted the training. The project also involved visits to rural and urban social service agencies and the Illinois state government.

EVOLVING PARTNERSHIPS

The collaboration quickly evolved beyond the relationship between SIUC and TSEC to include a number of other Russian academic institutions in the central Volga or Ural region, as well as the Togliatti city government, other government and nonprofit social service agencies, and a variety of professionals (educators, social pedagogues, psychologists, psychiatrists, and social workers). The development of such a broad-based partnership was made possible by a preexisting network of these entities, of which the TSEC president was an established leader. The subsequent workshops and seminars that were sponsored by this partnership soon led to a formal coalition of organizations involving SIPKRO and the government of Samara Oblast, as well as the municipal governments of Samara, Oktyabrsk, and Kynel Cherkaskyi. Later, academic faculty from Samara State University, Samara Professional College, and Tatishchev Volga University-Togliatti became involved.

Over time, the partnership was extended to include local nongovernmental organizations (NGOs), such as the Organization of Wheelchair Bound Invalids (Koliasochniki) in Togliatti and veterans organizations in Oktyabrsk and Togliatti, as well as school districts, religious organizations, and quasigovernmental organizations, such as the League for Defense of Motherhood and Childhood.

The U.S. Coalition

There was a similar evolution into a broad-based coalition among the U.S. partners. By 1997, the School of Social Work at SIUC had joined the SIUC College of Education and Human Services, which facilitated collaboration with other professional academic units. In particular, faculty at the Department of Health Education and Recreation (HER) were interested in the Russian project, and two such educators have become very active participants in the summer workshops in Russia with the support of the HER chair. Beginning in 2001, the Department of Educational Administration and Higher Education and the Rehabilitation Institute, both of which are in the SIUC College of Education and Human Services, became involved in helping develop programs and curricula to assist Russian colleagues in creating more democratic approaches to education.

The emphasis of the U.S. partners' training has been to expose the Russian participants to community programs and grassroots involvement in urban and rural areas through broad-based coalitions. Much of this training has focused on the functioning of groups of nongovernmental entities in the United States, such as school-based social services for needy children and families. The U.S. partnership now includes agencies and organizations in southern Illinois, western Kentucky, and St. Louis, as well as academic institutions (SIUC, St. Louis University, and Murray State University, in Murray Kentucky). The Regional Office of Education in southern Illinois and Southern Illinois Regional Social Services have also played a significant role in the project.

The U.S. coalition continues to expand. During the 2000 Russian—American Summer University (RASU), the chair of the Illinois state chapter of the National Association of Social Workers (NASW) participated in the training programs. Faculty from the University of North Dakota joined the project in the summer of 2001. An effort is also underway to involve a specialist in aging from the University of California at San Francisco and community-development specialists from Charles Sturt University, in New South Wales, Australia.

INSTITUTIONAL SUPPORT

The partnership has consistently received strong institutional and administrative support at SIUC, particularly from the current and past provosts, the chancellor, the dean of the College of Education and Human Services, the chair of the Department of Health Education and Recreation, and the director and associate director of the School of Social Work. In addition, the SIUC Public Policy Institute has provided invaluable assistance.

Financial backing for the various projects associated with this collaboration has been provided by direct funds and in-kind benefits. Direct funds, which have been used to cover the cost of airfare to Russia for the U.S. participants, have come primarily from the School of Social Work, the Department of Health Education and Recreation, the SIUC vice-chancellor for academic affairs and provost, and community practitioners who paid their own way. The Russian partners' contributions to the project have been in-kind, covering lodging, food, and local transportation. They have also covered the cost of their own transportation to Carbondale, with some expenses and in-kind benefits (such as housing) being covered by private and university sources during their stay. The SIUC Office of International Development and various TSEC and SIPKRO Russian interpreters have provided translation without charge. Although support has been sporadic, it has always been found. As discussed below, the approval of two federal grants in 2000 has made the current financial situation much more secure.

MUTUALITY AND WORK PLANS

The identification of mutual interests in the partnership reflects a lengthy process of formal discussions and informal networking among the broad-based coalitions from the United States and Russia. This process was critical in establishing the conditions of collaboration and partnership. It was mutually agreed that the formal training role of the U.S. partners was to be mainly limited to describing the current approaches to prevention and treatment in the United States and would take care to avoid prescribing interventions and solutions. Moreover, it was agreed that there should be a combination of joint classroom teaching, consultation, and observation in practice settings, and informal opportunities for learning about culture through interaction with a wide range of individuals. The partners were also in accord that the training should be interdisciplinary and should draw from the experiences of proven community-based social service agencies and organizations.

Work Plans

In 1997, the first work plan was designed to explore the development of school-based social services in Russia and was loosely modeled after the Family Resource Centers in Kentucky and Project Success in Illinois. These models were viewed as an attractive approach to addressing social service needs in the Volga region.

However, the idea of establishing school-based centers was soon determined to be unrealistic as an initial step because of both conceptual and logistical problems. Conceptually, there were issues with linking social service programs with educational programs. Logistically, there were problems in locating social service programs within schools with limited available space and personnel. Instead, the partners decided to conduct an ongoing program of training and workshops in a Russian-American Summer University. The curriculum for the first RASU was stimulated by survey research data, gathered by faculty at the Pedagogical and Psychological Center in Togliatti, which affirmed that the area of greatest need was adolescent substance

abuse prevention and treatment programs. In November 1997, before beginning the first RASU the following year, a special training program for college directors (and presidents) from seven locations in Russia (including Togliatti, Samara, Tyumen, and Orenburg) was organized and delivered by SIUC faculty and local social work practitioners.

The 1997 training program allowed the partners to establish a high level of trust based on frank discussions. This dialogue broke down many barriers and allowed the Russians to openly share their anxiety and fears about addressing a phenomenon very few individuals in the European part of Russia had been prepared to recognize or deal with: drug use among young people. This issue has been the major consolidating factor among the Russian partners, cutting across social strata and ethnic and religious boundaries. It has been the main reason for the broad involvement of community groups and concerned mothers in the RASU.

RASU 1998

The 1997 training program established the programmatic focus of RASU 1998 on two specific school-age populations: (1) children with disabilities, and (2) youth with addictions, especially youth addicted to alcohol and drugs. The training was to be targeted at local educators, health professionals, government civil servants, and employees of community-service agencies and organizations. Topics for future training and future target populations were to be negotiated between the partners in the fall of each year and refined during the winter and spring.

A faculty member from the SIUC School of Social Work was designated as the U.S. director of RASU with responsibility for recruiting the instructors, developing the curriculum, and ensuring that the technical support was in place. Staff from the Office of International Programs and Services at SIUC assisted this individual. The TSEC president, the SIPKRO rector, and the SIUC School of Social Work director, in collaboration with the head of the Samara Oblast Department of Education, collectively assumed overall responsibility for the project.

The first RASU was held in the summer of 1998 in Togliatti and Samara with workshops that were attended by over 400 people, including psychiatrists, psychologists, health care professionals, social service workers, elementary and high school teachers, school and local government administrators, community activists, and interested citizens. The instructors from the United States included six volunteers—four from SIUC and two from the practice community.

Initial Obstacles to Mutuality

Initially the U.S. pragmatic, "can-do" approach to individual or community problem solving was at odds with the more pessimistic Russian view that solutions are beyond individual and local control. Overcoming this obstacle required repeated dialogue between the instructors and the participants to work through these basic differences. Other problems in mutual understanding arose from the Russian participants who wanted the U.S. "experts" to give them a "magic bullet" that would solve the substance abuse problem. It also took time for both Russian instructors and participants to become used to interactive teaching methods that were more learner-centered than teacher-centered because the customary Russian method of instruction had been uninterrupted lecturing.

Additionally, the U.S. presenters had to fend off early isolated attempts from some participants to disrupt dialogue in the workshops by blaming the United States for the failures of Russia, including speculation that current substance abuse problems were a derivative of the introduction of Western-style democracy. Misunderstandings also developed from the widely held myth that the United States has a massive federal human-service budget for substance abuse prevention and treatment. Another myth that needed to be debunked during the first RASU was the belief that adopted Russian children were being used as organ donors in the United States. These issues were used as a method for discussing child abuse and the child protection framework in the United States, a topic of extremely high interest to the Russian participants.

RASU 1999

Preparation for RASU 1999 was aided by feedback from the first experience and by research that had been conducted by Russian faculty from the Pedagogical and Psychological Center in Togliatti. This study, which was developed through consultation with the U.S. RASU director, was conducted in 24 schools with 18,000 total students in the Komsomolsk district of Togliatti from 1996-1999. The study found that the use of hardcore narcotics among the students increased from 16% in 1997 to 27% in 1999, while the age of the users went down progressively. These results were jointly reported at the International School Social Work Conference in Chicago in April 1999. These findings reinforced the need for continuing education in this content area and formed the basis for the preparation and delivery of the second RASU in 1999.

The data also led to the agreement between the partners that it is critical to view the drug and alcohol problem from a comprehensive systemic perspective. Thus, the Russian partners designated two overall themes of "healthy living" for RASU 1999, which was conducted at TSEC and Togliatti Pedagogical College in Togliatti and at SIPKRO in Samara: Problems of Overcoming Drug Addiction and A Healthy Way of Life is the Important Factor of Survival in Humanity. The workshops consisted of training on: (1) cognitive therapy techniques, (2) educational and life skills strategies for substance abuse prevention, and (3) basics of therapeutic intervention.

In addition, the U.S. team was asked to conduct a needs assessment for building community-based social capital in the small town of Oktyabrsk, which was experiencing high levels of impoverishment and unemployment. This project was sponsored by SIPKRO and the Samara Oblast Department of Education and featured two Russian colleagues and three U.S. educators from SIUC working together to plan and conduct the project.

RASU 2000

The work plan for RASU 2000 was developed collaboratively with the head of the Samara Oblast Department of Education, the SIPKRO rector, and the TSEC president. Healthy lifestyles and adolescent drug prevention and treatment again emerged as the central focus. The specific workshops presented were the following: (1) drug prevention and rehabilitation, (2) working with children with learning disabilities, (3) substance abuse evaluation, (4) work with dysfunctional families, (5) supervision, and (6) in Oktyabrsk, community-based social service systems and social capital. The U.S. team consisted of three faculty from SIUC, the dean and one faculty member from the School of Social Service at St. Louis University, and the director of the Illinois state chapter of NASW. The U.S. RASU director and the SIUC School of Social Work director visited TSEC and SIPKRO the week before RASU 2000, participating in various workshops and visiting social service agencies.

RASU 2001

Beginning with RASU 2001, the project expanded beyond the summer university concept. Two grants from the U.S. State Department allowed the program an expansion and a change in direction.

One grant provided for an academic exchange that had eight Russian faculty and educational administrators visit the United States and four U.S. faculty visit Russia. The purpose of this exchange was to help the Oblast Ministry of Education implement a new law that required the development of school districts and school boards, and which was, in part, adopted to help address Russian misunderstandings about participatory democracy. Toward this end, the exchange program has helped to establish a faculty resource center with a specialized library and several computers at SIPKRO, a women's studies program cooperative endeavor between SIPKRO and the Jewish Foundation in Samara, and several specific courses funded through mini-grants for SIPKRO faculty.

The second grant funded a cultural exchange that was designed to increase women's participation in Russian civil society. Eight Russian women, who had been selected to develop projects for educating and assisting women, were brought to the United States during the winter of 2001 to learn about leadership programs for women. U.S. faculty worked with local community agencies to provide training in the fundamentals of women's leadership at economic and service organizations in southern Illinois and St. Louis. In addition, 14 faculty and practitioners from SIUC, St. Louis University, and the University of North Dakota conducted multiple seminars and conferences in Togliatti, Samara, and Oktyabrsk during the summer of 2001. These sessions covered issues of health education, substance abuse treatment and prevention, family therapy, and community empowerment.

EVALUATION

Evaluations from participants and organizers have been a part of each of the four summer universities. At the end of each year's activities, the collaboration partners evaluate feedback from the workshops to improve the design for the next year's program. In addition, the Russian program administrators provide a general assessment; these have been very positive. For example, in a July 25, 1998, letter to the director of the SIUC School of Social Work, the TSEC president comments on RASU 1998:

I am happy to inform you that our joint effort, the first Russian-American Summer University, was a tremendous success, thanks to the efforts of all your faculty and staff and to your support for this noble cause. The reactions were more than just enthusiastic. Everybody, including our Minister of Education, is already talking about the next Summer University. The media coverage was very extensive and very positive, both on TV and radio. Your colleagues had a permanent place in the anti-drug program of radio "August." I just want to say that the simple project we started with is developing into a great social program, assisting the process of democratic transitions in our part of Russia.

At RASU 1999, an evaluation session was conducted with Samara Oblast administrators, law enforcement and court officials, academicians, and NGO representatives in Samara. During this session, the head of the Samara Oblast's Department of Education observed that

The [RASU] program demonstrated a desperate need for professional training and education in modern ideas, methods, and practical skills, both in the educational leadership of our school system and in the specific [professional] areas, especially in teaching early school health education and substance abuse prevention. Also, we need the assistance of our American colleagues to develop programs in critical thinking skills, educational leadership, and community empowerment to deal with these new and troublesome phenomena that found us quite unprepared.

With regard to RASU 2000, the president of TSEC commented that the U.S. partners "delivered very valuable and helpful information." She expressed her appreciation for "new techniques" and noted, "our cooperation is bringing [fruitful] results."

RESULTS

Testimony to the effectiveness of the collaboration is also manifested in the development of spin-off initiatives. Indeed, the partnership demonstrates how a volunteer program with modest institutional support can create and implement a collaborative initiative to provide an exchange of knowledge and skills. This partnership has made a significant contribution to the training of a wide range of social service professionals and educators in the Samara Oblast regarding health, substance abuse prevention and treatment, and work with children with learning disabilities. It has also assisted in the development of formal and informal community-based networks, including women's leadership in social service programs, that will strengthen local social capital. The collaboration has also provided a constructive response to the critical social needs of the Samara Oblast population.

The partnership has had a number of specific benefits. For example, one SIPKRO faculty member now teaches rational emotional intervention techniques to students who are retraining to become psychologists. Social psychologists are using many of the behavioral techniques taught by the program and are developing them to fit Russian social service and education systems. Russian therapists have taken steps to develop a more effective field training program and a statement of professional ethics. One college in this region has hired a full-time social pedagogue to live in the dormitory and work with students who are struggling with stress or related mental health problems. SIPKRO has invited local social service NGOs to participate in planning and developing programs related to rehabilitation and drug abuse prevention. A training program that emphasizes understanding adolescent psychology and behavior is also underway for law enforcement officers who work with juveniles.

The Russian educators who attended the project's seminars have been exposed to an interactive, experiential teaching method which can be utilized in many settings to teach varied content and which is effective for teaching adolescents. Returning participants report using RASU methods to teach value clarification, time and stress management, and the problem-solving techniques needed for critical thinking.

The Women's Leadership for Community Empowerment grant, which was funded by the U.S. Department of State (DOS), was instrumental for the establishment of a women's counseling center in Togliatti in 2001. This center was created by a group of therapists, lawyers, and business professionals who had been active in RASU from the beginning. In Oktyabrsk, the U.S.-trained "instructors" founded several support programs: a group for mothers of addicts, a group for recovering addicts, and an educational course to help parents prevent substance abuse. Grant funds helped to purchase computers and Internet services for the Russian

partners in Togliatti (which are located in the Pedagogical and Psychological Center) and in Oktyabrsk (in the Municipal Department for Social Services). This equipment allows them to consult with U.S. colleagues on a regular basis.

The spring 2001 trip to SIUC offered Russian leaders the opportunity to exchange ideas and to visit with local social service agency staff over a month-long period. These meetings provided the Russian visitors with institution-strengthening activities that they put to use upon their return. During the summer of 2001, this "training-of-trainers" prepared eight Russian activists to develop a women's advocacy group in Togliatti. One of this group's activities was to pressure the city administration to convene a women's conference in November, 2001 that was attended by over 700 women. Another activity was to develop a mentoring program to help young women create successful businesses and other projects.

The other DOS-funded project in the Samara Oblast is the US-NIS Academic Partnership grant between SIUC and SIPKRO, which has supported the RASU since 1998. The rector of SIPKRO reported that several recent doctoral dissertations have used the healthy lifestyles information from the RASU and developed it into methods for teaching and supporting health education in Russia. It is clear that Russians are beginning to own Russian problems and develop Russian solutions.

Finally, it is important to note that the experiences of the U.S. academic participants inform their teaching and research. They are using the knowledge gained from their interactions with Russian scholars and practitioners to enrich their instruction and to enhance their scholarship.

LESSONS LEARNED AND FUTURE PROSPECTS

The lessons learned from this collaboration inform the task of sustaining those aspects of the partnership that have made it successful. These aspects include (1) describing knowledge and skills instead of prescribing approaches; (2) working jointly in planning, assessing needs, and delivering workshops and projects; (3) involving a broad spectrum of professional disciplines, academic institutions, social service agencies, municipal governments, practitioners, and consumers; (4) maintaining flexibility in instructional methods, curriculum content, and personnel; and (5) continuing to strengthen both informal and formal linkages among all participants.

After 8 years, the Russian participants have obtained a high level of skills and knowledge in education and social services practice. Educators and the practice community in both Russia and the United States fully appreciate the necessity of competencies, assessment, and verifiable outcomes. They recognize the need for adapting to societal changes and the benefits of instilling critical-thinking skills and problem-solving methods in professionals as well as students.

The continued success of this partnership will largely depend on how the participants respond to changes in social and educational needs, instructors, funding sources, administrative personnel, and leadership in both the United States and Russia. It is hoped that the substantial amount of trust and social capital that has developed from informal and formal interactions among the participants will be strong enough to withstand the pressures created by these inevitable transformations. Given the partners' strong commitment to improving education and social services in the United States and Russia, the collaboration is more than likely to continue to grow and prosper.

PRINCIPAL PARTICIPANTS IN TRAINING AND PROJECT DEVELOPMENT

U.S. Partners

Adrian Blow, PhD, assistant professor, School of Social Service, St. Louis University, St. Louis, Missouri.

Rosemarie Bogal-Albritten, PhD, chair, Social Work Program, Murray State University, Murray, Kentucky.

Wayne Evens, PhD, associate professor, School of Social Work, Bradley University, Peoria, Illinois. U.S. RASU program director (formerly on the faculty at the Southern Illinois University at Carbondale Social of Social Work).

Carol S. Goldbaum, PhD, director, Illinois State Chapter of NASW, Chicago, Illinois.

Donna Herndon, director, Calloway County Family Resource Center, East Elementary School, Murray, Kentucky.

Marjorie J. Malkin, EdD, professor, Department of Health Education and Recreation, Southern Illinois University at Carbondale.

Mizanur R. Miah, PhD, professor, School of Social Work, Southern Illinois University at Carbondale.

Ivan Nikolov, PhD, clinical faculty member and director, Global and International Education, College of Education and Human Services, Southern Illinois University at Carbondale.

John (Jack) Stretch, PhD, professor, School of Social Service, St. Louis University, St. Louis, Missouri.

Sue Tebb, PhD, dean, School of Social Service, St. Louis University, St. Louis, Missouri.

Tina Timm, PhD, assistant professor, School of Social Service, St. Louis University, St. Louis, Missouri.

Patsy D. Tracy, PhD, retired. Formerly clinical associate professor, School of Social Work, Southern Illinois University at Carbondale.

Martin B. Tracy, PhD, professor and associate dean for Research, University of Kentucky, Lexington, Kentucky. Formerly director and professor, the School of Social Work, Southern Illinois University at Carbondale.

Kathleen Welshimer, PhD, associate professor, Department of Health Education and Recreation, Southern Illinois University at Carbondale.

Jan Wilson, assistant clinical professor, School of Social Service, St. Louis University, St. Louis, Missouri.

Russian Partners

Elena Eremina, PhD, director, Togliatti Social and Economic College and dean of Social Technologies, Volga Tatishchev University, Togliatti, Russia.

Efim Kogan, PhD, head, Samara Oblast Department of Education, Samara, Russia.

Galena Moukanina, PhD, Pedagogical and Psychological Center, Togliatti, Russia.

Igor Noskov, PhD, rector, Samara Institute for Teacher Re-Training and Staff Development in Education, Samara, Russia.

Tatiana Saltykova, vice-president of academic affairs, Togliatti Social and Economic College, Togliatti, Russia.

Ludmilla Sultanova, lecturer, Togliatti Social and Economic College, Togliatti, Russia.

Margarita Zaitseva, ESL lecturer, Togliatti Social and Economic College, Togliatti, Russia.

FOURTEEN

Global Interdependence and International Exchange: Lessons for the Future

M. C. "Terry" Hokenstad

Today, it is difficult to function at any level of social work without an understanding of the global environment. Economic globalization, the tribalization of world politics, and the accelerating migration of the world's population all have implications for social welfare policy and social work practice. This changing context requires professionals who understand the impact of these forces on their clients, their agencies, and their practice.

In the introductory chapter of this volume, Asamoah reviews the recent literature that focuses on the need for social workers to think and act globally. This need includes the recognition of international interdependence and an awareness that social work at the local level is increasingly influenced by problems of global scope. For example, the high number of ethnic and religious conflicts in the past decade has produced a worldwide diaspora. As a result, a growing number of social workers in many countries, including the United States, are working with refugees.

Similarly, increasing economic disparity among nations, as well as within individual countries, is a major force behind recent patterns of migration that have produced multitudes of legal and illegal immigrants. These people, who are rarely fluent in the primary language of the host nation, provide a major clientele group for social workers. In working with these diverse populations, social workers need an understanding of their various cultural and geographical roots. This requires knowledge of the environment beyond the national borders of the social worker's home country.

International collaboration is one potentially effective method for preparing social workers to function in this context of global realities. Chapter 1 spells out a number of goals and objectives for such programs, which expose students, faculty, and professional practitioners to other countries and cultures and can expand the participants' understanding of interna-

tional interdependence. These experiences also have the potential for increasing the number of social workers with interest and beginning expertise in practice across national borders. Educational exchange programs hopefully will influence attitudes and produce both knowledge and skill outcomes.

Experiential learning is an essential component of professional education. Exchange programs offer an important experiential component for the internationalization of educational programs. They also present an added dimension in preparation for practice in the participant's own country. Although these programs result in information and insights about the practice of social work in different nations, the more important consequence is the knowledge and skills they provide for working with diverse populations. Thus, international exchange is a potentially valuable learning experience for students and professionals, regardless of the practice locale (Hokenstad & Midgley, 1997).

The case studies in this volume are examples of university-based collaborative programs. As such, they have specific objectives and functions beyond the general goal of promoting global understanding. While certainly implicit in all international exchange activities, increased understanding among nations and their peoples is most often a by-product of more tangible objectives. Some of the case studies have a goal of initiating expanded cultural linkages between countries, a less global but equally important general purpose. However, most of the programs have specific objectives that are focused on institutional change as well as individual enhancement.

Specific objectives for this group of social work exchange programs concentrate on both individual learning and institutional change. Individual-learning objectives emphasize student experiences in the partner country, but also recognize the mutual exchange of ideas and information between the host country and the visiting participants, be they students, faculty, or practitioners. Some projects have the objective of educating educators or developing continuing education for practitioners as the focus of the exchange.

Institutional-change objectives are diverse. Some programs are designed to help establish or build social work education in a particular country. Many participants see the exchange as contributing to an overall goal of internationalizing the social work curriculum, which can be an institutional objective for one or both partners in the program. Other participants aim for joint research and knowledge-building projects that can add an international dimension to existing subjects of expertise. These institutional-change purposes are usually coupled with individual-learning aspirations, and both sets of objectives need attention in project implementation and evaluation.

This final chapter will examine the case studies in this volume in order to illuminate the similarities and differences among the different collaborative programs. First, it will look at the contexts of the projects to determine which societal forces and institutional frameworks are conducive to international exchange. Then it will review the various types of collaboration identified in chapter 1, with an emphasis on program objectives and focus. This will include projects that concentrate on student learning, projects with a focus on program development, and projects with objectives that extend beyond social work education. Some attention also will be given to sources of financial support.

This chapter will then consider some principles of collaboration that may be helpful for the planning and implementation of future international exchange programs. These principles include mutuality, sustainability, and the ripple effect that were identified in chapter 1. Finally, the chapter explores the future of international exchange in social work education. What challenges and opportunities face educational collaboration in the 21st century? How can international exchange programs contribute to the preparation of social workers for work in an increasingly global society?

MODELS OF COLLABORATION: CONTEXT AND CONTENT

The 11 case studies in this book exemplify the programmatic diversity that exists in the field of international exchange. However, there are certainly commonalities. North American social work educators

are usually the initiators and are always key actors in these projects. Generally, the exchange is between two educational institutions. As indicated by Healy in chapter 2, international exchange relationships are fundamentally agreements between two organizations. But in one case, nongovernmental organizations (NGOs) serve as the partners abroad, and others are based on coalitions including, but not limited to, institutions of higher education.

Program diversity reflects each exchange's individual context. This context includes the developmental stage that social work education has reached in the partner country. The content of the collaboration is at least partially determined by the perceived need for consultation and technical assistance by one or both partners. Thus, some exchanges focus on developmental goals while others concentrate more directly on enriching student learning. The consultation project to develop the Center for Professional Education in Social Work in Kaunas, Lithuania (chapter 10) has a different focus and program from the collaboration between Boston University and the National Danish School of Social Work, Aarhus (chapter 7) collaboration. The first seeks to institutionalize social work education in a transitional country, while the second provides international learning experiences for students in two countries with established social work education traditions.

Context for Collaboration

These case studies demonstrate that educational exchange programs are influenced and shaped by their historical and social context. Historically, the 1990s produced more international collaborations than any decade since the 10 years following the Second World War. This first surge of international exchange programs followed the conclusion of a hot war and the second came after the Cold War ended. The political, economic, and social transitions in Central and Eastern Europe and the former Soviet Union were the major force in this new era of increased opportunities for international interaction in many fields. The profession of social work was no exception. The rapid initiation of social work exchange projects between institutions in North America and Western Europe and programs in former Soviet bloc countries reflected the mutually perceived need to instruct practitioners in a part of the world with limited or nonexistent social work education (Hokenstad & Kendall, 1995).

Several of the exchange programs described in this volume are a result of the social transformations in

Central and Eastern Europe following the collapse of the Soviet Union. The Lithuanian Center for Professional Education in Social Work (chapter 10) and the Russian-American Summer University (chapter 13) have been initiated in countries where social work was nonexistent prior to 1990. In both cases, the collaboration has centered on the educational and institutional needs of a former Soviet bloc country. The Augsburg College and the University of Ljubljana exchange (chapter 3) and the Eotvos Lorand University and Case Western Reserve University collaboration (chapter 5) have both involved a more mutual exchange of expertise because those participating Eastern European countries, Slovenia and Hungary, have had a longer, albeit limited, history of social work education.

Social change is also a powerful force behind the initiation of exchange programs in other parts of the world, and it creates a challenging environment for social work education. A revolutionary period in Central America provided the context in which the collaboration between the Escuela de Trabajo Social at the Universidad Centroamericana in Nicaragua and the University of Calgary (chapter 12) was initiated. The challenge for this project was to reconstitute the Nicaraguan social work program through the application of Freire's model of popular education. The concepts of empowerment and participation were emphasized throughout this exchange. In another case, the desire of the Sri Lanka School of Social Work to contribute to the country's social development led to a collaboration with the University of Toronto (chapter 11).

Cultural linkages are an important motivating factor for many collaborations. The cultural diversity of North America, particularly its immigration patterns, create potential connections with all parts of the world. The University of Connecticut–University of the West Indies, Mona Campus collaboration (chapter 6) was stimulated in part by the large West Indian immigrant population located in Hartford, Connecticut. One of the program's major objectives is outreach to this Caribbean American population.

Cultural connections also are evident motivators in the Tunghai University–San Jose State University (chapter 4) and the University of Texas at Arlington–Universidad Autónoma de Nuevo León (chapter 8) collaborations. These linkages were built on statewide patterns of immigration in California and Texas. Additionally, the Eotvos Lorand University–Case Western Reserve University connection was enhanced

by the fact that Cleveland was a major center of Hungarian immigration and still has a sizable Hungarian American population.

Institutional and organizational affiliations outside of the universities themselves are another important influence for international exchange programs. In addition to providing financial support, churches and NGOs sometimes provide the glue that holds these projects together. Of the cases in this volume, the most obvious example of this is the role of the Roman Catholic Church and its Caritas agency in coalescing the network needed to develop the Lithuanian Center for Professional Education in Social Work. The Church's involvement enabled social work educators from the United States to effectively work with a complex group of actors from various sectors of Lithuanian society. NGOs have also performed a key role in Grand Valley State University's service learning program in El Salvador (chapter 9).

International social work organizations have an important role to play as catalysts for bilateral and multilateral exchange programs. While small and financially fragile, both the International Association of Schools of Social Work (IASSW) and the International Federation of Social Workers offer communication networks and opportunities for interaction that can stimulate international collaborations. Contacts established through IASSW congresses, board meetings, and regional organizing meetings were key motivators in the United States–Caribbean and the United States–Eastern Europe collaborations. With their worldwide networks of social workers and social work educators, these organizations could assume a more central role in promoting exchange. But a lack of staff and a limited budget prevent them from doing so at the present time.

Of course, the universities and colleges that provide these programs of social work education are also part of the contexts for these exchanges. The cases in this volume report on projects that sprung from the interests and connections of social work schools and their faculties. Some collaborations, such as the Boston University–National Danish School of Social Work, Aarhus project, grew exclusively out of social work faculty members' interest and initiative, while others started as a component of a college- or university-wide plan. Augsburg College's exchange program with the University of Ljubljana is an interdisciplinary program that includes exchanges in education, business, and philosophy, in addition to social work. These kinds of projects involve a formal agreement between institutions and all components of the program are coordinated centrally. Social work shapes its exchange, but the program fits within the larger institutional structure. This may limit the autonomy of the social work component, but at the same time, lessens the pressure for finding resources for the ongoing project. It may also serve to increase the visibility of the social work program within the university.

Content of the Collaboration

International collaboration in social work education comes in a variety of forms. The case studies in this volume are difficult to categorize because they often have a mix of objectives and activities. But each does have a primary focus. Some programs concentrate on student learning, and others focus on the development of social work education in a particular country. Additionally, there are collaborations that include the purposes above, but also have objectives that extend beyond social work education. These are consortium programs whose overall goals are to develop social work and social welfare programs through international partnerships.

Programs with student learning as the primary objective often concentrate on expanding the global horizons and international knowledge of North American students. The Grand Valley State University programs in El Salvador and South Africa are examples of this kind of program. Alternatively, attention may be given to international learning for social work students on both sides of the collaboration. Examples of these kinds of projects include the exchange between Augsburg College and the University of Ljubljana and the exchange between Boston University and the National Danish School of Social Work, Aarhus. In both cases, students from each of the social work programs travel to the partner country for learning experiences.

Faculty exchanges also take place in some of these programs, but the emphasis is still on student learning. This instruction can take place through a number of modalities, including classes, seminars, short-term workshops, special summer schools, and field visits or practicum experiences. North American students are often at a disadvantage in these field-learning experiences because of language limitations. The Boston University–National Danish School of Social Work, Aarhus collaboration is a good example. U.S. student participants have less language facility than their Danish counterparts, therefore their contact with clients abroad is necessarily limited.

The University of Texas at Arlington–Universidad Autónoma de Nuevo León collaboration is a special case of student exchange. As a joint PhD program, it has a group of Mexican and U.S. students that learn together in both locations. Thus, fluency in both Spanish and English is essential for all students. This program exemplifies the mutuality highlighted by Healy in chapter 2 because both sides of the exchange collaborate on the educational program and students from both countries receive the same learning opportunities. It may well be the ideal form for student exchange, but it does require certain circumstances and substantial resources.

Collaborations with educational program development as the primary objective focus on faculty contributions, even though students may be involved in the project. Faculty from one or more of the collaborating institutions have a program-development responsibility. They may perform a number of roles, including teaching, but technical assistance, consultation, and sometimes organizing and management tasks are their primary functions. This type of collaboration matches North American institutions with those in transitional or developing countries.

Program-development collaborations may focus on one or both of the countries involved in the exchange. In this volume, the University of Toronto–Sri Lanka School of Social Work linkage had an overall goal of increasing the capacity of the Sri Lankan program to contribute to nationwide social development efforts. The Lithuanian consultation project was focused on the development of social work education in a transitional society. This involved building the social work profession from the ground up through the establishment of the Center for Professional Education in Social Work at Vytautas Magnus University. Educators from Canada and the United States took home increased international understanding, knowledge, and skills, but the focal points of the projects were the programs in Sri Lanka and Lithuania.

Other program-development cases in this volume place more emphasis on outcomes for both of the partners. One example is the collaboration between the University of Connecticut and the University of the West Indies, Mona Campus. The Caribbean partner has benefited through curriculum and faculty development, while the U.S. partner has received the same benefits, plus a greater understanding of and better connections with the local West Indian immigrant population. Dual outcomes also resulted from the Eotvos Lorand University and Case Western Reserve University connection. Curriculum development at both universities was improved by faculty visitors from the partner institution. This two-way exchange of faculty was a built-in feature of both collaborations.

Consortium programs often have objectives and activities broader than educational exchange, even when universities are the initiators and key actors in the collaboration. The Russian–American Summer University started as a dialogue and exchange between Southern Illinois University at Carbondale and the Togliatti Social and Economic University. However, it quickly grew to include more partners in Russia and eventually in the United States as well. These partners include local and regional governments and NGOs. The project has also become interdisciplinary in both the university and the community. While the exchange of social work faculty and students is part of the program, the focus is on broader training involving workshops for health-care professionals, social workers, school and local government administrators, community activists, and interested citizens. Needs-assessment studies and program development have also become part of the mix.

The collaboration between Tunghai University and San Jose State University, described in the case study as a linkage between cultures, is not as broad based in terms of sponsorship because the basic exchange agreement is only between the two universities. However, many of the project's programs are cosponsored by governmental and nongovernmental organizations. Emphasis is placed on short-term training involving professionals from a number of practice fields. Conferences are designed to provide an international forum for the exchange, and the discussion of social welfare issues, policies, and programs is another feature of the project. Because the collaboration includes faculty and student exchanges and program development, it is multifaceted in both objectives and content.

RESOURCES FOR COLLABORATION

Funding international exchange programs is a continual challenge for the institutions and individuals involved and it often requires piecing together funds from a number of sources. Usually some of the support comes from within the university and the rest from a variety of government and private agencies. Institutional support may be primarily in the form of released time or in-kind support. Outside funding may be programmatic or directed at individuals involved in the exchange. The case studies in this volume exemplify the ongoing struggle to find sufficient funds to achieve program objectives.

Student exchange programs often operate with little or no outside support. The Boston University–National Danish School of Social Work, Aarhus exchange is an example of this. The institutions involved in the project provide some released time and travel expenses for their faculty, but student travel is self-funded. This situation limits the number of students who can participate. It is possible to carry out an exchange between two affluent countries under such funding limitations, but students from the developing world would not be able to participate. The short distance between Monterrey, Mexico, and Arlington, Texas, plus student scholarships and other financial support from both universities, make the University of Texas at Arlington–Universidad Autónoma de Nuevo León joint doctoral program financially feasible.

Outside funding for the exchanges in this volume comes from a wide variety of sources, ranging from the United Nations Development Fund and the United Nations Children's Fund to national and local foundations. No single funding pattern is evident, but there is one interesting difference between programs initiated in Canada and the United States. The Canadian International Development Agency (CIDA) is the major funding source for both the University of Calgary–Escuela de Trabajo Social and the University of Toronto–Sri Lanka School of Social Work exchanges while its U.S. counterpart, the United States Agency for International Development provides only limited and circumscribed support for two of the nine U.S.-initiated programs. Although the sample is clearly too small to draw a conclusion, one wonders if social work education in Canada has better linkages to its international development agency.

Funding for the U.S.-based exchanges comes largely from nongovernmental sources. Only the Eotvos Lorand University–Case Western Reserve University collaboration received major funding from the United States Information Agency (USIA) through its University Affiliations Program, which is a significant source of financing for other university-based exchanges. While some individuals in other collaborations in this volume benefited from the Fulbright program, which is largely funded by USIA, there was no other project funding from this agency. On the other hand, independent foundations were an important source of support for many of the exchanges. The Russian–American Summer University received funds from the Eurasia Foundation. The Lithuanian Center for Professional Education in Social Work was supported by the Soros Foundation and the San Jose State University–Tunghai University collaboration was backed by the Chinese Fund for Families and Children. Other private funding, such as the support from the Lithuanian and U.S. bishops' conferences, was tied to the sponsorship of specific exchanges.

There are many sources of funding for international collaboration, but often resources are neither easy to locate nor to secure. It would be helpful to make more information about potential sources available to social work educators. A directory of government and nongovernment funders would offer a useful starting point for this process. But even with such information, the funding challenge will still require initiative and tenacity. Fortunately, the examples in this volume provide evidence that this obstacle can be successfully overcome.

LESSONS TO BE LEARNED

What can be learned from these case studies that might be useful in planning future international collaborations? Unfortunately, formal evaluations are seldom built into such projects. There may be final reports required by funding bodies or occasionally assessment questionnaires filled out by participants, but little systematic research is carried out to evaluate program effectiveness in achieving objectives. Built-in evaluation components are needed so that future exchange programs can learn from the accomplishments and limitations of past projects.

Each of the above cases has included some lessons that were learned from the specific experience. Rather than summarize those points, this final chapter will consider the concepts of mutuality, sustainability, and the ripple effect mentioned in chapter 1 and will draw examples from the cases to show how these concepts are incorporated into successful exchange programs. The uniqueness of these projects makes replication difficult, but there is much to be learned from the examples of collaboration longevity and networking.

Mutuality means that both partners contribute to and benefit from the exchange. The literature review in chapter 2 emphasizes the finding that the highest levels of satisfaction and interaction come from partners with substantial interdependence (Schmidt & Kochan,

1977). Although the partners may contribute different expertise or resources to the exchange, collaborative projects involve mutual contributions and mutual benefits.

In the past, social work exchange programs were usually based on the consultation model, which involves American social work educators travelling to another country to teach, to conduct research, and to provide program consultation. Student exchange went in the opposite direction, as students from around the world came to study in North America. This approach to international exchange raised serious issues about the appropriateness of knowledge transfer in both faculty consultation and foreign student education. While these programs may have been helpful in some cases, as a pattern of international interaction it was often inappropriate and sometimes very harmful (Hokenstad & Kendall, 1995).

Many of the cases in this book base the collaboration on a different model that emphasizes mutuality. This model starts with the premise that participants on each side of the exchange have a contribution to make. These contributions may be different, but they are equally important. Such mutuality is possible even if the participating countries are at different stages in the development of social work and social work education.

A good example of this is the Eotvos Lorand University and Case Western Reserve University collaboration. The U.S. partners contributed their expertise to the building of social work education in Hungary, including curriculum development at the professional level, training of practicum supervisors, and eventually, consultation in the creation of a doctoral program. At the same time, Hungarian social policy experts and social scientists assisted with both curriculum building and student education at Case Western Reserve University. These well-published scholars came to the United States with expertise in the macro theory as applied to social policy and in research methodology for cross-national comparisons of policy and programs. Participating faculty from both partners produced joint publications. This collaboration clearly benefited both institutions and social work education in both countries.

University of Connecticut–University of the West Indies, Mona Campus partnership has benefited both institutions in different ways. Visiting faculty from Jamaica have given workshops for U.S. social workers who serve Caribbean immigrants and have taught in the University of Connecticut social work program. Both partners have shared teaching materials and have contributed to curriculum development at the other school. Jointly planned conferences and resultant publications have enhanced the collaboration. The project has also produced increased publication opportunities for Jamaican faculty. Therefore, mutuality is again evidenced in this international exchange.

Many exchanges have a goal of internationalizing curricula, particularly for the North American partner. This is a benefit that ensures mutuality. Although it is certainly an appropriate outcome of collaboration, curriculum internationalization is too often an abstract goal without specific objectives or clear measures for evaluation. Exchange visits can allow for faculty workshops to discuss international content and methods for incorporating it into the curriculum. However, it is often difficult to involve faculty that are not directly part of the exchange. Attention must be given to careful implementation of the curriculum internationalization goal if it is to be more than window dressing for the project.

Exposure to social work in other countries is a useful experience for faculty and students involved in the exchange. After returning home, knowledge and insights gained can be shared with others through workshops and colloquia. However, it is very important that curriculum and course development proposals be part of the project. The incorporation of international content into the curriculum is one important measure of the collaboration's impact on the North American partner.

There are a number of other indicators of project sustainability. Project length is one such marker. The Tunghai University–San Jose State University exchange has an impressive history covering 2 decades. This ongoing linkage has included teaching and learning visits, joint workshops, and collaborative conferences involving practitioners and administrators in addition to educators and students. Mutual benefits have resulted from both the length and the content of this collaboration.

Development of program capacity and self-sufficiency are good social work principles that are reflected in some project outcomes. The University of Calgary–Escuela de Trabajo Social exchange focused on a participatory process to make the Southern partner the agent of its own change. Collaboration was designed to be nonintrusive and supportive of capacity building. This process was used to upgrade the teaching capabilities of the Nicaraguan faculty and to improve the programs and infrastructure needed to build social work

education in Nicaragua. The sustainability of this project is best indicated by the functioning of the Escuela de Trabajo Social after the conclusion of the collaboration. The sustainability of other projects is evidenced by the self-sufficient operation of social work education in Lithuania and Hungary and the improved focus of social work education in Sri Lanka.

The impact of the collaborations for a number of the cases in this volume has extended beyond social work education. This ripple effect may be built into the project's objectives or it may be almost serendipitous. Agency practice is enhanced by field education workshops and the professional organizations that are developed as a result of exchange visits. A network composed of various sectors of Lithuanian society was established to support the development of the Vytautas Magnus University Center for Professional Education in Social Work. In addition to serving a mediating function, it also enhanced the credibility of social work in Lithuania.

An example of an even wider ripple effect is the Russian–American Summer University. The initial exchange visits of this project expanded into a collaboration between two diverse coalitions that include universities, government bodies, and social service agencies. The project became multidisciplinary within the individual academic institutions and also among their collaborative partners. As the coalitions have grown, funding has also increased. While this type of expansion always risks blurring the project's focus, the larger network now reaches more people, institutions, and sectors of society. This growth is particularly relevant for transitional societies that need an expanded project impact. The ripple effect is a potentially positive outcome of a well-defined, but also flexible, project.

THE FUTURE OF EXCHANGE: COLLABORATION IN A CHANGING WORLD

International exchange programs are a key component for preparing social workers for the realities of global interdependence in the 21st century. Such programs can be sponsored by many different social institutions, but they are in particular an essential part of internationalism in higher education. Such global education includes many components, such as language programs and an internationalized curriculum. Some of these components can take place in one's own country. But the exchange of faculty and students is a cornerstone of higher education's global contribution to this changing world.

The models of collaboration presented in this volume are focused on social work but are generally based in educational programs in colleges and universities. Thus, in order to project the future of social work exchange, it is important to look at trends for international collaboration in higher education. Study abroad is not a new concept and various types of programs have been in existence for over a half century. In the United States, the Fulbright program for the exchange of both graduate students and faculty has been a major governmental program since 1946. It is the symbol of the United States' commitment to international education.

Unfortunately, in spite of the Fulbright program and a few other federally funded exchange programs, such as the University Affiliations Program of the USIA, there has been a post-Cold War decline in U.S. government support for educational collaborations. Allen Goodman (1999), president of the Institute of International Education, criticizes the inadequacy of this support and points out that the United States has fallen behind other nations in student exchange. Less than 1% of all U.S. college and university students study abroad annually. Even though the United States is still the top choice for students from other countries, Canada, Britain, France, and Australia have recently developed well-financed programs and launched recruitment efforts to increase enrollment of students from other countries.

There are some positive signs for the future of U.S. exchanges. In April of 2000, President Clinton issued an executive memorandum that renewed and strengthened the federal government's commitment to international education. This commitment includes emphasizing study abroad for U.S. students, encouraging students from other countries to study in the United States, and supporting teacher and scholar exchange programs. This executive policy was partly in response to the G-8 nations' official goal of doubling exchange opportunities in higher education in the next 10 years. It mandated joint action by the executive departments of the federal government and the private sector of U.S. society. While a slight increase in the funding of exchange programs was included in the 2001 federal budget, the long-term success of this policy initiative remains open to question. The Bush administration's commitment to international education is not yet clear and congressional funding continues to be problematic.

Other countries have put more governmental resources into international educational exchange programs and social work education has benefited by this commitment. As demonstrated by the cases in this volume, CIDA has been a major source of funding for social work exchange programs initiated in Canada. In chapter 1, Asamoah mentions some of the European Union (EU) programs that emphasize cross-national and intercultural learning. The TEMPUS and ERASMUS programs of the 1990s promoted exchanges between Western Europe and the transitional societies of Central and Eastern Europe, as well as collaboration among EU countries. Lyons (1999) points out that the EU's newer SOCRATES program focuses on exchange between entire educational institutions rather than individual disciplines such as social work. This has meant some redirection of resources, but consortium programs involving social work education continue to receive EU funding.

Resources will continue to be a major challenge for the future development of international exchange programs. Social work must compete for limited governmental and private-sector funding. It is imperative that information about potential funding sources be compiled and disseminated by national and international social work organizations as well as educational institutions. At the same time, the case studies in this volume demonstrate that ingenuity in program design coupled with industriousness in piecing together various types of support can lead to successful international collaboration. Because it is unlikely that funding will become easily available, scrambling for resources will continue to be a necessary part of future educational exchanges.

Twenty-first century technology offers one way of encouraging exchange within tight resource constraints. As Healy (2001) explains, technological tools such as listservs and computer bulletin boards bring together educators and students and allows them to share information and solve problems. Email and online communication is not limited by national borders. Lyons (1999) mentions the international computer network established by the National Institute of Social Work in London as one example of online communication. Additionally, a range of websites from the fields of social welfare and social work provide ready information access to students and faculty throughout the world. These electronic media give schools of social work the opportunity to incorporate comparative content and cross-national communications into their educational programs.

International exchange via distance education is already being implemented by social work educators.

One good example is the Email Partnership Project described by Johnson (1999). The program was part of an advanced methods course for students at Case Western Reserve University and it involved structured email exchanges with Romanian social workers and grassroots organizations. This interaction included sharing information about the countries, their social problems, and their social services. Reciprocity was built into the project. The U.S. students were expected to do research so that they could provide in-depth and up-to-date information about their own country while at the same time gaining knowledge about Romania. Students learned cross-cultural communication skills in addition to information and insights about the people and programs of another country.

Distance-learning modalities will be increasingly used to facilitate future international collaborations. In the future, visual as well as verbal interaction will be more readily available via improved technology. Electronic communication will become more universally available and affordable. Thus, faculty and students from all nations will have the opportunity to participate in this form of educational exchange. Of course, such distance learning cannot take the place of personally experiencing other countries and cultures. Virtual learning should supplement, not supplant, experiential learning.

International collaboration is an important way of energizing social work's response to the global realities of the 21st century. Increased opportunities for exchange experiences will create more social workers who are interested in and prepared for international practice (Hokenstad & Midgley, 1997). As this volume has shown, collaboration can take many forms. It might be primarily student exchange, faculty exchange, or a combination of the two. It might include teaching, research, consultation, in-service training, conferences, program planning, or practicum experiences. It may involve both virtual and actual exchanges. Hopefully, these collaborations will continue to contribute to the internationalization of social work curricula and to provide many students the opportunity to experience global diversity.

Programs of exchange will be truly collaborative if mutuality is an objective that is effectively implemented. This is a challenge that merits attention during program planning. Cases in this volume provide examples of how mutuality, as well as sustainability and the ripple effect, can be achieved. The effectiveness and the expansion of international exchange needs careful attention if social work is to remain relevant in a changing world.

REFERENCES

Goodman, A. E. (1999, March 12). America is devaluing international exchanges for students and scholars. *The Chronicle of Higher Education*, A56.

Healy, L. M. (2001). *International social work: Professional action in an interdependent world.* New York: Oxford University Press.

Hokenstad, M. C., & Kendall K. A. (1995). International social work education. In R. L. Richards (Ed.), *Encyclopedia of social work* (19th ed, pp. 1551-1520). Washington, DC: NASW Press.

Hokenstad, M. C., & Midgley, J. (1997). Realities of global interdependence: Challenge for social work in a new century. In M. C. Hokenstad & J. Midgley (Eds.), *Issues in international social work: Global challenges for a new century* (pp.1-10). Washington, DC: NASW Press.

Johnson, A. (1999). Globalization from below: Using the Internet to internationalize social work education. *Journal of Social Work Education*, 35, 377-393.

Lyons, K. (1999). *International social work: Themes and perspectives.* Aldershot, United Kingdom: Ashgate Publishing Company.

Schmidt, S. M., & Kochan, T. A. (1977). Interorganizational relationships: Patterns and motivations. *Administrative Science Quarterly*, 22, 220-234.

ABOUT THE EDITORS AND CONTRIBUTORS

EDITORS

Lynne M. Healy, PhD, is professor at the University of Connecticut School of Social Work and director of the school's Center for International Social Work Studies. She has published numerous articles and several books on international social work, including the recent *International Social Work: Professional Action in an Interdependent World*. Dr. Healy is currently president of the North American and Caribbean Association of Schools of Social Work and a vice president of the International Association of Schools of Social Work (IASSW); she serves on the editorial boards of the *Caribbean Journal of Social Work*, the *Asia-Pacific Journal of Social Work,* and the *Journal of Social Development in Africa*. She was chair of the Council on Social Work Education's (CSWE) International Commission for 5 years and has been a member of CSWE's board of directors. She has taught and consulted in Jamaica and Mauritius and has conducted many workshops on internationalizing social work curricula.

Yvonne Asamoah, PhD, is a retired professor from the Hunter College School of Social Work, in New York. Prior to her work at Hunter, she was director of all programs in social work at the University of Ghana for 15 years. Her teaching and research interests include human behavior in the social environment, research, international social policy, multicultural issues in policy, casework, community development, and administration. She was an exchange student in Europe and Africa and has traveled extensively on both continents as a consultant and as a presenter at conferences, seminars, and workshops. Dr. Asamoah's publications have included articles and chapters on curriculum development, homelessness, multiculturalism, aging, training and development, and issues before the United Nations (UN). She served as chair of CSWE's International Commission and as a UN representative for IASSW. She was extensively involved in supporting work for the UN Convention on the Rights of the Child.

M. C. "Terry" Hokenstad, PhD, is the Ralph S. and Dorothy P. Schmitt Professor at the Mandel School of Applied Social Sciences, Case Western Reserve University, Cleveland, Ohio. He also serves as professor of international health in the School of Medicine. Long active in international organizations, Dr. Hokenstad is a consultant to the UN and was a member of the U.S. Delegation to the UN Assembly on Ageing in 2002. He has served both as president and chair of CSWE's International Commission and as secretary of IASSW. Dr. Hokenstad has written extensively on international themes and served as the editor of the journal *International Social Work*. His books include *Issues in International Social Work: Global Challenges for a New Century* and *Gerontological Social Work: International Perspectives*. He has lectured and consulted in many countries, including serving as a Fulbright scholar at the Institute of Applied Social Research in Oslo, Norway, and as a senior Fulbright lecturer at Stockholm University in Sweden.

CONTRIBUTORS

Gabi Čačinovič Vogrinčič, PhD, is professor of family social work and family psychology, School of Social Work, University of Ljubljana, Slovenia. Dr. Čačinovič Vogrinčič is closely involved in the development of social work theory and practice in Slovenia. Her special fields of interest are effective concepts, methods, and skills for helping families. She has written several articles about the working relationship between the social worker and the family in the helping process. Dr. Čačinovič Vogrinčič is the author of *Family Psychology*.

Robert Constable, DSW, is professor emeritus at Loyola University, Chicago, Illinois, and visiting professor at the University of Navarra in Pamplona, Spain. His areas of interest for writing, research, and practice are school social work and school social work with families. He has taught and provided consultation in Lithuania, Poland, Spain, and Italy. He was codirector of the Center for Professional Social Work Education at Vytautas Magnus University in Lithuania from 1992 to 1997.

Héctor Luis Díaz, PhD, is on the faculty at the University of Texas at Arlington, where he is coordinator of the Joint Doctoral Program in International Comparative Social Welfare Policy. His areas of interest and expertise include international social work, social development, diversity, and comparative social policy. He has published on factors that impact the socioeconomic development of Hispanic families in the United States; on stress and alcohol use among Puerto Ricans; and on aspects of social capital and economic development in Peru, including food security and gender.

Doreen Elliott, PhD, is professor of social work at the University of Texas at Arlington (UTA), and previously taught at the University of Wales in the United Kingdom. She has published six books, including three coedited international books: *The World of Social Welfare: Social Welfare and Services in an International Context*; *The International Handbook on Social Work Education*; and *The International Handbook on Social Work Theory and Practice*. She is coeditor of the journal *Social Development Issues* and chair of CSWE's International Commission. She was instrumental in setting up the joint doctoral program between UTA and the Universidad Autónoma de Nuevo León in Monterrey, México.

Wayne Evens, PhD, is director of the Social Work Program at Bradley University, Peoria, Illinois. He holds an MSW and a PhD from the University of Iowa. He has been active in the Russian-American Summer University program for 6 years, serving as the U.S. director. His research interests are child welfare and spirituality.

Julia A. Guevara, PhD, teaches at the Grand Valley State University School of Social Work, Allendale, Michigan. She has taught social work at the University of Tirana, Albania, and at a special program in Merida, Mexico, and has conducted service learning and research projects throughout Central America since 1984. Most recently she returned from Cuba where she had been exploring social work opportunities for faculty and students.

W. David Harrison, PhD, is professor and dean at East Carolina University School of Social Work and Criminal Justice Studies, Greenville, North Carolina. He has been a practitioner in the United States and the United Kingdom. He has made over 30 consultation and teaching visits to Lithuania and he was given a Fulbright Senior Scholar appointment. He has specialized in chairing Lithuanian students' MSW and PhD theses and in building partnerships for developing appropriate research models.

Santos H. Hernández, PhD, is dean and professor, School of Social Work, University of Texas at Arlington. Dr. Hernández has published, presented, taught, and conducted research in the areas of cross-cultural social work practice, international social work, mental health, and generalist social work practice. He has an extensive record of professional involvement. Among his many leadership roles, he is on the boards of directors of CSWE, the Big Brothers Big Sisters of Arlington, the Fort Worth-based Family Services, Inc., and he is chair of the International Committee of the Texas Chapter of the National Association of Social Workers.

Catheleen Jordan, PhD, is professor of social work at the University of Texas at Arlington. Her areas of expertise are family assessment and treatment, clinical research, and family-work issues. Dr. Jordan has published in journals and books and is the coauthor of *Clinical Assessment for Social Workers*, *Family Practice*, and *Introduction to Family Social Work*.

Regina Kulys, PhD, is associate professor at the Jane Addams College of Social Work, University of Illinois at Chicago. Her areas of interest are policy, aging, health care, and international social work. Born in Lithuania, Dr. Kulys was codirector of the Center for Professional Education in Social Work at Vytautas Magnus University from 1992 to 1997. She continues to consult with nongovernmental organizations in Lithuania.

Terry Saunders Lane, MSS, is codirector of the Program Department and director of Policy, Research, and Evaluation at the Boston Foundation. Prior to 2001, she was associate dean at the Boston University School of Social Work. Her research interests include the effectiveness of services for vulnerable populations, including persons with HIV, young homeless women, pregnant teenagers, and immigrants and refugees.

Ole Langsted, Mag. art., is lektor of psychology at the National Danish School of Social Work in Aarhus, Denmark. He has published books and articles on young children's living conditions and everyday life, and on family care, public daycare, and the Danish public daycare system.

Peter Ching-Yung Lee, PhD, received his MSW from the University of Hawaii and both Master's of Public Health and PhD in Social Welfare from the University of California at Berkeley. He is professor of social work and Associate Vice-President for Faculty Affairs at San Jose State University, California. He is a member of CSWE's International Commission and serves as secretary-general of the Inter-University Consortium for International Social Development.

Rosemary J. Link, PhD, is professor of social work and chair, Professional Studies Division, at Augsburg College, Minneapolis, Minnesota. Dr. Link has a special interest in internationalizing social work curricula, sharing solutions to issues of child and family poverty, and parent participation for service planning. In addition to her articles on poverty, Dr. Link has recently coauthored with Dr. Chathapuram Ramanathan, *All Our Futures: Prinicples and Resources for Social Work Practice in a Global Era,* and a cross-national study of welfare reform with Dr. Anthony Bibus, *When Children Pay.*

Marjorie J. Malkin, EdD, is a professor of therapeutic recreation in the Department of Health Education and Recreation, College of Education and Human Services at Southern Illinois University at Carbondale. She has clinical and administrative experience in psychiatric and substance abuse treatment and has consulted with the Illinois Office of Mental Health for 7 years.

John A. Maxwell, Ph.D, is deputy dean, Faculty of Social Sciences, University of the West Indies, Mona Campus (UWI) in Jamaica. He also continues to teach and is involved in practicum coordination in the social work program at UWI, which he served as senior lecturer, coordinator of the social work program, and head of the Department of Sociology and Social Work over a 30-year period until his retirement in 2001. Dr. Maxwell has been extensively involved in social work organizations in the Caribbean region and throughout the world; he served as president of the North American and Caribbean Association of Schools of Social Work and as vice president of the International Association of Schools of Social Work. He is currently secretary of the Association of Caribbean Social Work Educators.

Mizanur R. Miah, PhD, is professor and graduate program director of social work at Southern Illinois University at Carbondale. His research interests center around social development, cultural diversity, and child welfare.

Ivan Nikolov, PhD, is research assistant professor and director of the Office of Global Education Projects at the College of Education and Human Services at Southern Illinois University at Carbondale. His research interests are international and community development and training.

Manuel Ribeiro Ferreira, PhD, holds a doctorate in education from Laval University, Quebec, Canada. He is the author of 11 books and approximately 40 articles on education, the family, and gender. Currently, he is a tenured professor in the School of Social Work at Universidad Autónoma de Nuevo León in Monterrey, México.

Wes Shera, PhD, is dean of the Faculty of Social Work, University of Toronto, Ontario, Canada. His major areas of research and publication include mental health, community development, social policy, evaluation research, and multicultural and international social work. More recently his work has focused on operationalizing and testing concepts of empowerment with individuals, organizations, and communities.

Lee H. Staples, PhD, is clinical professor at the Boston University School of Social Work and has extensive experience as a community organizer, supervisor, staff director, trainer, and consultant with a wide variety of grassroots social change organizations. He continues practice, research, and publication in the areas of consumer and community empowerment, leadership development, direct action strategy, task oriented groups, and community-responsive health care.

Sue Tebb, PhD, is dean, School of Social Service, Saint Louis University, Missouri. She writes and studies in the area of family caregiving, using both national and international approaches.

Patsy D. Tracy, PhD, is a retired social work clinical associate professor and is currently vice president and research associate with Social Insurance Research International, an international organization that provides consultation on developing social capital and civil society.

Martin B. Tracy, PhD, is professor and associate dean for research, College of Social Work, University of Kentucky. He is involved in various initiatives related to community-based social services and has most recently been engaged in a program with the International Labor Organization and the Albanian government to improve social assistance and social capital in Albania.

Kathleen Welshimer, PhD, is associate professor in the Department of Health Education and Recreation at Southern Illinois University at Carbondale. She specializes in organizing communities around public health issues and also conducts research into the psychology of health-protective behaviors.

Maureen Wilson, PhD, is on the Faculty of Social Work, University of Calgary, Alberta, Canada. She is currently involved in a three-country Central American water resource project and a social development project in Mexico and Belize. She has served as a consultant to programs of the Inter-American Development Bank and the Pan American Health Organization, and is a vice president of the Inter-University Consortium for International Social Development. Professor Wilson has taught in Mexico, Costa Rica, Nicaragua, and Cuba. She is interested in popular responses to the human impact of globalization and is coauthor, with Elizabeth Whitmore, of *Seeds of Fire: Social Development in an Era of Globalism.*

Ruth S. Ylvisaker, PhD, has her doctorate from the University of Minnesota and an MSSW from the University of Wisconsin-Madison. Her international interests focus on different models for the distribution of welfare benefits and on student opportunities for international experiences in South Africa, the United Kingdom, and Greece. She is the author of *The Impact of Tax Legislation on Corporate Income Security Planning for Retirees.*